P9-CDK-586

Complete Works of
Abraham Lincoln

Abraham Lincoln

The Celebrated Chicago Photograph.

*Photogravure from the Original Photograph
taken about 1860 by Hesler, of Chicago,
Illinois (O. II. Oldroyd Lincoln
Memorial Collection, Washington, D. C.)*

Abraham Lincoln

The Celebrated Chicago Photograph.

Photogravure from the Original Photograph taken about 1860 by Hesler, of Chicago, Illinois (O. H. Oldroyd Lincoln Memorial Collection, Washington, D. C.)

Copyright, 1894, by
JOHN G. NICOLAY *and* JOHN HAY

Complete Works *of*

Abraham Lincoln

Edited by

JOHN G. NICOLAY *and* JOHN HAY

With a Foreword *by*
HERBERT HOOVER
and Appreciations
by OTHER EMINENT PERSONS

New and Enlarged Edition

VOLUME V

PUBLISHED BY
LINCOLN MEMORIAL UNIVERSITY

viii Abraham Lincoln

main elements of Lincoln's character and the qualities which made his great career possible are revealed with startling distinctness. It expresses the experience of the noble young man of to-day equally as well as then. We see therein " that brave old wisdom of sincerity," that oneness in feeling with the common people, and that supreme confidence in them, which formed the foundation of his political faith.

Among the statesmen of America, Lincoln is the true Democrat; and, Franklin perhaps excepted, the first great one. He had no illustrious ancestry, no inherited place or wealth, and none of the prestige, power, training, or culture which were assured to the gentry or landed class of our own Colonial times. Nor did Lincoln believe that these classes, respectable and patriotic however they might be, should, as a matter of abstract right, have the controlling influence in our government. Instead, he believed in the all-pervading power of public opinion.

Lincoln had little or no instruction in the common school; but, as the eminent Dr. Cuyler has said, he was graduated from " the grand college of free labor, whose works were the flat-boat, the farm, and the backwoods lawyer's office." He had a broad comprehension of the central idea of popular government. The Declaration of Independence was his handbook; time and again he expressed his belief in freedom and equality. On July 1, 1854, he wrote:

" Most governments have been based, practically, on the denial of the equal rights of men. Ours began by affirming those rights. They said ' some men

George Bancroft, the historian, alluding to this characteristic, which was never so conspicuously manifested as during the darker hours of the war, beautifully illustrated it in these memorable words: "As a child, in a dark night, on a rugged way, catches hold of the hand of its father for guidance and support, Lincoln clung fast to the hand of the people, and moved calmly through the gloom."

His earliest public utterances were marked by this confidence. On March 9, 1832, when announcing himself as a candidate for Representative in the Illinois Legislature, he said that he felt it his duty to make known to the people his sentiments upon the questions of the day:

"Every man is said to have his precious ambition," he observed, "and whether it be true or not, I can say, for one, that I have no other so great as that of being truly esteemed by my fellow men by rendering myself worthy of their esteem. How far I shall succeed in gratifying this ambition is yet to be developed. I am young and unknown to many of you. I was born, and have ever remained, in the humblest walks of life. I have no wealthy or popular relatives or friends to recommend me. My case is thrown exclusively upon the independent voters of the county. . . . But if the good people, in their wisdom, shall see fit to keep me in the background, I have been too familiar with disappointments to be very much chagrined."

In this remarkable address — to me always pathetic — made when he was only twenty-three, the ination and criticism. He submitted his plans and purposes, as far as practicable, to public consideration with perfect frankness and sincerity. There was such homely simplicity in his character that it could not be hedged in by the pomp of place, nor the ceremonials of high official station. He was so accessible to the public that he seemed to take the whole people into his confidence. Here, perhaps, was one secret of his power. The people never lost their confidence in him, however much they unconsciously added to his personal discomfort and trials. His patience was almost superhuman; and who will say that he was mistaken in his treatment of the thousands who thronged continually about him? More than once when reproached for permitting visitors to crowd upon him, he asked, in pained surprise: " Why, what harm does this confidence in men do me? I get only good and inspiration from it."

Horace Greeley once said: " I doubt whether man, woman or child, white or black, bond or free, virtuous or vicious, ever accosted, or reached forth a hand to Abraham Lincoln, and detected in his countenance or manner, any repugnance or shrinking from the proffered contact, any assumption of superiority, or betrayal of disdain."

Frederick Douglass, the orator and patriot, is credited with saying: " Mr. Lincoln is the only white man with whom I have ever talked, or in whose presence I have ever been, who did not consciously or unconsciously betray to me that he recognized my color."

Abraham Lincoln, the Great Republican.[1]

IT requires the most gracious pages in the world's history to record what one American achieved. The story of this simple life is the story of a plain, honest, manly citizen, true patriot, and profound statesman, who believing with all the strength of his mighty soul in the institutions of his country, won because of them the highest place in its government — then fell a precious sacrifice to the Union he held so dear, which Providence had spared his life long enough to save.

.   .   .   .

What were the traits of character which made Abraham Lincoln prophet and master, without a rival, in the greatest crisis in our history? What gave him such mighty power? To me the answer is simple: Lincoln had sublime faith in the people. He walked with and among them. He recognized the importance and power of an enlightened public sentiment and was guided by it. Even amid the vicissitudes of war, he concealed little from public review and inspection. In all he did, he invited, rather than evaded, exam-

[1] From an Address by William McKinley, before the Marquette Club, Chicago, February 12, 1896.

are too ignorant and vicious to share in government.'
' Possibly so,' said we, ' and by your system you
would always keep them ignorant and vicious. We
proposed to give all a chance; and we expected the
weak to grow stronger, the ignorant wiser, and all
better and happier together.' We made the experiment, and the fruit is before us. Look at it, think of
it! Look at it in its aggregate grandeur, extent of
country, and numbers of population."

Lincoln believed in the uplifting influences of free
government, and that by giving all a chance we could
get higher average results for the people than where
governments are exclusive and opportunities are limited to the few. No American ever did so much as
he to enlarge these opportunities, or tear down the
barriers which excluded a free participation in them.
In his first message to Congress, at the special session
convening on July 4, 1861, he gave signal evidence of
his faith in our institutions, and their elevating influences, in most impressive language. He said:

" It may be affirmed without extravagance that the
free institutions we enjoy have developed the powers
and improved the condition of our whole people beyond any example in the world. Of this we now
have a striking and an impressive illustration. So
large an army as the Government has now on foot
was never before known without a soldier in it but
who has taken his place there of his own free choice."
(Then what followed in his message is, to me, the
highest and most touching tribute ever spoken or
written of our matchless Volunteer Army of 1861–65

by any American statesman, soldier, or citizen from that day to this:) " But more than this, there are many single regiments whose members, one and another, possess full practical knowledge of all the arts, sciences, and professions, and whatever else, whether useful or elegant, is known in the world; and there is scarcely one from which there could not be selected a President, a Cabinet, a Congress, and perhaps a Court, abundantly competent to administer the Government itself."

What a noble, self-sacrificing army of freemen he describes! The like of it mankind never saw before and will not look upon soon again. Their service and sacrifice were not in vain — the Union is stronger, freer and better than ever before because they lived, and the peace, fraternity and harmony, which Lincoln prayed might come, and which he prophesied would come, is happily here. And now that the wounds of the war are healed, may we not, with grateful hearts, resolve, in the words of Lincoln, that we will " care for him who shall have borne the battle, and for his widow, and his orphan."

Lincoln's antecedent life seems to have been one of unconscious preparation for the great responsibilities which were committed to him in 1860. As one of the masses himself, and living with them, sharing their feelings, and sympathizing with their daily trials, their hopes and aspirations, he was better fitted to lead them than any other man of his age. He recognized more clearly than any one else that the plain people he met in his daily life, and knew so familiarly, were, according to the dictates of justice and our theory of government, its ultimate rulers and the arbiters of its destiny. He knew this not as a theory, but from his own personal experience.

Born in poverty, and surrounded by obstacles on every hand seemingly insurmountable but for the intervening hand of Providence, Lincoln grew every year into greater and grander intellectual power and vigor. His life, until he was twelve years old, was spent either in a " half-faced camp " or cabin. Yet amid such surroundings the boy learned to read, write, and cipher, to think, declaim, and speak, in a manner far beyond his years and time. All his days in the school-house " added together would not make a single year." But every day of his life from infancy to manhood was a constant drill in the school of nature and experience. His study of books and newspapers was beyond that of any other person in his town or neighorhood, and perhaps of his county or section. He did not read many books, but he learned more from them than any other reader. It was strength of body as well as of mind that made Lincoln's career possible. Ill success only spurred him into making himself more worthy of trust and confidence. Nothing could daunt him. He might have but a single tow-linen shirt, or only one pair of jeans pantaloons, he often did not know where his next dollar was to come from, but he mastered English grammar and composition, arithmetic, geometry, surveying, logic, and the law.

How well he mastered the art of expression, is

shown by the incident of the Yale professor who heard his Cooper Institute speech and called on him at his hotel, to inquire where he had learned his matchless power as a public speaker. The modest country lawyer was in turn surprised to be suspected of possessing unusual talents as an orator, and could only answer that his sole training had been in the school of experience.

Eight years' service in the Illinois Legislature, two years in Congress and nearly thirty years' political campaigning, in the most exciting period of American politics, gave scope for the development of his powers, and that tact, readiness, and self-reliance, which were invaluable to a modest, backward man, such as Lincoln naturally was. Added to these qualities, he had the genius, which communizes, which puts a man on a level, not only with the highest, but with the lowest of his kind. By dint of patient industry, and by using wisely his limited opportunities, he became the most popular orator, the best political manager, and the ablest leader of his party in Illinois.

But the best training he had for the Presidency, after all, was his twenty-three years' arduous experience as a lawyer traveling the circuit of the courts of his district and State. Here he met in forensic contests, and frequently defeated some of the most powerful legal minds of the West. In the higher courts he won still greater distinction in the important cases committed to his charge.

With this preparation, it is not surprising that Lincoln entered upon the Presidency peculiarly well

equipped for its vast responsibilities. His contemporaries, however, did not realize this. The leading statesmen of the country were not prepossessed in his favor. They appear to have had no conception of the remarkable powers latent beneath that uncouth and rugged exterior. It seemed to them strangely out of place that the people should at this, the greatest crisis of their history, entrust the supreme executive power of the Nation to one whom they presumptuously called " this ignorant rail-splitter from the prairies of Illinois." Many predicted failure from the beginning.

Lincoln was essentially a man of peace. He inherited from his Quaker forefathers an intense opposition to war. During his brief service in Congress he found occasion more than once to express it. He opposed the Mexican war from principle, but voted men and supplies after hostilities actually began. In one of his few speeches in the House, he characterized military glory as " that rainbow that rises in showers of blood — that serpent that charms but to destroy." When he became responsible for the welfare of the country, he was none the less earnest for peace. He felt that even in the most righteous cause, war is a fearful thing, and he was actuated by the feeling that it ought not to be begun except as a last resort, and then only after it had been precipitated by the enemies of the country. He said in Philadelphia, on February 22, 1861:

" There is no need of bloodshed and war. There is no necessity for it. I am not in favor of such a

course; and I may say in advance that there will be no bloodshed unless it is forced upon the Government. The Government will not use force unless force is used against it."

In the selection of his Cabinet, he at once showed his greatness and magnanimity. His principal rivals for the Presidential nomination were invited to seats in his council chamber. No one but a great man, conscious of his own strength, would have done this. It was soon perceived that his greatness was in no sense obscured by the presence of the distinguished men who sat about him. The most gifted statesmen of the country: Seward, Chase, Cameron, Stanton, Blair, Bates, Welles, Fessenden, and Dennison, some of whom had been leaders in the Senate of the United States, composed that historic Cabinet, and the man who had been sneered at as "the rail-splitter" suffered nothing by such association and comparison. He was a leader in fact as well as name.

Magnanimity was one of Lincoln's most striking traits. Patriotism moved him at every step. At the beginning of the war he placed at the head of three most important military departments three of his political opponents — Patterson, Butler and McClellan. He did not propose to make it a partisan war. He sought by every means in his power to enlist all who were patriots.

In his message of July 4, 1861, he stated his purpose in these words:

"I desire to preserve the Government that it may be administered for all, as it was administered by the

men who made it. On the side of the Union
it is a struggle to maintain in the world that form
and substance of Government whose leading object
is to elevate the condition of men, lift artificial burdens from all shoulders and clear the paths of lauda-
ble pursuits for all, to afford all an unfettered start
and a fair chance in the race of life. This is the
leading object of the Government for whose existence
we contend."

Many people were impatient at Lincoln's conservatism. He gave the South every chance possible. He
pleaded with them with an earnestness that was pathetic. He recognized that the South was not alone
to blame for the existence of slavery, but that the
sin was a National one. He sought to impress upon
the South that he would not use his office as President
to take away from them any constitutional right, great
or small.

In his first inaugural he addressed the men of the
South as well as the North, as his " countrymen,"
one and all, and with an outburst of indescribable
tenderness, exclaimed: " We are not enemies, but
friends. We must not be enemies." And then in
those wondrously sweet and touching words which
even yet thrill the heart, he said:

" Though passion may have strained, it must not
break our bonds of affection. The mystic chords of
memory, stretching from every battlefield and patriot
grave to every living heart and hearthstone all over
this broad land, will yet swell the chorus of the Union

when again touched, as surely they will be, by the better angels of our nature."

But his words were unheeded. The mighty war came with its dreadful train. Knowing no wrong, he dreaded no evil for himself. He had done all he could to save the country by peaceful means. He had entreated and expostulated, now he would do and dare. He had in words of solemn import warned the men of the South. He had appealed to their patriotism by the sacred memories of the battle-fields of the Revolution, on which the patriot blood of their ancestors had been so bravely shed, not to break up the Union. Yet all in vain. "Both parties deprecated war; but one would make war rather than let the Nation survive; and the other would accept war rather than let it perish. And the war came."

Lincoln did all he could to avert it, but there was no hesitation on his part when the sword of rebellion flashed from its scabbard. He was from that moment until the close of his life unceasingly devoted and consecrated to the great purpose of saving the Union. All other matters he regarded as trivial, and every movement, of whatever character, whether important or unimportant of itself, was bent to that end.

The world now regards with wonder the infinite patience, gentleness and kindness, with which he bore the terrible burdens of that four years' struggle. Humane, forgiving and long-suffering himself, he was always especially tender and considerate of the poor, and in his treatment of them was full of those

" kind little acts which are of the same blood as great
and holy deeds." As Charles Sumner so well said:
" With him as President, the idea of republican institutions, where no place is too high for the humblest, was perpetually manifest, so that his simple
presence was a proclamation of the equality of all
men."

During the whole of the struggle, he was a tower
of strength to the Union. Whether in defeat or victory, he kept right on, dismayed at nothing, and never
to be diverted from the pathway of duty. Always
cool and determined, all learned to gain renewed
courage, calmness and wisdom from him, and to lean
upon his strong arm for support. The proud des-
ignation, " Father of His Country," was not more ap-
propriately bestowed upon Washington, than the af-
fectionate title " Father Abraham " was given to
Lincoln by the soldiers and loyal people of the North.

The crowning glory of Lincoln's administration,
and the greatest executive act in American history,
was his immortal Proclamation of Emancipation.
Perhaps more clearly than anyone else Lincoln had
realized years before he was called to the Presidency,
that the country could not continue half slave and
half free. He declared it before Seward proclaimed
the " irrepressible conflict." The contest between
freedom and slavery was inevitable; it was written in
the stars. The Nation must be either all slave, or
all free. Lincoln with almost supernatural prescience
foresaw it. His prophetic vision is manifested
through all his utterances, notably in the great de-

bate between himself and Douglas. To him was given the duty and responsibility of making that great classic of liberty, the Declaration of Independence, no longer an empty promise, but a glorious fulfillment.

Many long and thorny steps were to be taken before this great act of justice could be performed. Patience and forbearance had to be exercised. It had to be demonstrated that the Union could be saved in no other way.

Lincoln, much as he abhorred slavery, felt that his chief duty was to save the Union, under the Constitution, and within the Constitution. He did not assume the duties of his great office with the purpose of abolishing slavery, nor changing the Constitution, but as a servant of the Constitution and the laws of the country then existing. In a speech delivered in Ohio, in 1859, he said: "The people of the United States are the rightful masters of both Congress and the Courts — not to overthrow the Constitution, but to overthrow the men who would overthrow the Constitution."

This was the principle which governed him, and which he applied in his official conduct when he reached the Presidency. We now know that he had emancipation constantly in his mind's eye for nearly two years after his first inauguration. It is true, he said at the start, "I believe I have no lawful right to interfere with slavery where it now exists, and have no intention of doing so;" and that the public had little reason to think he was meditating general eman-

cipation until he issued his preliminary proclamation, September 22, 1862.

Just a month before, exactly, he had written to the editor of the New York Tribune:

" My paramount object is to save the Union, and not either to save or destroy slavery. If I could save the Union without freeing any slave, I would do it; if I could save it by freeing all the slaves, I would do it; and if I could do it by freeing some and leaving others alone, I would also do that."

The difference in his thought and purpose about " the divine institution " is very apparent in these two expressions. Both were made in absolute honor and sincerity. Public sentiment had undergone a great change, and Lincoln, valiant defender of the Constitution that he was, and faithful tribune of the people that he always was, changed with the people. The war had brought them and him to a nearer realization of our absolute dependence upon a Higher Power, and had quickened his conceptions of duty more acutely than the public could realize. The purposes of God, working through the ages, were perhaps more clearly revealed to him than to any other.

Besides, it was as he himself once said: " It is a quality of revolutions not to go by old lines or old laws, but to break up both and make new ones." He was " naturally anti-slavery," and the determination he formed when as a young man he witnessed an auction in the slave shambles of New Orleans, never forsook him. It is recorded how his soul burned with indignation, and that he then exclaimed, " If I

ever get a chance to hit that thing, I'll hit it hard." He " hit it hard " when as a member of the Illinois Legislature he protested that " the institution of slavery is founded on both injustice and bad policy."

He " hit it hard " when as a member of Congress he " voted for the Wilmot Proviso as good as forty times." He " hit it hard " when he stumped his state against the Kansas-Nebraska bill, and on the direct issue carried Illinois in favor of the restriction of slavery by a majority of 4,414 votes. He " hit it hard " when he approved the law abolishing slavery in the District of Columbia, an anti-slavery measure that he had voted for in Congress. He " hit it hard " when he signed the acts abolishing slavery in all the Territories, and for the repeal of the Fugitive Slave Law. But it still remained for him to strike slavery its death-blow. He did that in his glorious Proclamation of Freedom.

It was in this light that Lincoln himself viewed these great events. He wrote a mass-meeting of unconditional Union men at Springfield, Ill., August 26, 1863, as follows:

" The emancipation policy and the use of colored troops constitute the heaviest blow yet dealt to the Rebellion, and at least one of these important successes could not have been achieved when it was but for the aid of black soldiers. . . . The job was a great National one, and let none be banned who bore an honorable part in it. . . . Peace does not appear so distant as it did. I hope it will come soon, and come to stay; and so come as to be worth

the keeping in all future time. It will then have
proved that among the free men there can be no successful appeal from the ballot to the bullet, and that
they who take such appeal are sure to lose their case
and pay the cost. And then there will be some black
men who can remember that with silent tongue, and
clenched teeth, and steady eye, and well-poised bay-
onet, they have helped mankind on to this great consummation, while I fear there will be some white
ones unable to forget that with malignant heart and
deceitful speech they strove to hinder it."

Secretary Seward tells how when he carried the
historic Proclamation to the President for signature
at noon on the first day of January, 1863, he said:
" I have been shaking hands since nine o'clock this
morning, and my right hand is almost paralyzed. If
my name ever goes into history, it will be for this
act, and my whole soul is in it. If my hand trem-
bles when I sign the Proclamation all who examine
the document hereafter, will say, ' he hesitated.' "
He turned to the table, took up his pen and slowly,
firmly wrote that ' *Abraham Lincoln* ' with which the
whole world is now familiar. Then he looked up
and said: " That will do."

In all the long years of slavery agitation, unlike
any of the other anti-slavery leaders, Lincoln always
carried the people with him. In 1854 Illinois cast
loose from her old Democratic moorings and followed his leadership in a most emphatic protest
against the repeal of the Missouri Compromise. In
1858 the people of Illinois endorsed his opposition

to the aggressions of slavery, in a state usually Democratic, even against so popular a leader as " the Little Giant."   In 1860 the whole country endorsed his position on slavery, even when the people were continually harangued that his election meant the dissolution of the Union.   During the war the people advanced with him step by step to its final overthrow. Indeed, in the election of 1864 the people not only endorsed emancipation, but went far towards recognizing the political equality of the negro.   They heartily justified the President in having enlisted colored soldiers to fight side by side with the white man in the noble cause of union and liberty.   Aye, they did more, they endorsed his position on another and vastly more important phase of the race problem. They approved his course as President in reorganizing the government of Louisiana, and a hostile press did not fail to call attention to the fact that this meant eventually negro suffrage in that State.

Perhaps, however, it was not known then that Lincoln had written the new Free State Governor, on March 13, 1864, as follows:

" Now you are about to have a convention, which, among other things, will probably define the elective franchise.   I barely suggest for your private consideration, whether some of the colored people may not be let in — as for instance, the very intelligent, and especially those who have fought gallantly in our ranks.   They would probably help, in some trying time to come, to keep the jewel of liberty within the family of freedom."

Lincoln had that happy, peculiar habit, which few public men have attained, of looking away from the deceptive and misleading influences about him, and none are more deceptive than those of public life in our capitals, straight into the hearts of the people. He could not be deceived by the self-interested host of eager counselors who sought to enforce their own particular views upon him as the voice of the country. He chose to determine for himself what the people were thinking about and wanting him to do, and no man ever lived who was a more accurate judge of their opinions and wishes.

The battle of Gettysburg turned the scale of the war in favor of the Union, and it has always seemed to me most fortunate that Lincoln declared for emancipation before rather than after that decisive contest. A later Proclamation might have been construed as a tame and cowardly performance, not a challenge of Truth to Error for mortal combat. The ground on which that battle was fought is held sacred by every friend of freedom. But important as the battle itself was the dedication of it as a National Cemetery is celebrated for a grander thing. The words Lincoln spoke there will live " until time shall be no more," through all eternity. Well may they be forever preserved on tablets of bronze upon the spot where he spoke, but how infinitely better it would be if they could find a permanent lodging place in the soul of every American!

Lincoln was a man of moderation. He was neither an autocrat nor a tyrant. If he moved slowly some-

times, it was because it was better to move slowly,
and, like the successful general that he was, he was
only waiting for his reserves to come up.   Possessing
almost unlimited power, he yet carried himself like
one of the humblest of men.   He weighed every
subject.   He considered and reflected upon every
phase of public duty.   He got the average judgment
of the plain people.   He had a high sense of justice, a clear understanding of the rights of others,
and never needlessly inflicted an injury upon any man.

He said, in response to a serenade, November 10,
1864, just after his triumphal election for a second
term to the great office of President:

" Now that the election is over, may not all having a common interest reunite in a common effort to
save our common country?   For my own part, I
have striven and shall strive to avoid placing any
obstacle in the way.   So long as I have been here I
have not willingly planted a thorn in any man's
bosom.   While I am deeply sensible to the high compliment of a re-election, and duly grateful, as I trust,
to Almighty God for having directed my countrymen
to a right conclusion, as I think, for their own good,
it adds nothing to my satisfaction that any other man
may be disappointed or pained by the result."

It is pleasant to note that in the very last public
speech by President Lincoln, on April 11, 1865, he
uttered noble sentiments of charity and good-will similar to those of his sublime second inaugural, which
were of peculiar interest to the people of the South.
In discussing the question of reconstruction, he said:

"We all agree that the seceded States, so called, are out of their proper practical relation with the Union, and that the sole object of the government, civil and military, in regard to those States, is to again get them into that proper practical relation. I believe that it is not only possible, but in fact easier, to do this without deciding or even considering whether these States have ever been out of the Union, than with it. Finding themselves safely at home, it would be utterly immaterial whether they had ever been abroad. Let us all join in doing the acts necessary to restoring the proper practical relations between these States and the Union, and each forever after innocently indulge his own opinion whether in doing the acts he brought the States from without into the Union, or only gave them proper assistance, they never having been out of it."

It is not difficult to place a correct estimate upon the character of Lincoln. He was the greatest man of his time, especially approved of God for the work He gave him to do. History abundantly proves his superiority as a leader, and establishes his constant reliance upon a Higher power for guidance and support. The tendency of this age is to exaggeration, but of Lincoln certainly none have spoken more highly than those who knew him best.

A distinguished orator has said: "Lincoln surpassed all orators in eloquence; all diplomatists in wisdom; all statesmen in foresight; and the most ambitious in fame."

This is in accord with the estimate of Stanton who

pronounced him " the most perfect ruler of men the world had ever seen."

Seward, too, declared Lincoln " a man of destiny, with character made and molded by Divine Power to save a nation from perdition."

Ralph Waldo Emerson characterized him as " the true representative of this continent; an entirely public man; father of his country; the pulse of twenty millions throbbing in his heart, the thought of their minds articulated by his tongue.

Bancroft wisely observed: " Lincoln thought always of mankind, as well as his own country, and served human nature itself; he finished a work which all time cannot overthrow."

Sumner said that in Lincoln " the West spoke to the East, pleading for human rights, as declared by our fathers."

Horace Greeley, in speaking of the events which led up to and embraced the Rebellion, declared: " Other men were helpful, and nobly did their part; yet, looking back through the lifting mists of those seven eventful, tragic, trying, glorious years, I clearly discern the one providential leader, the indispensable hero of the great drama, Abraham Lincoln."

James Russell Lowell was quick to perceive and proclaim Lincoln's greatness. In December, 1863, in a review of the " President's Policy," in the Atlantic Monthly, he said: " Perhaps none of our Presidents since Washington has stood so firm in the confidence of the people as Lincoln, after three years' stormy administration. . . . A profound common sense is the best genius for statesmanship. Hitherto the wisdom of the President's measures has been justified by the fact that they always resulted in more firmly uniting public opinion."

Lincoln is certainly the most sagacious and far-seeing statesman in the annals of American history. His entire public life justifies this estimate of him. It is notable that his stand upon all public questions in his earlier as well as his later career stamp him as the wisest exponent of political truths we have ever had.

.   .   .   .

The greatest names in American history are Washington and Lincoln. One is forever associated with the independence of the States and formation of the Federal Union; the other with universal freedom and the preservation of that Union. Washington enforced the Declaration of Independence as against England; Lincoln proclaimed its fulfillment not only to a downtrodden race in America, but to all people for all time, who may seek the protection of our flag. These illustrious men achieved grander results for mankind within a single century — from 1775 to 1865 — than any other men ever accomplished in all the years since first the flight of time began. Washington engaged in no ordinary revolution. With him it was not who should rule, but what should rule. He drew his sword, not for a change of rulers upon an established throne, but to establish a new government, which should acknowledge no throne but the

tribune of the people.   Lincoln accepted war to save
the Union, the safeguard of our liberties, and re-es-
tablished it on " indestructible foundations " as forever " one and indivisible."   To quote his own grand
words :

" Now we are contending that this Nation under
God, shall have a new birth of freedom; and that
government of the people, by the people, for the people, shall not perish from the earth."

Each lived to accomplish his appointed task.   Each
received the unbounded gratitude of the people of
his time, and each is held in great and ever-increas-
ing reverence by posterity.   The fame of each will
never die.   It will grow with the ages, because it is
based upon imperishable service to humanity — not
to the people of a single generation or country, but
to the whole human family, wherever scattered, forever.

The present generation knows Washington only
from history, and by that alone can judge him.   Lincoln we know by history also; but thousands are still
living who participated in the great events in which he
was leader and master.   Many of his contemporaries
survived him; some are here yet in almost every locality.   So Lincoln is not far removed from us.   Indeed, he may be said to be still known to the millions; not surrounded by the mists of antiquity, nor
by a halo of idolatry that is impenetrable.

He never was inaccessible to the people.   Thousands carry with them yet the words which he spoke
in their hearing; thousands remember the pressure of

his hand; and I remember, as though it were but yesterday, and thousands of my comrades will recall, how, when he reviewed the Army of the Potomac immediately after the battle of Antietam, his indescribably sad, thoughtful, far-seeing expression pierced every man's soul. Nobody could keep the people away from him, and when they came to him he would suffer no one to drive them back. So it is that an unusually large number of the American people came to know this great man, and that he is still so well remembered by them. It can not be said that they are mistaken about him, or that they misinterpreted his character and greatness.

. . . .

This host of witnesses, without exception, agree as to the true nobility and intellectual greatness of Lincoln. All proudly claim for Lincoln the highest abilities and the most distinguished and self-sacrificing patriotism. Lincoln taught them, and has taught us, that no party or partisan can escape responsibility to the people; that no party advantage, or presumed party advantage, should ever swerve us from the plain path of duty, which is ever the path of honor and distinction. He emphasized his words by his daily life and deeds. He showed to the world by his lofty example, as well as by precept and maxim that there are times when the voice of partisanship should be hushed and that of patriotism only be heeded. He taught that a good service done for the country, even in aid of an unfriendly Administration, brings to the

men and the party who rise above the temptation of
temporary partisan advantage, a lasting gain in the
respect and confidence of the people. He showed
that such patriotic devotion is usually rewarded, not
only with retention in power and the consciousness
of duty well and bravely done, but with the gratifica-
tion of beholding the blessings of relief and prosperity, not of a party, or section, but of the whole
country. This, he held, should be the first and great
consideration of all public servants.

When Lincoln died, a grateful people, moved by
a common impulse, immediately placed him side by
side with the immortal Washington, and unanimously
proclaimed them the two greatest and best Ameri-
cans. That verdict has not changed, and will not
change, nor can we conceive how the historians of this
or any age will ever determine what is so clearly a
matter of pure personal opinion as to which of these
noble men is entitled to greatest honor and homage
from the people of America.

A recent writer says: " The amazing growth Lincoln made in the esteem of his countrymen and the
world, while he was doing his great work, has been
paralleled by the increase of his fame in the years since
he died." He might have added that, like every important event of his life, Lincoln's fame rests upon
a severer test than that of any other American.
Never, in all the ages of men, have the acts, words,
motives — even thoughts — of any statesman been so
scrutinized, analyzed, studied, or speculated upon, as
his. Yet from all inquirers, without distinction as to

party, church, section, or country, from friend and foe alike, comes the unanimous verdict that Abraham Lincoln must have no second place in American history, and that he will never be second to any in the reverent affections of the American people.

.   .   .   .

My fellow citizens, a noble manhood, nobly consecrated to man, never dies. The Martyr to Liberty, the Emancipator of a Race, the Savior of the only free Government among men, may be buried from human sight, but his deeds will live in human gratitude forever.

" Great captains, with their guns and drums,
　　Disturb our judgment for the hour,
But at last silence comes;
　　These are all gone, and, standing like a tower,
Our children shall behold his fame;
　　The kindly-earnest, brave, far-seeing man,
Sagacious, patient, dreading praise, not blame,
　　New birth of our new soil, the first American."

Wm McKinley

Sonnet in 1862

BY JOHN JAMES PIATT.

Stern be the Pilot in the dreadful hour
   When a great nation, like a ship at sea
   With the wroth breakers whitening at her lee,
Feels her last shudder if her Helsman cower;
A godlike manhood be his mighty dower!
   Such and so gifted, Lincoln may'st thou be
   With thy high wisdom's low simplicity
And awful tenderness of voted power:
From our hot records then thy name shall stand
   On time's calm ledger out of passionate days —
With the pure debt of gratitude begun,
   And only paid in never-ending praise —
One of the many of a mighty Land,
Made by God's providence the Anointed One.

Illustrations

Complete Works of Abraham Lincoln

Volume V

[1858---1860]

Complete Works of Abraham Lincoln

THE SEVENTH AND LAST JOINT DEBATE, AT ALTON, ILLINOIS, October 15, 1858.

Senator Douglas's Opening Speech.

LADIES AND GENTLEMEN: It is now nearly four months since the canvass between Mr. Lincoln and myself commenced. On the 16th of June the Republican convention assembled at Springfield, and nominated Mr. Lincoln as their candidate for the United States Senate, and he, on that occasion, delivered a speech in which he laid down what he understood to be the Republican creed, and the platform on which he proposed to stand during the contest. The principal points in that speech of Mr. Lincoln's were: First, that this government could not endure permanently divided into free and slave States, as our fathers made it; that they must all become free or all become slave; all become one thing or all become the other, otherwise this Union could not continue to exist. I give you his opinions almost in the identical language he used. His second proposition was a crusade against the Supreme Court of the United States, because of the Dred Scott decision; urging as an especial reason for his opposition to that decision that it deprived the negroes of the rights and benefits of that clause in the Constitution of the United States which guarantees to the citizens of each State all the rights, privileges, and immunities of the citizens of the several States. On the 10th of July I returned home, and delivered a speech to the people of Chicago, in which I announced it to be my purpose to appeal to the people of Illinois to sustain the course I had pursued in Congress. In that speech I joined issue with Mr. Lincoln on the points which he had presented. Thus there was an issue clear and distinct made up between us on these two propositions laid down in the speech of Mr. Lincoln at Springfield, and controverted by me in my reply to him at Chicago. On the next day, the 11th of July, Mr. Lincoln replied to me at Chicago, explaining at some length, and reaffirming the positions which he had taken in his Springfield speech. In that Chicago speech he even went further than he had before, and uttered sentiments in regard to the negro being on an equality with the white man. He adopted in support of this position the argument which Lovejoy, and Codding, and other Abolition lecturers had made familiar in the northern and central portions of the State, to wit: that the Declaration of Independence having declared all men free and equal by Divine law, negro equality was also an inalienable right, of which they could not be deprived. He insisted, in that speech, that the Declaration of Independence included the negro in the clause asserting that all men were created equal, and went so far as to say that if one man was allowed to take the position that it did not include the negro, others might take the position that it did not include other men. He said that all these distinctions between this man and that man, this race and the other race, must be discarded, and we must all stand by the Declaration of Independence, declaring that all men were created equal.

The issue thus being made up between Mr. Lincoln and myself on three points, we went before the people of the State. During the following seven weeks, between the Chicago speeches and our first meeting at Ottawa, he and I addressed large assemblages of the people in many of the central counties. In my speeches

I confined myself closely to those three positions which he had taken, controverting his
proposition that this Union could not exist as
our fathers made it, divided into free and slave
States, controverting his proposition of a crusade against the Supreme Court because of the
Dred Scott decision, and controverting his
proposition that the Declaration of Independence included and meant the negroes as well
as the white men, when it declared all men to
be created equal. I supposed at that time that
these propositions constituted a distinct issue between us, and that the opposite positions we had
taken upon them we would be willing to be held
to in every part of the State. I never intended
to waver one hair's breadth from that issue either
in the north or the south, or wherever I should
address the people of Illinois. I hold that when
the time arrives that I cannot proclaim my political creed in the same terms not only in the
northern but the southern part of Illinois, not
only in the Northern but the Southern States,
and wherever the American flag waves over
American soil, that then there must be something wrong in that creed—so long as we live
under a common Constitution, so long as we
live in a confederacy of sovereign and equal
States, joined together as one for certain purposes, that any political creed is radically wrong

which cannot be proclaimed in every State and
every section of that Union, alike. I took up
Mr. Lincoln's three propositions in my several
speeches, analyzed them, and pointed out what
I believed to be the radical errors contained in
them. First, in regard to his doctrine that this
government was in violation of the law of God,
which says that a house divided against itself
cannot stand; I repudiated it as a slander upon
the immortal framers of our Constitution. I
then said, I have often repeated, and now again
assert, that in my opinion our government can
endure forever, divided into free and slave
States as our fathers made it—each State having
the right to prohibit, abolish, or sustain slavery,
just as it pleases. This government was made
upon the great basis of the sovereignty of the
States, the right of each State to regulate its
own domestic institutions to suit itself, and that
right was conferred with the understanding and
expectation that inasmuch as each locality had
separate interests, each locality must have different and distinct local and domestic institutions, corresponding to its wants and interests.
Our fathers knew, when they made the government, that the laws and institutions which were
well adapted to the green mountains of Ver-
mont were unsuited to the rice plantations of
South Carolina. They knew then, as well as

we know now, that the laws and institutions
which would be well adapted to the beautiful
prairies of Illinois would not be suited to the
mining regions of California.   They knew that
in a republic as broad as this, having such a
variety of soil, climate, and interest, there must
necessarily be a corresponding variety of local
laws—the policy and institutions of each State
adapted to its condition and wants.   For this
reason this Union was established on the right
of each State to do as it pleased on the question
of slavery, and every other question, and the
various States were not allowed to complain of,
much less interfere with, the policy of their
neighbors.

Suppose the doctrine advocated by Mr. Lincoln and the Abolitionists of this day had prevailed when the Constitution was made, what
would have been the result?   Imagine for a moment that Mr. Lincoln had been a member of
the convention that framed the Constitution of
the United States, and that when its members
were about to sign that wonderful document,
he had arisen in that convention, as he did at
Springfield this summer, and addressing himself to the President, had said: "A house divided against itself cannot stand; this government, divided into free and slave States, cannot
endure; they must all be free or all be slave,

they must all be one thing or all the other; otherwise, it is a violation of the law of God, and cannot continue to exist"—suppose Mr. Lincoln had convinced that body of sages that that doctrine was sound, what would have been the result? Remember that the Union was then composed of thirteen States, twelve of which were slaveholding and one free. Do you think that the one free State would have out-voted the twelve slave-holding States, and thus have secured the abolition of slavery? On the other hand, would not the twelve slave-holding States have out-voted the one free State, and thus have fastened slavery, by a constitutional provision, on every foot of the American republic forever? You see that if this Abolition doctrine of Mr. Lincoln had prevailed when the government was made, it would have established slavery as a permanent institution, in all the States, whether they wanted it or not; and the question for us to determine in Illinois now, as one of the free States, is whether or not we are willing, having become the majority section, to enforce a doctrine on the minority which we would have resisted with our heart's blood had it been attempted on us when we were in a minority. How has the South lost her power as the majority section in this Union, and how have the free States gained it, except under the operation of that principle which declares the right of the people of each State and each Territory to form and regulate their domestic institutions in their own way? It was under that principle that slavery was abolished in New Hampshire, Rhode Island, Connecticut, New York, New Jersey, and Pennsylvania; it was under that principle that one half of the slave-holding States became free; it was under that principle that the number of free States increased until, from being one out of twelve States, we have grown to be the majority of States of the whole Union, with the power to control the House of Representatives and Senate, and the power, consequently, to elect a President by Northern votes without the aid of a Southern State. Having obtained this power under the operation of that great principle, are you now prepared to abandon the principle, and declare that merely because we have the power you will wage a war against the Southern States and their institutions until you force them to abolish slavery everywhere?

After having pressed these arguments home on Mr. Lincoln for seven weeks, publishing a number of my speeches, we met at Ottawa in joint discussion, and he then began to crawfish a little, and let himself down. I there propounded certain questions to him. Amongst

others, I asked him whether he would vote for
the admission of any more slave States in the
event the people wanted them.   He would not
answer.   I then told him that if he did not answer the question there I would renew it at
Freeport, and would then trot him down into
Egypt and again put it to him.   Well, at Freeport, knowing that the next joint discussion took
place in Egypt, and being in dread of it, he did
answer my question in regard to no more slave
States in a mode which he hoped would be satisfactory to me, and accomplish the object he
had in view.   I will show you what his answer
was.   After saying that he was not pledged to
the Republican doctrine of "no more slave
States," he declared:

I state to you freely, frankly, that I should be
exceedingly sorry to ever be put in the position of
having to pass upon that question.   I should be exceedingly glad to know that there never would be
another slave State admitted into this Union.

Here permit me to remark that I do not think
the people will ever force him into a position
against his will.   He went on to say:

But I must add, in regard to this, that if slavery
shall be kept out of the Territory during the territorial existence of any one given Territory, and then
the people should —— having a fair chance and a clear

field when they come to adopt a constitution — if
they should do the extraordinary thing of adopting
a slave constitution, uninfluenced by the actual presence of the institution among them, I see no alter-
native, if we own the country, but we must admit it
into this Union.

That answer Mr. Lincoln supposed would
satisfy the old-line Whigs, composed of Kentuckians and Virginians, down in the southern
part of the State. Now, what does it amount
to? I desired to know whether he would vote
to allow Kansas to come into the Union with
slavery or not, as her people desired. He would
not answer, but in a roundabout way said that
if slavery should be kept out of a Territory during the whole of its territorial existence, and
then the people, when they adopted a State constitution, asked admission as a slave State, he
supposed he would have to let the State come
in. The case I put to him was an entirely different one. I desired to know whether he
would vote to admit a State if Congress had
not prohibited slavery in it during its territorial
existence, as Congress never pretended to do
under Clay's compromise measures of 1850. He
would not answer, and I have not yet been able
to get an answer from him. I have asked him
whether he would vote to admit Nebraska if
her people asked to come in as a State with a

constitution recognizing slavery, and he refused
to answer. I have put the question to him with
reference to New Mexico, and he has not uttered a word in answer. I have enumerated
the Territories, one after another, putting the
same question to him with reference to each,
and he has not said, and will not say, whether,
if elected to Congress, he will vote to admit any
Territory now in existence with such a constitution as her people may adopt. He invents
a case which does not exist, and cannot exist,
under this government, and answers it; but he
will not answer the question I put to him in
connection with any of the Territories now in
existence. The contract we entered into with
Texas when she entered the Union obliges us
to allow four States to be formed out of the old
State, and admitted with or without slavery, as
the respective inhabitants of each may determine. I have asked Mr. Lincoln three times
in our joint discussions whether he would vote
to redeem that pledge, and he has never yet
answered. He is as silent as the grave on the
subject. He would rather answer as to a state
of the case which will never arise than commit
himself by telling what he would do in a case
which would come up for his action soon after
his election to Congress. Why can he not say
whether he is willing to allow the people of

each State to have slavery or not, as they please, and to come into the Union when they have the requisite population as a slave or a free State, as they decide? I have no trouble in answering the question. I have said everywhere, and now repeat to you, that if the people of Kansas want a slave State they have a right, under the Constitution of the United States, to form such a State, and I will let them come into the Union with slavery or without it, as they determine. If the people of any other Territory desire slavery, let them have it. If they do not want it, let them prohibit it. It is their business, not mine. It is none of our business in Illinois whether Kansas is a free State or a slave State. It is none of your business in Missouri whether Kansas shall adopt slavery or reject it. It is the business of her people, and none of yours. The people of Kansas have as much right to decide that question for themselves as you have in Missouri to decide it for yourselves, or we in Illinois to decide it for ourselves.

And here I may repeat what I have said in every speech I have made in Illinois, that I fought the Lecompton constitution to its death, not because of the slavery clause in it, but because it was not the act and deed of the people of Kansas. I said then in Congress, and I say now, that if the people of Kansas want a slave

State, they have a right to have it. If they
wanted the Lecompton constitution, they had
a right to have it. I was opposed to that constitution because I did not believe that it was
the act and deed of the people, but, on the contrary, the act of a small, pitiful minority, acting
in the name of the majority. When at last it
was determined to send that constitution back
to the people, and accordingly, in August last,
the question of admission under it was submitted to a popular vote, the citizens rejected it
by nearly ten to one, thus showing conclusively
that I was right when I said that the Lecompton constitution was not the act and deed of the
people of Kansas, and did not embody their
will.

I hold that there is no power on earth, under
our system of government, which has the right
to force a constitution upon an unwilling people. Suppose that there had been a majority
of ten to one in favor of slavery in Kansas, and
suppose there had been an Abolition President,
and an Abolition administration, and by some
means the Abolitionists succeeded in forcing an
Abolition constitution on those slave-holding
people, would the people of the South have submitted to that act for one instant? Well, if you
of the South would not have submitted to it a
day, how can you, as fair, honorable, and honest

men, insist on putting a slave constitution on a
people who desire a free State? Your safety
and ours depend upon both of us acting in good
faith, and living up to that great principle
which asserts the right of every people to form
and regulate their domestic institutions to suit
themselves, subject only to the Constitution of
the United States.

Most of the men who denounced my course
on the Lecompton question objected to it not
because I was not right, but because they thought
it expedient at that time, for the sake of keeping the party together, to do wrong. I never
knew the Democratic party to violate any one
of its principles out of policy or expediency,
that it did not pay the debt with sorrow. There
is no safety or success for our party unless we
always do right, and trust the consequences to
God and the people. I chose not to depart from
principle for the sake of expediency in the Lecompton question, and I never intend to do it
on that or any other question.

But I am told that I would have been all right
if I had only voted for the English bill after
Lecompton was killed. You know a general
pardon was granted to all political offenders on
the Lecompton question, provided they would
only vote for the English bill. I did not accept
the benefits of that pardon, for the reason that

I had been right in the course I had pursued, and hence did not require any forgiveness. Let us see how the result has been worked out. English brought in his bill referring the Lecompton constitution back to the people, with the provision that if it was rejected Kansas should be kept out of the Union until she had the full ratio of population required for a member of Congress, thus in effect declaring that if the people of Kansas would only consent to come into the Union under the Lecompton constitution, and have a slave State when they did not want it, they should be admitted with a population of 35,000; but that if they were so obstinate as to insist upon having just such a constitution as they thought best, and to desire admission as a free State, then they should be kept out until they had 93,420 inhabitants.

I then said, and I now repeat to you, that whenever Kansas has people enough for a slave State she has people enough for a free State. I was, and am, willing to adopt the rule that no State shall ever come into the Union until she has the full ratio of population for a member of Congress, provided that rule is made uniform.

I made that proposition in the Senate last winter, but a majority of the senators would not agree to it; and I then said to them, "If you will not adopt the general rule, I will not consent to make an exception of Kansas."

I hold that it is a violation of the fundamental principles of this government to throw the weight of federal power into the scale, either in favor of the free or the slave States. Equality among all the States of this Union is a fundamental principle in our political system. We have no more right to throw the weight of the Federal Government into the scale in favor of the slave-holding than of the free States, and, least of all, should our friends in the South consent for a moment that Congress should withhold its powers either way when they know that there is a majority against them in both houses of Congress.

Fellow-citizens, how have the supporters of the English bill stood up to their pledges not to admit Kansas until she obtained a population of 93,420 in the event she rejected the Lecompton constitution? How? The newspapers inform us that English himself, whilst conducting his canvass for reëlection, and in order to secure it, pledged himself to his constituents that if returned he would disregard his own bill and vote to admit Kansas into the Union with such population as she hight have when she made application. We are informed that every Democratic candidate for Congress in all the

States where elections have recently been held was pledged against the English bill, with perhaps one or two exceptions. Now, if I had only done as these anti-Lecompton men who voted for the English bill in Congress, pledging themselves to refuse to admit Kansas if she refused to become a slave State until she had a population of 93,420, and then returned to their people, forfeited their pledge, and made a new pledge to admit Kansas any time she applied, without regard to population, I would have had no trouble. You saw the whole power and patronage of the Federal Government wielded in Indiana, Ohio, and Pennsylvania to elect anti-Lecompton men to Congress, who voted against Lecompton, then voted for the English bill, and then denounced the English bill, and pledged themselves to their people to disregard it. My sin consists in not having given a pledge, and then in not having afterward forfeited it. For that reason, in this State, every postmaster, every route agent, every collector of the ports, and every federal office-holder, forfeits his head the moment he expresses a preference for the Democratic candidates against Lincoln and his Abolition associates. A Democratic administration, which we helped to bring into power, deems it consistent with its fidelity to principle, and its regard to duty, to wield its power in this

State in behalf of the Republican Abolition candidates in every county and every congressional district against the Democratic party. All I have to say in reference to the matter is that if that administration have not regard enough for principle, if they are not sufficiently attached to the creed of the Democratic party to bury forever their personal hostilities in order to succeed in carrying out our glorious principles, I have. I have no personal difficulty with Mr. Buchanan or his cabinet. He chose to make certain recommendations to Congress, as he had a right to do, on the Lecompton question. I could not vote in favor of them. I had as much right to judge for myself how I should vote as he had how he should recommend. He undertook to say to me, "If you do not vote as I tell you, I will take off the heads of your friends." I replied to him, "You did not elect me; I represent Illinois, and I am accountable to Illinois, as my constituency, and to God, but not to the President or to any other power on earth."

And now this warfare is made on me because I would not surrender my convictions of duty, because I would not abandon my constituency, and receive the orders of the executive authorities how I should vote in the Senate of the United States. I hold that an attempt to control the Senate on the part of the executive is subversive of the principles of our Constitution. The executive department is independent of the Senate, and the Senate is independent of the President. In matters of legislation the President has a veto on the action of the Senate, and in appointments and treaties the Senate has a veto on the President. He has no more right to tell me how I shall vote on his appointments than I have to tell him whether he shall veto or approve a bill that the Senate has passed. Whenever you recognize the right of the executive to say to a senator, "Do this, or I will take off the heads of your friends," you convert this government from a republic into a despotism. Whenever you recognize the right of a President to say to a member of Congress, "Vote as I tell you, or I will bring a power to bear against you at home which will crush you," you destroy the independence of the representative, and convert him into a tool of executive power. I resisted this invasion of the constitutional rights of a senator, and I intend to resist it as long as I have a voice to speak, or a vote to give. Yet Mr. Buchanan cannot provoke me to abandon one iota of Democratic principles out of revenge or hostility to his course. I stand by the platform of the Democratic party, and by its organization, and support its nominees. If there are any who choose to bolt, the fact only shows that they are not as good Democrats as I am.

My friends, there never was a time when it was as important for the Democratic party, for all national men, to rally and stand together as it is to-day. We find all sectional men giving up past differences and uniting on the one question of slavery, and when we find sectional men thus uniting, we should unite to resist them and their treasonable designs. Such was the case in 1850, when Clay left the quiet and peace of his home, and again entered upon public life to quell agitation and restore peace to a distracted Union. Then we Democrats, with Cass at our head, welcomed Henry Clay, whom the whole nation regarded as having been preserved by God for the times. He became our leader in that great fight, and we rallied around him the same as the Whigs rallied around Old Hickory in 1832 to put down nullification. Thus you see that while Whigs and Democrats fought fearlessly in old times about banks, the tariff, distribution, the specie circular, and the subtreasury, all united as a band of brothers when the peace, harmony, or integrity of the Union was imperiled. It was so in 1850, when Abolitionism had even so far divided this country, North and South, as to endanger the peace of the Union. Whigs and Democrats united in

establishing the compromise measures of that
year, and restoring tranquillity and good feeling. These measures passed on the joint action
of the two parties. They rested on the great
principle that the people of each State and each
Territory should be left perfectly free to form
and regulate their domestic institutions to suit
themselves. You Whigs and we Democrats
justified them in that principle. In 1854, when
it became necessary to organize the Territories
of Kansas and Nebraska, I brought forward the
bill on the same principle. In the Kansas-Nebraska bill you find it declared to be the true
intent and meaning of the act not to legislate
slavery into any State or Territory, nor to exclude it therefrom, but to leave the people thereof perfectly free to form and regulate their domestic institutions in their own way.

I stand on that same platform in 1858 that I
did in 1850, 1854, and 1856. The Washington
"Union," pretending to be the organ of the administration, in the number of the 5th of this
month, devotes three columns and a half to establish these propositions: first, that Douglas
in his Freeport speech held the same doctrine
that he did in his Nebraska bill in 1854; second, that in 1854 Douglas justified the Nebraska
bill upon the ground that it was based upon the
same principle as Clay's compromise measures

of 1850. The "Union" thus proved that Douglas was the same in 1858 that he was in 1856,
1854, and 1850, and consequently argued that
he was never a Democrat. Is it not funny that
I was never a Democrat? There is no pretense
that I have changed a hair's-breadth. The
"Union" proves by my speeches that I explained
the compromise measures of 1850 just as I do
now, and that I explained the Kansas and Nebraska bill in 1854 just as I did in my Freeport
speech, and yet says that I am not a Democrat,
and cannot be trusted, because I have not
changed during the whole of that time. It has
occurred to me that in 1854 the author of the
Kansas and Nebraska bill was considered a
pretty good Democrat. It has occurred to me
that in 1856, when I was exerting every nerve
and every energy for James Buchanan, standing
on the same platform then that I do now, that
I was a pretty good Democrat. They now tell
me that I am not a Democrat, because I assert
that the people of a Territory, as well as those
of a State, have the right to decide for themselves whether slavery can or cannot exist in
such Territory. Let me read what James Buchanan said on that point when he accepted the
Democratic nomination for the presidency in
1856. In his letter of acceptance, he used the
following language:

The recent legislation of Congress respecting domestic slavery, derived as it has been from the original and pure fountain of legitimate political power, the will of the majority, promises ere long to allay the dangerous excitement. This legislation is founded upon principles as ancient as free government itself, and in accordance with them has simply declared that the people of a Territory, like those of a State, shall decide for themselves whether slavery shall or shall not exist within their limits.

Doctor Hope will there find my answer to the question he propounded to me before I commenced speaking. Of course no man will consider it an answer, who is outside of the Democratic organization, bolts Democratic nominations, and indirectly aids to put Abolitionists into power over Democrats. But whether Dr. Hope considers it an answer or not, every fairminded man will see that James Buchanan has answered the question, and has asserted that the people of a Territory, like those of a State, shall decide for themselves whether slavery shall or shall not exist within their limits. I answer specifically, if you want a further answer, and say that while under the decision of the Supreme Court, as recorded in the opinion of Chief Justice Taney, slaves are property like all other property, and can be carried into any Territory of the United States the same as any other description of property, yet when you get them there they are subject to the local law of the Territory just like all other property. You will find in a recent speech delivered by that able and eloquent statesman, Hon. Jefferson Davis, at Bangor, Maine, that he took the same view of this subject that I did in my Freeport speech. He there said:

If the inhabitants of any Territory should refuse to enact such laws and police regulations as would give security to their property or to his, it would be rendered more or less valueless in proportion to the difficulties of holding it without such protection. In the case of property in the labor of man, or what is usually called slave property, the insecurity would be so great that the owner could not ordinarily retain it. Therefore, though the right would remain, the remedy being withheld, it would follow that the owner would be practically debarred, by the circumstances of the case, from taking slave property into a Territory where the sense of the inhabitants was opposed to its introduction. So much for the oft-repeated fallacy of forcing slavery upon any community.

You will also find that the distinguished Speaker of the present House of Representatives, Hon. James L. Orr, construed the Kansas and Nebraska bill in this same way in 1856, and also that great intellect of the South, Alexander

H. Stephens, put the same construction upon it
in Congress that I did in my Freeport speech.
The whole South is rallying to the support of
the doctrine that if the people of a Territory
want slavery they have a right to have it, and if
they do not want it that no power on earth can
force it upon them. I hold that there is no
principle on earth more sacred to all the friends
of freedom than that which says that no institution, no law, no constitution, should be forced
on an unwilling people contrary to their wishes;
and I assert that the Kansas and Nebraska bill
contains that principle. It is the great principle contained in that bill. It is the principle
on which James Buchanan was made President.
Without that principle he never would have
been made President of the United States. I
will never violate or abandon that doctrine, if
I have to stand alone. I have resisted the blan-
dishments and threats of power on the one side,
and seduction on the other, and have stood immovably for that principle, fighting for it when
assailed by Northern mobs, or threatened by
Southern hostility. I have defended it against
the North and the South, and I will defend it
against whoever assails it, and I will follow it
wherever its logical conclusions lead me. I say
to you that there is but one hope, one safety for
this country, and that is to stand immovably by

that principle which declares the right of each
State and each Territory to decide these questions for themselves. This government was
founded on that principle, and must be administered in the same sense in which it was founded.

But the Abolition party really think that under the Declaration of Independence the negro
is equal to the white man, and that negro equality is an inalienable right conferred by the Almighty, and hence that all human laws in violation of it are null and void. With such men
it is no use for me to argue. I hold that the
signers of the Declaration of Independence had
no reference to negroes at all when they declared all men to be created equal. They did
not mean negroes, nor the savage Indians, nor
the Feejee Islanders, nor any other barbarous
race. They were speaking of white men. They
alluded to men of European birth and European descent—to white men, and to none others,
when they declared that doctrine. I hold that
this government was established on the white
basis. It was established by white men, for
the benefit of white men and their posterity forever, and should be administered by white men,
and none others. But it does not follow, by
any means, that merely because the negro is not
a citizen, and merely because he is not our equal,
that therefore he should be a slave. On the

contrary, it does follow that we ought to extend
to the negro race, and to all other dependent
races, all the rights, all the privileges, and all
the immunities which they can exercise con-
sistently with the safety of society. Humanity
requires that we should give them all those privileges; Christianity commands that we should
extend those privileges to them. The question
then arises, What are those privileges, and what
is the nature and extent of them? My answer
is that that is a question which each State must
answer for itself. We in Illinois have decided
it for ourselves. We tried slavery, kept it up
for twelve years, and finding that it was not
profitable, we abolished it for that reason, and
became a free State. We adopted in its stead
the policy that a negro in this State shall not
be a slave and shall not be a citizen. We have
a right to adopt that policy. For my part, I
think it is a wise and sound policy for us. You
in Missouri must judge for yourselves whether
it is a wise policy for you. If you choose to
follow our example, very good; if you reject
it, still well; it is your business, not ours. So
with Kentucky. Let Kentucky adopt a policy
to suit herself. If we do not like it, we will
keep away from it; and if she does not like ours,
let her stay at home, mind her own business,
and let us alone. If the people of all the States

will act on that great principle, and each State mind its own business, attend to its own affairs, take care of its own negroes, and not meddle with its neighbors, then there will be peace between the North and the South, the East and the West, throughout the whole Union. Why can we not thus have peace? Why should we thus allow a sectional party to agitate this country, to array the North against the South, and convert us into enemies instead of friends, merely that a few ambitious men may ride into power on a sectional hobby? How long is it since these ambitious Northern men wished for a sectional organization? Did any one of them dream of a sectional party as long as the North was the weaker section and the South the stronger? Then all were opposed to sectional parties. But the moment the North obtained the majority in the House and Senate by the admission of California, and could elect a President without the aid of Southern votes, that moment ambitious Northern men formed a scheme to excite the North against the South, and make the people be governed in their votes by geographical lines, thinking that the North, being the stronger section, would outvote the South, and consequently they, the leaders, would ride into office on a sectional hobby. I am told that my hour is out. It was very short.

Mr. Lincoln's Reply in the Alton Joint Debate.

LADIES AND GENTLEMEN: I have been somewhat, in my own mind, complimented by a large portion of Judge Douglas's speech—I mean that portion which he devotes to the controversy between himself and the present administration. This is the seventh time Judge Douglas and myself have met in these joint discussions, and he has been gradually improving in regard to his war with the administration. At Quincy, day before yesterday, he was a little more severe upon the administration than I had heard him upon any occasion, and I took pains to compliment him for it. I then told him to "give it to them with all the power he had"; and as some of them were present, I told them I would be very much obliged if they would give it to him in about the same way. I take it that he has now vastly improved upon the attack he made then upon the administration. I flatter myself he has really taken my advice on this subject. All I can say now is to re-commend to him and to them what I then commended—to prosecute the war against one another in the most vigorous manner. I say to them again, "Go it, husband; go it, bear!"

There is one other thing I will mention before I leave this branch of the discussion—although I do not consider it much of my business, anyway. I refer to that part of the judge's remarks where he undertakes to involve Mr. Buchanan in an inconsistency. He reads something from Mr. Buchanan, from which he undertakes to involve him in an inconsistency; and he gets something of a cheer for having done so. I would only remind the judge that while he is very valiantly fighting for the Nebraska bill and the repeal of the Missouri Compromise, it has been but a little while since he was the valiant advocate of the Missouri Compromise. I want to know if Buchanan has not as much right to be inconsistent as Douglas has? Has Douglas the exclusive right in this country of being on all sides of all questions? Is nobody allowed that high privilege but himself? Is he to have an entire monopoly on that subject?

So far as Judge Douglas addressed his speech to me, or so far as it was about me, it is my business to pay some attention to it. I have heard the judge state two or three times what he has stated to-day—that in a speech which I made at Springfield, Illinois, I had in a very especial manner complained that the Supreme

Court in the Dred Scott case had decided that
a negro could never be a citizen of the United
States. I have omitted, by some accident, heretofore to analyze this statement, and it is required of me to notice it now. In point of fact
it is untrue. I never have complained especially of the Dred Scott decision, because it
held that a negro could not be a citizen, and
the judge is always wrong when he says I ever
did so complain of it. I have the speech here,
and I will thank him or any of his friends to
show where I said that a negro should be a
citizen, and complained especially of the Dred
Scott decision because it declared he could not
be one. I have done no such thing, and Judge
Douglas so persistently insisting that I have
done so has strongly impressed me with the belief of a predetermination on his part to mis-
represent me. He could not get his foundation
for insisting that I was in favor of this negro
equality anywhere else as well as he could by
assuming that untrue proposition. Let me tell
this audience what is true in regard to that matter; and the means by which they may correct
me if I do not tell them truly is by a recurrence
to the speech itself. I spoke of the Dred Scott
decision in my Springfield speech, and I was
then endeavoring to prove that the Dred Scott
decision was a portion of a system or scheme to

make slavery national in this country. I pointed out what things had been decided by the
court. I mentioned as a fact that they had decided that a negro could not be a citizen—that
they had done so, as I supposed, to deprive the
negro, under all circumstances, of the remotest
possibility of ever becoming a citizen and claiming the rights of a citizen of the United States
under a certain clause of the Constitution. I
stated that, without making any complaint of
it at all. I then went on and stated the other
points decided in the case,—namely, that the
bringing of a negro into the State of Illinois,
and holding him in slavery for two years here,
was a matter in regard to which they would
not decide whether it would make him free or
not; that they decided the further point that
taking him into a United States Territroy where
slavery was prohibited by act of Congress, did
not make him free, because that act of Congress, as they held, was unconstitutional. I mentioned these three things as making up the points
decided in that case. I mentioned them in a
lump taken in connection with the introduction
of the Nebraska bill, and the amendment of
Chase, offered at the time, declaratory of the
right of the people of the Territories to exclude
slavery, which was voted down by the friends
of the bill. I mentioned all these things to-

gether, as evidence tending to prove a combination and conspiracy to make the institution of slavery national.   In that connection and in that way I mentioned the decision on the point that a negro could not be a citizen, and in no other connection.

Out of this, Judge Douglas builds up his beautiful fabrication—of my purpose to introduce a perfect social and political equality between the white and the black races. His assertion that I made an "especial objection" (that is his exact language) to the decision on this account, is untrue in point of fact.

Now, while I am upon this subject, and as Henry Clay has been alluded to, I desire to place myself, in connection with Mr. Clay, as nearly right before this people as may be. I am quite aware what the judge's object is here by all these allusions. He knows that we are before an audience having strong sympathies southward by relationship, place of birth, and so on. He desires to place me in an extremely Abolition attitude. He read upon a former occasion, and alludes without reading to-day, to a portion of a speech which I delivered in Chicago. In his quotations from that speech, as he has made them upon former occasions, the extracts were taken in such a way as, I suppose, brings them within the definition of what is

called garbling—taking portions of a speech
which, when taken by themselves, do not present the entire sense of the speaker as expressed
at the time. I propose, therefore, out of that
same speech, to show how one portion of it
which he skipped over (taking an extract before
and an extract after) will give a different idea,
and the true idea I intended to convey. It will
take me some little time to read it, but I believe
I will occupy the time that way.

You have heard him frequently allude to my
controversy with him in regard to the Declaration of Independence. I confess that I have
had a struggle with Judge Douglas on that matter, and I will try briefly to place myself right
in regard to it on this occasion. I said—and
it is between the extracts Judge Douglas has
taken from this speech, and put in his published
speeches:

It may be argued that there are certain conditions
that make necessities and impose them upon us, and
to the extent that a necessity is imposed upon a man
he must submit to it. I think that was the condition in which we found ourselves when we established this government. We had slaves among us;
we could not get our Constitution unless we permitted them to remain in slavery; we could not secure
the good we did secure if we grasped for more: and
having by necessity submitted to that much, it does

not destroy the principle that is the charter of our liberties.   Let that charter remain as our standard.

Now I have upon all occasions declared as strongly as Judge Douglas against the disposition to interfere with the existing institution of slavery.   You hear me read it from the same speech from which he takes garbled extracts for the purpose of proving upon me a disposition to interfere with the institution of slavery, and establish a perfect social and political equality between negroes and white people.

Allow me, while upon this subject, briefly to present one other extract from a speech of mine, made more than a year ago, at Springfield, in discussing this very same question, soon after Judge Douglas took his ground that negroes were not included in the Declaration of Independence:

I think the authors of that notable instrument intended to include all men, but they did not intend to declare all men equal in all respects.   They did not mean to say that all men were equal in color, size, intellect, moral development, or social capacity. They defined with tolerable distinctness in what respects they did consider all men created equal — equal in certain inalienable rights, among which are life, liberty, and the pursuit of happiness.   This they said, and this they meant.   They did not mean to

assert the obvious untruth, that all were then actually
enjoying that equality, nor yet that they were about
to confer it immediately upon them.   In fact, they
had no power to confer such a boon.   They meant
simply to declare the right, so that the enforcement of
it might follow as fast as circumstances should permit.

They meant to set up a standard maxim for free
society which should be familiar to all and revered
by all — constantly looked to, constantly labored for,
and even, though never perfectly attained, constantly
approximated; and thereby constantly spreading and
deepening its influence and augmenting the happiness
and value of life to all people, of all colors, everywhere.

There, again, are the sentiments I have expressed in regard to the Declaration of Independence upon a former occasion—sentiments
which have been put in print and read wherever
anybody cared to know what so humble an individual as myself chose to say in regard to it.

At Galesburg the other day, I said, in answer
to Judge Douglas, that three years ago there
never had been a man, so far as I knew or believed, in the whole world, who had said that
the Declaration of Independence did not include negroes in the term "all men."   I reas-
sert it to-day.   I assert that Judge Douglas and
all his friends may search the whole records of

the country, and it will be a matter of great astonishment to me if they shall be able to find that one human being three years ago had ever uttered the astounding sentiment that the term "all men" in the Declaration did not include the negro. Do not let me be misunderstood. I know that more than three years ago there were men who, finding this assertion constantly in the way of their schemes to bring about the ascendancy and perpetuation of slavery, denied the truth of it. I know that Mr. Calhoun and all the politicians of his school denied the truth of the Declaration. I know that it ran along in the mouth of some Southern men for a period of years, ending at last in that shameful though rather forcible declaration of Pettit of Indiana, upon the floor of the United States Senate, that the Declaration of Independence was in that respect "a self-evident lie," rather than a self-evident truth. But I say, with a perfect knowledge of all this hawking at the Declaration without directly attacking it, that three years ago there never had lived a man who had ventured to assail it in the sneaking way of pretending to believe it and then asserting it did not include the negro. I believe the first man who ever said it was Chief Justice Taney in the Dred Scott case, and the next to him was our friend, Stephen A. Douglas. And now it has become the catchword of the entire party. I would like to call upon his friends everywhere, to consider how they have come in so short a time to view this matter in a way so entirely different from their former belief; to ask whether they are not being borne along by an irresistible current— whither, they know not.

In answer to my proposition at Galesburg last week, I see that some man in Chicago has got up a letter addressed to the Chicago "Times," to show, as he professes, that somebody had said so before; and he signs himself "An Old-Line Whig," if I remember correctly. In the first place I would say he was not an old-line Whig. I am somewhat acquainted with the old-line Whigs. I was with the old-line Whigs from the origin to the end of that party; I became pretty well acquainted with them, and I know they always had some sense, whatever else you could ascribe to them. I know there never was one who had not more sense than to try to show by the evidence he produces that some man had, prior to the time I named, said that negroes were not included in the term "all men" in the Declaration of Independence. What is the evidence he produces? I will bring forward his evidence, and let you see what he offers by way of showing that somebody more than three years ago had said negroes were not in-

cluded in the Declaration. He brings forward
part of a speech from Henry Clay—the part of
the speech of Henry Clay which I used to bring
forward to prove precisely the contrary. I
guess we are surrounded to some extent to-day
by the old friends of Mr. Clay, and they will
be glad to hear anything from that authority.
While he was in Indiana a man presented a
petition to liberate his negroes, and he (Mr.
Clay) made a speech in answer to it, which I
suppose he carefully wrote himself and caused
to be published. I have before me an extract
from that speech which constitutes the evidence
this pretended "Old-Line Whig" at Chicago
brought forward to show that Mr. Clay didn't
suppose the negro was included in the Declaration of Independence. Hear what Mr. Clay
said:

And what is the foundation of this appeal to me
in Indiana, to liberate the slaves under my care in
Kentucky? It is a general declaration in the act
announcing to the world the independence of the
thirteen American colonies, that all men are created
equal. Now, as an abstract principle, there is no
doubt of the truth of that declaration; and it is desirable, in the original construction of society, and
in organized societies, to keep it in view as a great
fundamental principle. But then I apprehend that
in no society that ever did exist, or ever shall be

formed, was or can the equality asserted among the members of the human race be practically enforced and carried out.   There are portions, large portions, — women, minors, insane, culprits, transient so-journers,— that will always probably remain subject to the government of another portion of the com-munity.

That declaration, whatever may be the extent of its import, was made by the delegations of the thir-teen States.   In most of them slavery existed, and had long existed, and was established by law.   It was introduced and forced upon the colonies by the paramount law of England.   Do you believe that in making that declaration the States that concurred in it intended that it should be tortured into a virtual emancipation of all the slaves within their respective limits?   Would Virginia and other Southern States have ever united in a declaration which was to be interpreted into an abolition of slavery among them? Did any one of the thirteen colonies entertain such a design or expectation?   To impute such a secret and unavowed purpose would be to charge a political fraud upon the noblest band of patriots that ever assembled in council — a fraud upon the confederacy of the Revolution — a fraud upon the union of those States whose constitution not only recognized the lawfulness of slavery, but permitted the importation of slaves from Africa until the year 1808.

This is the entire quotation brought forward to prove that somebody previous to three years

ago had said the negro was not included in the
term "all men" in the Declaration. How does
it do so? In what way has it a tendency to
prove that? Mr. Clay says it is true as an abstract principle that all men are created equal,
but that we cannot practically apply it in all
cases. He illustrates this by bringing forward
the cases of females, minors, and insane persons, with whom it cannot be enforced; but he
says that it is true as an abstract principle in the
organization of society, as well as in organized
society, and it should be kept in view as a fundamental principle. Let me read a few words
more before I add some comments of my own.
Mr. Clay says a little further on:

I desire no concealment of my opinions in regard
to the institution of slavery. I look upon it as a
great evil, and deeply lament that we have derived
it from the parent government, and from our ancestors. I wish every slave in the United States was
in the country of his ancestors. But here they are,
and the question is, how can they be best dealt with?
If a state of nature existed, and we were about to
lay the foundations of society, no man would be more
strongly opposed than I should be, to incorporating
the institution of slavery among its elements.

Now, here in this same book—in this same
speech—in this same extract brought forward

to prove that Mr. Clay held that the negro was
not included in the Declaration of Independence—we find no such statement on his part,
but instead the declaration that it is a great
fundamental truth, which should be constantly
kept in view in the organization of society and
in societies already organized. But if I say a
word about it; if I attempt, as Mr. Clay said
all good men ought to do, to keep it in view; if,
in this "organized society," I ask to have the
public eye turned upon it; if I ask, in relation to the organization of new Territories, that
the public eye should be turned upon it,—forthwith I am vilified as you hear me to-day. What
have I done that I have not the license of Henry
Clay's illustrious example here in doing? Have
I done aught that I have not his authority for,
while maintaining that in organizing new Territories and societies, this fundamental principle should be regarded, and in organized society holding it up to the public view and recognizing what he recognized as the great principle of free government?

And when this new principle—this new
proposition that no human being ever thought
of three years ago—is brought forward, I combat it as having an evil tendency, if not an evil
design. I combat it as having a tendency to
dehumanize the negro—to take away from him

the right of ever striving to be a man. I combat it as being one of the thousand things constantly done in these days to prepare the public
mind to make property, and nothing but property, of the negro in all the States in this Union.

But there is a point that I wish, before leaving this part of the discussion, to ask attention
to. I have read, and I repeat, the words of
Henry Clay:

I desire no concealment of my opinions in regard
to the institution of slavery. I look upon it as a
great evil, and deeply lament that we have derived
it from the parent government, and from our ancestors. I wish every slave in the United States was
in the country of his ancestors. But here they are,
and the question is, how can they best be dealt with?
If a state of nature existed, and we were about to lay
the foundations of society, no man would be more
strongly opposed than I should be, to incorporating
the institution of slavery among its elements.

The principle upon which I have insisted in
this canvass, is in relation to laying the foundations of new societies. I have never sought to
apply these principles to the old States for the
purpose of abolishing slavery in those States.
It is nothing but a miserable perversion of what
I have said, to assume that I have declared Missouri, or any other slave State, shall emancipate

her slaves. I have proposed no such thing. But when Mr. Clay says that in laying the foundations of societies in our Territories where it does not exist, he would be opposed to the introduction of slavery as an element, I insist that we have his warrant—his license for insisting upon the exclusion of that element which he declared in such strong and emphatic language was most hateful to him.

Judge Douglas has again referred to a Springfield speech in which I said, "A house divided against itself cannot stand." The judge has so often made the entire quotation from that speech that I can make it from memory. I used this language:

We are now far into the fifth year since a policy was initiated with the avowed object and confident promise of putting an end to the slavery agitation. Under the operation of this policy, that agitation has not only not ceased, but has constantly augmented. In my opinion it will not cease until a crisis shall have been reached and passed. "A house divided against itself cannot stand." I believe this government cannot endure permanently half slave and half free. I do not expect the house to fall — but I do expect it will cease to be divided. It will become all one thing, or all the other. Either the opponents of slavery will arrest the further spread of it, and place it where the public mind shall rest in the belief

that it is in the course of ultimate extinction, or its
advocates will push it forward till it shall become
alike lawful in all the States — old as well as new,
North as well as South.

That extract, and the sentiments expressed in
it, have been extremely offensive to Judge Douglas.   He has warred upon them as Satan wars
upon the Bible.   His perversions upon it are
endless.   Here now are my views upon it in
brief.

I said we were now far into the fifth year
since a policy was initiated with the avowed object and confident promise of putting an end to
the slavery agitation.   Is it not so?   When that
Nebraska bill was brought forward four years
ago last January, was it not for the "avowed object" of putting an end to the slavery agitation?
We were to have no more agitation in Congress; it was all to be banished to the Territories.
By the way, I will remark here that, as Judge
Douglas is very fond of complimenting Mr.
Crittenden in these days, Mr. Crittenden has
said there was a falsehood in that whole business, for there was no slavery agitation at that
time to allay.   We were for a little while quiet
on the troublesome thing, and that very allay-
ing-plaster of Judge Douglas's stirred it up
again.   But was it not undertaken or initiated
with the "confident promise" of putting an end

to the slavery agitation? Surely it was. In every speech you heard Judge Douglas make, until he got into this "imbroglio," as they call it, with the administration about the Lecompton constitution, every speech on that Nebraska bill was full of his felicitations that we were just at the end of the slavery agitation. The last tip of the last joint of the old serpent's tail was just drawing out of view. But has it proved so? I have asserted that under that policy that agitation "has not only ceased, but has constantly augmented." When was there ever a greater agitation in Congress than last winter? When was it as great in the country as to-day?

There was a collateral object in the introduction of that Nebraska policy which was to clothe the people of the Territories with a superior degree of self-government, beyond what they had ever had before. The first object and the main one of conferring upon the people a higher degree of self-government, is a question of fact to be determined by you in answer to a single question. Have you ever heard or known of a people anywhere on earth who had as little to do as, in the first instance of its use, the people of Kansas had with this same right of self-government? In its main policy and in its collateral object, it has been nothing but a living, creeping lie from the time of its introduction till to-day.

I have intimated that I thought the agitation
would not cease until a crisis should have been
reached and passed. I have stated in what way
I thought it would be reached and passed. I
have said that it might go one way or the other.
We might, by arresting the further spread of it,
and placing it where the fathers originally
placed it, put it where the public mind should
rest in the belief that it was in the course of ultimate extinction. Thus the agitation may cease.
It may be pushed forward until it shall become
alike lawful in all the States, old as well as new,
North as well as South. I have said, and I repeat, my wish is that the further spread of it
may be arrested, and that it may be placed where
the public mind shall rest in the belief that it is
in the course of ultimate extinction. I have expressed that as my wish. I entertain the opinion, upon evidence sufficient to my mind, that
the fathers of this government placed that institution where the public mind did rest in the
belief that it was in the course of ultimate extinction. Let me ask why they made provision
that the source of slavery—the African slave-
trade—should be cut off at the end of twenty
years? Why did they make provision that in
all the new territory we owned at that time,
slavery should be forever inhibited? Why stop
its spread in one direction and cut off its source

in another, if they did not look to its being placed in the course of ultimate extinction?

Again, the institution of slavery is only mentioned in the Constitution of the United States two or three times, and in neither of these cases does the word "slavery" or "negro race" occur; but covert language is used each time, and for a purpose full of significance. What is the language in regard to the prohibition of the African slave-trade? It runs in about this way: "The migration or importation of such persons as any of the States now existing shall think proper to admit, shall not be prohibited by the Congress prior to the year 1808."

The next allusion in the Constitution to the question of slavery and the black race, is on the subject of the basis of representation, and there the language used is: "Representatives and direct taxes shall be apportioned among the several States which may be included within this Union, according to their respective numbers, which shall be determined by adding to the whole number of free persons, including those bound to service for a term of years, and excluding Indians not taxed, three fifths of all other persons."

It says "persons," not slaves, not negroes; but this "three fifths" can be applied to no other class among us than the negroes.

Lastly, in the provision for the reclamation of fugitive slaves, it is said: "No person held to service or labor in one State, under the laws thereof, escaping into another, shall in consequence of any law or regulation therein be discharged from such service or labor, but shall be delivered up, on claim of the party to whom such service or labor may be due." There, again, there is no mention of the word "negro," or of slavery. In all three of these places, being the only allusion to slavery in the instrument, covert language is used. Language is used not suggesting that slavery existed or that the black race were among us. And I understand the contemporaneous history of those times to be that covert language was used with a purpose, and that purpose was that in our Constitution, which it was hoped, and is still hoped, will endure forever,—when it should be read by intelligent and patriotic men, after the institution of slavery had passed from among us,—there should be nothing on the face of the great charter of liberty suggesting that such a thing as negro slavery had ever existed among us.

This is part of the evidence that the fathers of the government expected and intended the institution of slavery to come to an end. They expected and intended that it should be in the

course of ultimate extinction. And when I say
that I desire to see the further spread of it arrested, I only say I desire to see that done which
the fathers have first done. When I say I desire to see it placed where the public mind will
rest in the belief that it is in the course of ultimate extinction, I only say I desire to see it
placed where they placed it. It is not true that
our fathers, as Judge Douglas assumes, made
this government part slave and part free. Understand the sense in which he puts it. He assumes that slavery is a rightful thing within itself—was introduced by the framers of the Constitution.

The exact truth is that they found the institution existing among us, and they left it as
they found it. But in making the government they left this institution with many clear
marks of disapprobation upon it. They found
slavery among them, and they left it among them
because of the difficulty — the absolute impossibility—of its immediate removal. And when
Judge Douglas asks me why we cannot let it
remain part slave and part free, as the fathers
of the government made it, he asks a question
based upon an assumption which is itself a falsehood; and I turn upon him and ask him the
question, when the policy that the fathers of the
government had adopted in relation to this ele-

ment among us was the best policy in the world,
—the only wise policy, the only policy that we
can ever safely continue upon, that will ever
give us peace, unless this dangerous element
masters us all and becomes a national institution,
—I turn upon him and ask him why he could
not leave it alone.   I turn and ask him why he
was driven to the necessity of introducing a new
policy in regard to it.   He has himself said
he introduced a new policy.   He said so in his
speech on the 22d of March of the present year,
1858.   I ask him why he could not let it remain
where our fathers placed it.   I ask, too, of
Judge Douglas and his friends, why we shall
not again place this institution upon the basis
on which the fathers left it?   I ask you, when
he infers that I am in favor of setting the free
and the slave States at war, when the institution
was placed in that attitude by those who made
the Constitution, did they make any war?   If
we had no war out of it when thus placed, where-
in is the ground of belief that we shall have war
out of it if we return to that policy?   Have we
had any peace upon this matter springing from
any other basis?   I maintain that we have not.
I have proposed nothing more than a return to
the policy of the fathers.

I confess, when I propose a certain measure
of policy, it is not enough for me that I do not

intend anything evil in the result, but it is incumbent on me to show that it has not a tendency to that result. I have met Judge Douglas in that point of view. I have not only made the declaration that I do not mean to produce a conflict between the States, but I have tried to show by fair reasoning, and I think I have shown to the minds of fair men, that I propose nothing but what has a most peaceful tendency. The quotation that I happened to make in that Springfield speech, that "a house divided against itself cannot stand," and which has proved so offensive to the judge, was part and parcel of the same thing. He tries to show that variety in the domestic institutions of the different States is necessary and indispensable. I do not dispute it. I have no controversy with Judge Douglas about that. I shall very readily agree with him that it would be foolish for us to insist upon having a cranberry law here, in Illinois, where he have no cranberries, because they have a cranberry law in Indiana, where they have cranberries. I should insist that it would be exceedingly wrong in us to deny to Virginia the right to enact oyster laws, where they have oysters, because we want no such laws here. I understand, I hope, quite as well as Judge Douglas, or anybody else, that the variety in the soil and climate and face of the country, and conse-

quent variety in the industrial pursuits and productions of a country, require systems of laws
conforming to this variety in the natural features
of the country. I understand quite as well as
Judge Douglas, that if we here raise a barrel of
flour more than we want, and the Louisianians
raise a barrel of sugar more than they want, it is
of mutual advantage to exchange. That produces commerce, brings us together, and makes
us better friends. We like one another the more
for it. And I understand as well as Judge Douglas, or anybody else, that these mutual accommodations are the cements which bind together the
different parts of this Union; that instead of
being a thing to "divide the house"—figuratively expressing the Union—they tend to sustain it; they are the props of the house tending
always to hold it up.

But when I have admitted all this, I ask if
there is any parallel between these things and
this institution of slavery? I do not see that
there is any parallel at all between them. Consider it. When have we had any difficulty
or quarrel amongst ourselves about the cranberry laws of Indiana, or the oyster laws of Virginia, or the pine-lumber laws of Maine, or the
fact that Louisiana produces sugar, and Illinois
flour? When have we had any quarrels over
these things? When have we had perfect peace

in regard to this thing which I say is an element
of discord in this Union? We have sometimes
had peace, but when was it? It was when the
institution of slavery remained quiet where it
was. We have had difficulty and turmoil whenever it has made a struggle to spread itself where
it was not. I ask, then, if experience does not
speak in thunder-tones, telling us that the policy
which has given peace to the country heretofore,
being returned to, gives the greatest promise
of peace again. You may say, and Judge Douglas has intimated the same thing, that all this
difficulty in regard to the institution of slavery
is the mere agitation of office-seekers and ambitious northern politicians. He thinks we want
to get "his place," I suppose. I agree that there
are office-seekers among us. The Bible says
somewhere that we are desperately selfish. I
think we would have discovered that fact without the Bible. I do not claim that I am any less
so than the average of men, but I do claim that
I am not more selfish than Judge Douglas.

But is it true that all the difficulty and agitation we have in regard to this institution of
slavery springs from office-seeking—from the
mere ambition of politicians? Is that the truth?
How many times have we had danger from this
question? Go back to the day of the Missouri
Compromise. Go back to the nullification

question, at the bottom of which lay this same slavery question. Go back to the time of the annexation of Texas. Go back to the troubles that led to the compromise of 1850. You will find that every time, with the single exception of the nullification question, they sprang from an endeavor to spread this institution. There never was a party in the history of this country, and there probably never will be, of sufficient strength to disturb the general peace of the country. Parties themselves may be divided and quarrel on minor questions, yet it extends not beyond the parties themselves. But does not this question make a disturbance outside of political circles? Does it not enter into the churches and rend them asunder? What divided the great Methodist Church into two parts, North and South? What has raised this constant disturbance in every Presbyterian general assembly that meets? What disturbed the Unitarian Church in this very city two years ago? What has jarred and shaken the great American Tract Society recently—not yet splitting it, but sure to divide it in the end? Is it not this same mighty, deepseated power that somehow operates on the minds of men, exciting and stirring them up in every avenue of society—in politics, in religion, in literature, in morals, in all the manifold relations of life? Is this the work of politicians? Is that irresistible power, which for fifty years has shaken the government and agitated the people, to be stilled and subdued by pretending that it is an exceedingly simple thing, and we ought not to talk about it? If you will get everybody else to stop talking about it, I assure you I will quit before they have half done so. But where is the philosophy or statesmanship which assumes that you can quiet that disturbing element in our society which has disturbed us for more than half a century, which has been the only serious danger that has threatened our institutions—I say, where is the philosophy or the statesmanship based on the assumption that we are to quit talking about it, and that the public mind is all at once to cease being agitated by it? Yet this is the policy here in the North that Douglas is advocating—that we are to care nothing about it! I ask you if it is not a false philosophy? Is it not a false statesmanship that undertakes to build up a system of policy upon the basis of caring nothing about the very thing that everybody does care the most about—a thing which all experience has shown we care a very great deal about?

The judge alludes very often in the course of his remarks to the exclusive right which the States have to decide the whole thing for themselves. I agree with him very readily that the

different States have that right.   He is but fighting a man of straw when he assumes that I am
contending against the rights of the States to do
as they please about it.   Our controversy with
him is in regard to the new Territories.   We
agree that when the States come in as States they
have the right and the power to do as they please.
We have no power as citizens of the free States,
or in our federal capacity as members of the
Federal Union through the General Government, to disturb slavery in the States where it
exists.   We profess constantly that we have no
more inclination than belief in the power of the
government to disturb it; yet we are driven constantly to defend ourselves from the assumption
that we are warring upon the rights of the States.
What I insist upon is, that the new Territories
shall be kept free from it while in the territorial
condition.   Judge Douglas assumes that we have
no interest in them—that we have no right whatever to interfere.   I think we have some interest.
I think that as white men we have.   Do we
wish for an outlet for our surplus population,
if I may so express myself?   Do we not feel an
interest in getting to that outlet with such institutions as we would like to have prevail there?
If you go to the Territory opposed to slavery,
and another man comes upon the same ground
with his slave, upon the assumption that the

things are equal, it turns out that he has the
equal right all his way, and you have no part of
it your way.   If he goes in and makes it a slave
Territory, and by consequence a slave State, is
it not time that those who desire to have it a
free State were on equal ground?   Let me suggest it in a different way.   How many Democrats are there about here ["A thousand"] who
have left slave States and come into the free
State of Illinois to get rid of the institution of
slavery? [Another voice: "A thousand and
one."]   I reckon there are a thousand and one.
I will ask you, if the policy you are now advocating had prevailed when this country was in
a territorial condition, where would you have
gone to get rid of it?   Where would you have
found your free State or Territory to go to?
And when hereafter, for any cause, the people
in this place shall desire to find new homes, if
they wish to be rid of the institution, where will
they find the place to go to?

Now, irrespective of the moral aspect of this
question as to whether there is a right or wrong
in enslaving a negro, I am still in favor of our
new Territories being in such a condition that
white men may find a home—may find some
spot where they can better their condition—
where they can settle upon new soil, and better
their condition in life.   I am in favor of this

not merely (I must say it here as I have elsewhere) for our own people who are born
amongst us, but as an outlet for free white people everywhere, the world over—in which Hans,
and Baptiste, and Patrick, and all other men
from all the world, may find new homes and
better their condition in life.

I have stated upon former occasions, and I
may as well state again, what I understand to be
the real issue of this controversy between Judge
Douglas and myself.   On the point of my wanting to make war between the free and the slave
States, there has been no issue between us.   So,
too, when he assumes that I am in favor of introducing a perfect social and political equality
between the white and black races.   These are
false issues, upon which Judge Douglas has tried
to force the controversy.   There is no foundation in truth for the charge that I maintain
either of these propositions.   The real issue in
this controversy—the one pressing upon every
mind—is the sentiment on the part of one class
that looks upon the institution of slavery as a
wrong, and of another class that does not look
upon it as a wrong.   The sentiment that con-
templates the institution of slavery in this country as a wrong is the sentiment of the Republican party.   It is the sentiment around which all
their actions, all their arguments, circle; from

which all their propositions radiate. They look
upon it as being a moral, social, and political
wrong; and while they contemplate it as such,
they nevertheless have due regard for its actual
existence among us, and the difficulties of getting rid of it in any satisfactory way, and to all
the constitutional obligations thrown about it.
Yet having a due regard for these, they desire
a policy in regard to it that looks to its not cre-
ating any more danger. They insist that it, as
far as may be, be treated as a wrong, and one of
the methods of treating it as a wrong is to make
provision that it shall grow no larger. They
also desire a policy that looks to a peaceful end
of slavery some time, as being a wrong. These
are the views they entertain in regard to it, as
I understand them; and all their sentiments, all
their arguments and propositions, are brought
within this range. I have said, and I repeat it
here, that if there be a man amongst us who does
not think that the institution of slavery is wrong
in any one of the aspects of which I have spoken,
he is misplaced, and ought not to be with us.
And if there be a man amongst us who is so impatient of it as a wrong as to disregard its actual
presence among us and the difficulty of getting
rid of it suddenly in a satisfactory way, and to
disregard the constitutional obligations thrown
about it, that man is misplaced if he is on our

platform. We disclaim sympathy with him in practical action. He is not placed properly with us.

On this subect of treating it as a wrong, and limiting its spread, let me say a word. Has anything ever threatened the existence of this Union save and except this very institution of slavery? What is it that we hold most dear amongst us? Our own liberty and prosperity. What has ever threatened our liberty and prosperity save and except this institution of slavery? If this is true, how do you propose to improve the condition of things by enlarging slavery— by spreading it out and making it bigger? You may have a wen or cancer upon your person, and not be able to cut it out lest you bleed to death; but surely it is no way to cure it, to engraft it and spread it over your whole body. That is no proper way of treating what you regard as a wrong. You see this peaceful way of dealing with it as a wrong—restricting the spread of it, and not allowing it to go into new countries where it has not already existed. That is the peaceful way, the old-fashioned way, the way in which the fathers themselves set us the example.

On the other hand, I have said there is a sentiment which treats it as not being wrong. That is the Democratic sentiment of this day. I do not mean to say that every man who stands within that range positively asserts that it is right. That class will include all who positively assert that it is right, and all who, like Judge Douglas, treat it as indifferent, and do not say it is either right or wrong. These two classes of men fall within the general class of those who do not look upon it as a wrong. And if there be among you anybody who supposes that he, as a Democrat, can consider himself "as much opposed to slavery as anybody," I would like to reason with him. You never treat it as a wrong. What other thing that you consider as a wrong do you deal with as you deal with that? Perhaps you say it is wrong, but your leader never does, and you quarrel with anybody who says it is wrong. Although you pretend to say so yourself, you can find no fit place to deal with it as a wrong. You must not say anything about it in the free States, because it is not here. You must not say anything about it in the slave States, because it is there. You must not say anything about it in the pulpit, because that is religion, and has nothing to do with it. You must not say anything about it in politics, because that will disturb the security of "my place." There is no place to talk about it as being a wrong, although you say yourself it is a wrong. But finally you will screw yourself up to the belief that if the people of the slave States should adopt a system of gradual emancipation on the slavery question, you would be in favor of it. You would be in favor of it! You say that is getting it in the right place, and you would be glad to see it succeed. But you are deceiving yourself. You all know that Frank Blair and Gratz Brown, down there in St. Louis, undertook to introduce that system in Missouri. They fought as valiantly as they could for the system of gradual emancipation which you pretend you would be glad to see succeed. Now I will bring you to the test. After a hard fight, they were beaten; and when the news came over here, you threw up your hats and hurrahed for Democracy. More than that, take all the argument made in favor of the system you have proposed, and it carefully excludes the idea that there is anything wrong in the institution of slavery. The arguments to sustain that policy carefully exclude it. Even here to-day you heard Judge Douglas quarrel with me because I uttered a wish that it might some time come to an end. Although Henry Clay could say he wished every slave in the United States was in the country of his ancestors, I am denounced by those pretending to respect Henry Clay, for uttering a wish that it might some time, in some peaceful way, come to an end.

The Democratic policy in regard to that institution will not tolerate the merest breath, the slightest hint, of the least degree of wrong about it. Try it by some of Judge Douglas's arguments. He says he "don't care whether it is voted up or voted down" in the Territories. I do not care myself, in dealing with that expression, whether it is intended to be expressive of his individual sentiments on the subject, or only of the national policy he desires to have established. It is alike valuable for my purpose. Any man can say that who does not see anything wrong in slavery, but no man can logically say it who does see a wrong in it; because no man can logically say he don't care whether a wrong is voted up or voted down. He may say he don't care whether an indifferent thing is voted up or down, but he must logically have a choice between a right thing and a wrong thing. He contends that whatever community wants slaves has a right to have them. So they have if it is not a wrong. But if it is a wrong, he cannot say people have a right to do wrong.

He says that, upon the score of equality, slaves should be allowed to go into a new Territory like other property. This is strictly logical if there is no difference between it and other property. If it and other property are equal, his argument is entirely logical. But if you insist that one is wrong and the other right, there is no use to institute a comparison between right and wrong. You may turn over everything in the Democratic policy from beginning to end, whether in the shape it takes on the statute-book, in the shape it takes in the Dred Scott decision, in the shape it takes in conversation, or the shape it takes in short maxim-like arguments—it everywhere carefully excludes the idea that there is anything wrong in it.

That is the real issue. That is the issue that will continue in this country when these poor tongues of Judge Douglas and myself shall be silent. It is the eternal struggle between these two principles—right and wrong—throughout the world. They are the two principles that have stood face to face from the beginning of time; and will ever continue to struggle. The one is the common right of humanity, and the other the divine right of kings. It is the same principle in whatever shape it develops itself. It is the same spirit that says, "You toil and work and earn bread, and I'll eat it." No matter in what shape it comes, whether from the mouth of a king who seeks to bestride the people of his own nation and live by the fruit of their labor, or from one race of men as an apology for enslaving another race, it is the same tyrannical principle. I was glad to express my gratitude at Quincy, and I reëxpress it here to Judge

Douglas—that he looks to no end of the institution of slavery. That will help the people to see where the struggle really is. It will hereafter place with us all men who really do wish the wrong may have an end. And whenever we can get rid of the fog which obscures the real question,—when we can get Judge Douglas and his friends to avow a policy looking to its perpetuation,—we can get out from among them that class of men and bring them to the side of those who treat it as a wrong. Then there will soon be an end of it, and that end will be its "ultimate extinction." Whenever the issue can be distinctly made, and all extraneous matter thrown out, so that men can fairly see the real difference between the parties, this controversy will soon be settled, and it will be done peaceably too. There will be no war, no violence. It will be placed again where the wisest and best men of the world placed it.

Brooks of South Carolina once declared that when this Constitution was framed, its framers did not look to the institution existing until this day. When he said this, I think he stated a fact that is fully borne out by the history of the times. But he also said they were better and wiser men than the men of these days; yet the men of these days had experience which they had not, and by the invention of the cotton-gin it became a necessity in this country that slavery should be perpetual. I now say that, willingly or unwillingly, purposely or without purpose, Judge Douglas has been the most prominent instrument in changing the position of the institution of slavery,—which the fathers of the government expected to come to an end 'ere this,—and putting it upon Brook's cotton-gin basis—placing it where he openly confesses he has no desire there shall ever be an end of it.

I understand I have ten minutes yet. I will employ it in saying something about this argument Judge Douglas uses, while he sustains the Dred Scott decision, that the people of the Territories can still somehow exclude slavery. The first thing I ask attention to is the fact that Judge Douglas constantly said, before the decision, that whether they could or not, was a question for the Supreme Court. But after the court has made the decision, he virtually says it is not a question for the Supreme Court, but for the people. And how is it he tells us they can exclude it? He says it needs "police regulations," and that admits of "unfriendly legislation." Although it is a right established by the Constitution of the United States to take a slave into a Territory of the United States and hold him as property, yet unless the territorial legislature will give friendly legislation, and, more especially, if they adopt unfriendly legislation, they can practically exclude him.   Now, without meeting this proposition as a matter of fact, I pass to consider the real constitutional obligation.   Let me take the gentleman who looks me in the face before me, and let us suppose that he is a member of the territorial legislature.   The first thing he will do will be to swear that he will support the Constitution of the United States.   His neighbor by his side in the Territory has slaves and needs territorial legislation to enable him to enjoy that constitutional right.   Can he withhold the legislation which his neighbor needs for the enjoyment of a right which is fixed in his favor in the Constitution of the United States which he has sworn to support?   Can he withhold it without violating his oath?   And more especially, can he pass unfriendly legislation to violate his oath?

Why, this is a monstrous sort of talk about the Constitution of the United States!   There has never been as outlandish or lawless a doctrine from the mouth of any respectable man on earth.   I do not believe it is a constitutional right to hold slaves in a Territory of the United States.   I believe the decision was improperly made, and I go for reversing it.   Judge Douglas is furious against those who go for reversing a decision.   But he is for legislating it

out of all force while the law itself stands. I
repeat that there has never been so monstrous a
doctrine uttered from the mouth of a respectable
man.

I suppose most of us (I know it of myself)
believe that the people of the Southern States
are entitled to a congressional fugitive-slave
law; that it is a right fixed in the Constitution.
But it cannot be made available to them without
congressional legislation. In the judge's language, it is a "barren right" which needs legislation before it can become efficient and valuable
to the persons to whom it is guaranteed. And,
as the right is constitutional, I agree that the
legislation shall be granted to it. Not that we
like the institution of slavery; we profess to have
no taste for running and catching negroes—at
least, I profess no taste for that job at all. Why
then do I yield support to a fugitive-slave law?
Because I do not understand that the Constitution, which guarantees that right, can be supported without it. And if I believed that the
right to hold a slave in a Territory was equally
fixed in the Constitution with the right to reclaim fugitives, I should be bound to give it the
legislation necessary to support it. I say that no
man can deny his obligation to give the necessary legislation to support slavery in a Territory,
who believes it is a constitutional right to have it

there. No man can, who does not give the Abolitionists an argument to deny the obligation enjoined by the Constitution to enact a fugitive-slave law. Try it now. It is the strongest Abolition argument ever made. I say, if that Dred Scott decision is correct, then the right to hold slaves in a Territory is equally a constitutional right with the right of a slaveholder to have his runaway returned. No one can show the distinction between them. The one is express, so that we cannot deny it; the other is construed to be in the Constitution, so that he who believes the decision to be correct believes in the right. And the man who argues that by unfriendly legislation, in spite of that constitutional right, slavery may be driven from the Territories, cannot avoid furnishing an argument by which Abolitionists may deny the obligation to return fugitives, and claim the power to pass laws unfriendly to the right of the slaveholder to reclaim his fugitive.

I do not know how such an argument may strike a popular assembly like this, but I defy anybody to go before a body of men whose minds are educated to estimating evidence and reasoning, and show that there is an iota of difference between the constitutional right to reclaim a fugitive, and the constitutional right to hold a slave, in a Territory, provided this Dred Scott decision is correct. I defy any man to make an

argument that will justify unfriendly legislation
to deprive a slaveholder of his right to hold his
slave in a Territory, that will not equally, in all
its length, breadth, and thickness, furnish an argument for nullifying the fugitive-slave law.
Why, there is not such an Abolitionist in the
nation as Douglas, after all.

Mr. Douglas's Rejoinder in the Alton Joint Debate.

MR. LINCOLN has concluded his remarks by saying that there is not such an Abolitionist as I am in all America. If he could make the Abolitionists of Illinois believe that, he would not have much show for the Senate. Let him make the Abolitionists believe the truth of that statement, and his political back is broken.

His first criticism upon me is the expression of his hope that the war of the administration will be prosecuted against me and the Democratic party of this State with vigor. He wants that war prosecuted with vigor; I have no doubt of it. His hopes of success, and the hopes of his party, depend solely upon it. They have no chance of destroying the Democracy of this State except by the aid of federal patronage. He has all the federal office-holders here as his allies, running separate tickets against the Democracy to divide the party, although the leaders all intend to vote directly the Abolition ticket, and only leave the greenhorns to vote this separate ticket who refuse to go into the Abolition

camp. There is something really refreshing in
the thought that Mr. Lincoln is in favor of prosecuting one war vigorously. It is the first war
I ever knew him to be in favor of prosecuting.
It is the first war that I ever knew him to believe
to be just or constitutional. When the Mexican
war was being waged, and the American army
was surrounded by the enemy in Mexico, he
thought the war was unconstitutional, unnecessary, and unjust. He thought it was not commenced on the right spot.

When I made an incidental allusion of that
kind in the joint discussion over at Charleston,
some weeks ago, Lincoln, in replying, said that
I, Douglas, had charged him with voting against
supplies for the Mexican war, and then he
reared up, full length, and swore that he never
voted against the supplies,—that it was a slander,—and caught hold of Ficklin, who sat on
the stand, and said, "Here, Ficklin, tell the people that it is a lie." Well, Ficklin, who had
served in Congress with him, stood up and told
them all he recollected about it. It was that
when George Ashmun, of Massachusetts,
brought forward a resolution declaring the war
unconstitutional, unnecessary, and unjust, Lincoln had voted for it. "Yes," said Lincoln, "I
did." Thus he confessed that he voted that the
war was wrong, that our country was in the

wrong, and consequently that the Mexicans were in the right; but charged that I had slandered him by saying that he voted against the supplies. I never charged him with voting against the supplies in my life, because I knew that he was not in Congress when they were voted. The war was commenced on the 13th day of May, 1846, and on that day we appropriated in Congress ten millions of dollars and fifty thousand men to prosecute it. During the same session we voted more men and more money, and at the next session we voted more men and more money, so that by the time Mr. Lincoln entered Congress we had enough men and enough money to carry on the war, and had no occasion to vote for any more. When he got into the House, being opposed to the war, and not being able to stop the supplies, because they had all gone forward, all he could do was to follow the lead of Corwin, and prove that the war was not begun on the right spot, and that it was unconstitutional, unnecessary and wrong. Remember, too, that this he did after the war had been begun. It is one thing to be opposed to the declaration of a war, another and very different thing to take sides with the enemy against your own country after the war has been commenced. Our army was in Mexico at the time, many battles had been fought; our citizens, who were defending the

honor of their country's flag, were surrounded
by the daggers, the guns, and the poison of the
enemy. Then it was that Corwin made his
speech in which he declared that the American
soldiers ought to be welcomed by the Mexicans
with bloody hands and hospitable graves; then it
was that Ashmun and Lincoln voted in the House
of Representatives that the war was unconstitutional and unjust; and Ashmun's resolution, Corwin's speech, and Lincoln's vote were sent to
Mexico and read at the head of the Mexican
army, to prove to them that there was a Mexican
party in the Congress of the United States who
were doing all in their power to aid them. That
a man who takes sides with the common enemy
against his own country in time of war should
rejoice in a war being made on me now, is very
natural. And in my opinion, no other kind of
a man would rejoice in it.

Mr. Lincoln has told you a great deal to-day
about his being an old-line Clay Whig. Bear
in mind that there are a great many old Clay
Whigs down in this region. It is more agreeable, therefore, for him to talk about the old
Clay Whig party than it is for him to talk Abolitionism. We did not hear much about the
old Clay Whig party up in the Abolition districts. How much of an old-line Henry Clay
Whig was he? Have you read General Single-

ton's speech at Jacksonville? You know that
General Singleton was, for twenty-five years, the
confidential friend of Henry Clay in Illinois,
and he testified that in 1847, when the constitutional convention of this State was in session,
the Whig members were invited to a Whig caucus at the house of Mr. Lincoln's brother-in-
law, where Mr. Lincoln proposed to throw Henry Clay overboard and take up General Taylor
in his place, giving, as his reason, that if the
Whigs did not take up General Taylor, the
Democrats would.

Singleton testifies that Lincoln, in that speech,
urged, as another reason for throwing Henry
Clay overboard, that the Whigs had fought
long enough for principle, and ought to begin
to fight for success. Singleton also testifies that
Lincoln's speech did have the effect of cutting Clay's throat, and that he (Singleton)
and others withdrew from the caucus in indignation. He further states that when they got
to Philadelphia to attend the national convention of the Whig party, that Lincoln was
there, the bitter and deadly enemy of Clay, and
that he tried to keep him (Singleton) out of the
convention because he insisted on voting for
Clay, and Lincoln was determined to have Taylor. Singleton says that Lincoln rejoiced with
very great joy when he found the mangled re-

mains of the murdered Whig statesman lying
cold before him.   Now Mr. Lincoln tells you
that he is an old-line Clay Whig!   General
Singleton testifies to the facts I have narrated,
in a public speech which has been printed and
circulated broadcast over the State for weeks,
yet not a lisp have we heard from Mr. Lincoln
on the subject, except that he is an old Clay
Whig.

What part of Henry Clay's policy did Lincoln
ever advocate?   He was in Congress in 1848-49,
when the Wilmot proviso warfare disturbed the
peace and harmony of the country, until it shook
the foundation of the republic from its center
to its circumference.   It was that agitation that
brought Clay forth from his retirement at Ash-
land again to occupy his seat in the Senate of
the United States, to see if he could not, by his
great wisdom and experience, and the renown
of his name, do something to restore peace
and quiet to a disturbed country.   Who got up
that sectional strife that Clay had to be called
upon to quell?   I have heard Lincoln boast that
he voted forty-two times for the Wilmot proviso,
and that he would have voted as many more
times if he could.   Lincoln is the man, in connection with Seward, Chase, Giddings, and
other Abolitionists, who got up that strife that
I helped Clay to put down.   Henry Clay came

back to the Senate in 1849, and saw that he must
do something to restore peace to the country.
The Union Whigs and the Union Democrats
welcomed him the moment he arrived, as the
man for the occasion. We believed that he, of
all men on earth, had been preserved by divine
providence to guide us out of our difficulties,
and we Democrats rallied under Clay then, as
you Whigs in nullification times rallied under
the banner of old Jackson, forgetting party
when the country was in danger, in order that
we might have a country first and parties afterward.

And this reminds me that Mr. Lincoln told
you that the slavery question was the only thing
that ever disturbed the peace and harmony of
the Union. Did not nullification once raise its
head and disturb the peace of this Union in
1832? Was that the slavery question, Mr. Lincoln? Did not disunion raise its monster head
during the last war with Great Britain? Was
that the slavery question, Mr. Lincoln? The
peace of this country has been disturbed three
times, once during the war with Great Britain,
once on the tariff question, and once on the slavery question. His argument, therefore, that
slavery is the only question that has ever created
dissention in the Union falls to the ground. It
is true that agitators are enabled now to use this

slavery question for the purpose of sectional strife. He admits that, in regard to all things else, the principle that I advocate, making each State and Territory free to decide for itself, ought to prevail. He instances the cranberry laws, and the oyster laws, and he might have gone through the whole list with the same effect. I say that all these laws are local and domestic, and that local and domestic concerns should be left to each State and Territory to manage for itself. If agitators would acquiesce in that principle, there never would be any danger to the peace and harmony of the Union.

Mr. Lincoln tries to avoid the main issue by attacking the truth of my proposition, that our fathers made this government divided into free and slave States, recognizing the right of each to decide all its local questions for itself. Did they not thus make it? It is true that they did not establish slavery in any of the States, or abolish it in any of them; but finding thirteen States, twelve of which were slave and one free, they agreed to form a government uniting them together, as they stood, divided into free and slave States, and to guarantee forever to each State the right to do as it pleased on the slavery question. Having thus made the government, and conferred this right upon each State forever, I assert that this government can exist as they made it, divided into free and slave States, if any one State choses to retain slavery. He says that he looks forward to a time when slavery shall be abolished everywhere. I look forward to the time when each State shall be allowed to do as it pleases. If it chooses to keep slavery forever, it is not my business, but its own; if it chooses to abolish slavery, it is its own business, not mine. I care more for the great principle of self-government, the right of the people to rule, than I do for all the negroes in Christendom. I would not endanger the perpetuity of this Union; I would not blot out the great inalienable rights of the white men for all the negroes that ever existed. Hence, I say, let us maintain this government on the principles on which our fathers made it, recognizing the right of each State to keep slavery as long as its people determine, or to abolish it when they please. But Mr. Lincoln says that when our fathers made this government they did not look forward to the state of things now existing, and therefore he thinks the doctrine was wrong; and he quotes Brooks, of South Carolina, to prove that our fathers then thought that probably slavery would be abolished by each State acting for itself before this time. Suppose they did; suppose they did not foresee what has occurred—does that change the principles of our govern-

ment? They did not probably foresee the tele-
graph that transmits intelligence by lightning;
nor did they foresee the railroads that now form
the bonds of union between the different States;
or the thousand mechanical inventions that have
elevated mankind. But do these things change
the principles of the government? Our fathers,
I say, made this government on the principle of
the right of each State to do as it pleases in its
own domestic affairs, subject to the Constitution, and allowed the people of each to apply
to every new change of circumstances such remedy as they may see fit to improve their condition.
This right they have for all time to come.

Mr. Lincoln went on to tell you that he does
not at all desire to interfere with slavery in the
States where it exists, nor does his party. I expected him to say that down here. Let me ask
him then how he expects to put slavery in the
course of ultimate extinction everywhere, if he
does not intend to interfere with it in the States
where it exists? He says that he will prohibit
it in all Territories, and the inference is, then,
that unless they make free States out of them he
will keep them out of the Union; for, mark you,
he did not say whether or not he would vote to
admit Kansas with slavery or not, as her people
might apply (he forgot that, as usual); he did
not say whether or not he was in favor of bring-

ing the Territories now in existence into the
Union on the principle of Clay's compromise
measures on the slavery question. I told you
that he would not.   His idea is that he will prohibit slavery in all the Territories, and thus force
them all to become free States, surrounding the
slave States with a cordon of free States and
hemming them in, keeping the slaves confined
to their present limits whilst they go on multiplying until the soil on which they live will
no longer feed them, and he will thus be able
to put slavery in a course of ultimate extinction
by starvation. He will extinguish slavery in
the Southern States as the French general extin-
guished the Algerines when he smoked them
out. He is going to extinguish slavery by surrounding the slave States, hemming in the slaves,
and starving them out of existence, as you smoke
a fox out of his hole. He intends to do that in
the name of humanity and Christianity, in order
that we may get rid of the terrible crime and
sin entailed upon our fathers of holding slaves.
Mr. Lincoln makes out that line of policy, and
appeals to the moral sense of justice and to the
Christian feeling of the community to sustain
him. He says that any man who holds to the
contrary doctrine is in the position of the king
who claimed to govern by divine right. Let
us examine for a moment and see what principle

it was that overthrew the divine right of George III. to govern us. Did not these colonies rebel because the British parliament had no right to pass laws concerning our property and domestic and private institutions without our consent? We demanded that the British government should not pass such laws unless they gave us representation in the body passing them—and this the British government insisting on doing, we went to war, on the principle that the home government should not control and govern distant colonies without giving them a representation. Now Mr. Lincoln proposes to govern the Territories without giving them a representation, and calls on Congress to pass laws controlling their property and domestic concerns without their consent and against their will. Thus he asserts for his party the identical principle asserted by George III. and the Tories of the Revolution.

I ask you to look into these things, and then tell me whether the Democracy or the Abolitionists are right. I hold the people of a Territory, like those of a State (I use the language of Mr. Buchanan in his letter of acceptance), have the right to decide for themselves whether slavery shall or shall not exist within their limits. The point upon which Chief Justice Taney expresses his opinion is simply this, that slaves, being property, stand on an equal footing with other property, and consequently that the owner has the same right to carry that property into a Territory that he has any other, subject to the same conditions. Suppose that one of your merchants was to take fifty or one hundred thousand dollars' worth of liquors to Kansas. He has a right to go there under that decision, but when he gets there he finds the Maine liquor-law in force, and what can he do with his property after he gets it there?   He cannot sell it, he cannot use it, it is subject to the local law, and that law is against him, and the best thing he can do with it is to bring it back into Missouri or Illinois and sell it.

If you take negroes to Kansas, as Colonel Jefferson Davis said in his Bangor speech, from which I have quoted to-day, you must take them there subject to the local law. If the people want the institution of slavery, they will protect and encourage it; but if they do not want it, they will withhold that protection, and the absence of local legislation protecting slavery excludes it as completely as a positive prohibition. You slaveholders of Missouri might as well understand what you know practically, that you cannot carry slavery where the people do not want it.   All you have a right to ask is that the people shall do as they please; if they want slavery, let them have it; if they do not want it, allow them to refuse to encourage it.

My friends, if, as I have said before, we will only live up to this great fundamental principle, there will be peace between the North and the South. Mr. Lincoln admits that under the Constitution, on all domestic questions except slavery, we ought not to interfere with the people of each State. What right have we to interfere with slavery any more than we have to interfere with any other question? He says that this slavery question is now the bone of contention. Why? Simply because agitators have combined in all the free States to make war upon it. Suppose the agitators in the States should combine in one half of the Union to make war upon the railroad system of the other half. They would thus be driven to the same sectional strife. Suppose one section makes war upon any other peculiar institution of the opposite section, and the same strife is produced. The only remedy and safety is that we shall stand by the Constitution as our fathers made it, obey the laws as they are passed, while they stand the proper test, and sustain the decisions of the Supreme Court and the constituted authorities.

FRAGMENT: OPINION ON ELECTION LAWS OF
ILLINOIS. [October 15?] 1858

It is made a question whether, under our laws,
a person offering to vote, and being challenged,
and having taken the oath prescribed by the act
of 1849, is then absolutely entitled to vote, or
whether his oath may be disproved, and his vote
thereon lawfully rejected. In Purple's Statutes,
Volume I, all our existing election laws are
brought together, commencing on page 514 and
extending to page 532. They consist of acts
and parts of acts passed at different times. The
true way of reading so much of the law as applies to the above question, is to first read (64)
section x, including the form of the oath on page
528. Then turn back and read (19) section xix,
on page 518. If it be said that the section last
mentioned is not now in force, turn forward to
(75) section xxi, on page 530, where it is expressly declared to be in force.

The result is that when a person has taken the
oath, his oath may still be proved to be false, and
his vote thereupon rejected. It may be proved
to be false by cross-examining the proposed voter
himself, or by any other person, or competent
testimony known to the general law of evidence.
On page 532 is an extract of a Supreme Court
decision on the very section xix, on page 518,

in which, among other things, the court says: "If such person takes the oath prescribed by law, the judges must receive his vote, unless the oath be proved false." Something of a definition of residence is therein given.

*LETTER TO JAMES N. BROWN [1]

SPRINGFIELD, October 18, 1858.

My dear Sir: I do not perceive how I can express myself, more plainly, than I have done in the foregoing extracts. In four of them I have expressly disclaimed all intentions to bring about social and political equality between the white and black races, and, in all the rest, I have done the same thing by clear implication.

I have made it equally plain that I think the negro is included in the word "men" used in the Declaration of Independence.

I believe the declaration that "all men are cre-

[1] This letter accompanied a little book from the hand of Lincoln, containing newspaper-clippings of portions of his speeches, compiled to aid Captain Brown in the campaign of 1858. Brown had been an Old-Line Whig and became a Lincoln Republican. Upon the change he found he needed something to refute the cry of "negro equality" brought against his new party, and for that purpose Lincoln put together the booklet. Lincoln further wrote: "The following extracts are taken from various speeches of mine delivered at various times and places; and I believe they contain the substance of all I have ever said about 'negro equality.' The first three are from my answer to Judge Douglas, Oct. 16, 1854, at Peoria."

ated equal" is the great fundamental principle upon which our free institutions rest; that negro slavery is violative of that principle; but that, by our form of government, that principle has not been made one of legal obligation; that by our form of government, the States which have slavery are to retain it, or surrender it at their own pleasure; and that all others—individuals, free-states and national government—are constitutionally bound to leave them alone about it.

I believe our government was thus framed because of the *necessity* springing from the actual presence of slavery, when it was framed.

That such necessity does not exist in the territories, where slavery is not present.

In his Mendenhall speech Mr. Clay says:

" Now, as an abstract principle, there is no doubt of the truth of that declaration (all men are created equal) and it is desirable, in the original construction of society, and in organized societies, to keep it in view as a great fundamental principle."

Again, in the same speech Mr. Clay says:

" If a state of nature existed, and we were about to lay the foundations of society, no man would be more strongly opposed than I would to incorporate the institutions of slavery among its elements."

Exactly so. In our new free territories, a state of nature *does* exist. In them Congress lays the foundations of society; and, in laying those foundations, I say, with Mr. Clay, it is desirable that the declaration of the equality of all men shall be kept in view, as a great fundamental principle; and that Congress, which lays the foundations of society, should, like Mr. Clay, be strongly opposed to the incorporation of slavery among its elements.

But it does not follow that social and political equality between white and black, *must* be incorporated, because slavery must *not*. The declaration does not so require.

Yours as ever,

A. LINCOLN.

*LETTER TO ALEXANDER SYMPSON

BLANDINSVILLE, October 26, 1858.

Dear Sir: Since parting with you this morning I heard some things which make me believe that Edmunds and Morrill will spend this week among the National Democrats trying to induce them to content themselves by voting for Jake Davis, and then to vote for the Douglas candidates for Senator and Representative. Have this headed off, if you can. Call Wagley's attention to it, and have him and the National Democrat for Rep. to counteract it as far as they can.   Yours as ever,

A. LINCOLN.

LETTER TO EDWARD LUSK

SPRINGFIELD, October 30, 1858.

Dear Sir: I understand the story is still being told and insisted upon that I have been a
Know-nothing. I repeat what I stated in a
public speech at Meredosia, that I am not, nor
ever have been, connected with the party called
the Know-nothing party, or party calling themselves the American party. Certainly no man
of truth, and I believe no man of good character
for truth, can be found to say on his own knowledge that I ever was connected with that party.

Yours very truly,

A. LINCOLN.

LETTER TO J. J. CRITTENDEN

SPRINGFIELD, November 4, 1858.

My dear Sir: Yours of the 27th was taken
from the office by my law partner, and in the
confusion consequent upon the recent election,
was handed to me only this moment. I am
sorry the allusion made in the "Missouri Republican" to the private correspondence between
yourself and me has given you any pain. It
gave me scarcely a thought, perhaps for the reason that, being away from home, I did not see
it until two days before the election. It never
occurred to me to cast any blame upon you. I

have been told that the correspondence has been alluded to in the "Missouri Republican" several times; but I only saw one of the allusions made, in which it was stated, as I remember, that a gentleman of St. Louis had seen a copy of your letter to me. As I have given no copy, nor ever shown the original, of course I inferred he had seen it in your hands; but it did not occur to me to blame you for showing what you had written yourself. It was not said that the gentleman had seen a copy, or the original, of my letter to you.

The emotions of defeat at the close of a struggle in which I felt more than a merely selfish interest, and to which defeat the use of your name contributed largely, are fresh upon me; but even in this mood I cannot for a moment suspect you of anything dishonorable.

Your obedient servant,
A. LINCOLN.

LETTER TO N. B. JUDD

SPRINGFIELD, November 15, 1858.

My dear Sir: I have the pleasure to inform you that I am convalescent, and hoping these lines may find you in the same improving state of health. Doubtless you have suspected for some time that I entertain a personal wish for a term in the United States Senate; and had the suspicion taken the shape of a direct charge, I think I could not have truthfully denied it. But let the past as nothing be.

For the future, my view is that the fight must go on. The returns here are not yet completed; but it is believed that Dougherty's vote will be slightly greater than Miller's majority over Tracy.

We have some hundred and twenty thousand clear Republican votes. That pile is worth keeping together. It will elect a State treasurer two years hence.

In that day I shall fight in the ranks, but I shall be in no one's way for any of the places. I am especially for Trumbull's reëlection; and, by the way, this brings me to the principal object of this letter. Can you not take your draft of an apportionment law, and carefully revise it till it shall be strictly and obviously just in all particulars, and then by an early and persistent effort get enough of the enemy's men to enable you to pass it? I believe if you and Peck make a job of it, begin early, and work earnestly and quietly, you can succeed in it. Unless something be done, Trumbull is eventually beaten two years hence. Take this into serious consideration.

Yours as ever,

A. LINCOLN.

LETTER TO N. B. JUDD

SPRINGFIELD, November 16, 1858.

Dear Sir: Yours of the 15th is just received. I wrote you the same day. As to the pecuniary matter, I am willing to pay according to my ability; but I am the poorest hand living to get others to pay.

I have been on expenses so long without earning anything that I am absolutely without money now for even household purposes. Still, if you can put in two hundred and fifty dollars for me toward discharging the debt of the committee, I will allow it when you and I settle the private matter between us.

This, with what I have already paid, and with an outstanding note of mine, will exceed my subscription of five hundred dollars. This, too, is exclusive of my ordinary expenses during the campaign, all of which being added to my loss of time and business, bears pretty heavily upon one no better off in [this] world's goods than I; but as I had the post of honor, it is not for me to be over nice. You are feeling badly,—"And this too shall pass away," never fear.

Yours as ever,

A. LINCOLN.

LETTER TO HENRY ASBURY

SPRINGFIELD, November 19, 1858.

Dear Sir: Yours of the 13th was received
some days ago. The fight must go on. The
cause of civil liberty must not be surrendered at
the end of one or even one hundred defeats.
Douglas had the ingenuity to be supported in
the late contest both as the best means to break
down and to uphold the slave interest. No ingenuity can keep these antagonistic elements in
harmony long. Another explosion will soon
come.   Yours truly,

A. LINCOLN.

LETTER TO A. G. HENRY

SPRINGFIELD, ILLINOIS, November 19, 1858.

My dear Sir: Yours of the 27th of September was received two days ago. I was at Oquaw-
ka, Henderson County, on the 9th of October;
and I may then have seen Major A. N. Arm-
strong; but having nothing then to fix my attention, I do not remember such a man. I have
concluded, as the best way of serving you, to
inclose your letter to E. A. Paine, Esq., of Mon-
mouth, Ill., a reliable lawyer, asking him to do
what you ask of me. If a suit is to be brought,
he will correspond directly with you.

You doubtless have seen ere this the result of the election here. Of course I wished, but I did not much expect, a better result. The popular vote of the State is with us; so that the seat in the

. . . .

(Lower portion of page cut off.)

. . . .

whole canvass. On the contrary, John and George Weber, and several such old Democrats, were furiously for me. As a general rule, out of Sangamon as well as in it, much of the plain old Democracy is with us, while nearly all the old exclusive silk-stocking Whiggery is against us. I don't mean nearly all the Old Whig party, but nearly all of the nice exclusive sort. And why not? There has been nothing in politics since the Revolution so congenial to their nature as the present position of the great Democratic party.

I am glad I made the late race. It gave me a hearing on the great and durable question of the age, which I could have had in no other way; and though I now sink out of view, and shall be forgotten, I believe I have made some marks which will tell for the cause of civil liberty long after I am gone. Mary joins me in sending our best wishes to Mrs. Henry and others of your family.

LETTER TO JOEL A. MATTESON

SPRINGFIELD, November 25, 1858.

Dear Sir: Last summer, when a movement was made in court against your road, you engaged us to be on your side. It has so happened that, so far, we have performed no service in the case; but we lost a cash fee offered us on the other side. Now, being hard run, we propose a little compromise. We will claim nothing for the matter just mentioned, if you will relieve us at once from the old matter at the Marine and Fire Insurance Company, and be greatly obliged to boot. Can you not do it?

Yours truly,

A. LINCOLN.

*LETTER TO H. D. SHARPE

SPRINGFIELD, December 8, 1858.

Dear Sir: Your very kind letter of November 9th was duly received. I do not know that you expected or desired an answer; but glancing over the contents of yours again, I am prompted to say that, while I desired the result of the late canvass to have been different, I still regard it as an exceeding small matter. I think we have fairly entered upon a durable struggle as to whether this nation is to ultimately become all slave or all free, and though I fall early in the contest, it is nothing if I shall have contributed, in the least degree, to the final rightful result.

Respectfully yours,
A. LINCOLN.

*LETTER TO ALEXANDER SYMPSON

SPRINGFIELD, December 12, 1858.

My dear Sir: I expect the result of the election went hard with you. So it did with me, too, perhaps not quite so hard as you may have supposed. I have an abiding faith that we shall beat them in the long run. Step by step the objects of the leaders will become too plain for the people to stand them. I write merely to let you know that I am neither dead nor dying. Please give my respects to your good family, and all inquiring friends.

Yours as ever,   A. LINCOLN.

*LEGAL OPINION, JANUARY 6, 1859

The 11th Section of the Act of Congress, approved Feb. 11, 1805, prescribing rules for the subdivision of Sections of land within the United States system of Surveys, standing unrepealed, in my opinion, is binding on the respective purchasers of different parts of the same section, and furnishes the true rule for Surveyors in establishing lines between them. That law, being in force at this time each became a purchaser, becomes a condition of the purchase.

And by that law, I think the true rule for dividing into quarters, any interior Section, or Sections, which is not fractional, is to run straight lines through the Section from the opposite quarter section corners, fixing the point where such straight lines cross, or intersect each other, as the middle or center of the Section.

Nearly, perhaps quite, all the original surveys are to some extent, erroneous, and in some of the Sections, greatly so. In each of the latter, it is obvious that a more equitable mode of division than the above, might be adopted; but as error is infinitely various perhaps no better single rules can be prescribed.

At all events I think the above has been prescribed by the competent authority.

A. Lincoln.

Springfield, Jany. 6, 1859.

Edwin M. Stanton

Wood Engraving from a Photograph.

LECTURE ON " DISCOVERIES, INVENTIONS, AND
IMPROVEMENTS" [FEBRUARY 22 ? 1859], DE-
LIVERED IN NEIGHBORING TOWNS IN 1859,
AND BEFORE THE SPRINGFIELD LIBRARY ASSO-
CIATION, SPRINGFIELD, ILLINOIS, FEBRUARY
22, 1860 [1]

WE have all heard of Young America.
He is the most current youth of the
age. Some think him conceited and
arrogant; but has he not reason to entertain a
rather extensive opinion of himself? Is he not
the inventor and owner of the present, and
sole hope of the future? Men and things,
everywhere, are ministering unto him. Look
at his apparel, and you shall see cotton fabrics
from Manchester and Lowell; flax linen from
Ireland; wool cloth from Spain; silk from
France; furs from the arctic region; with a
buffalo-robe from the Rocky Mountains, as
a general outsider. At his table, besides plain
bread and meat made at home, are sugar from
Louisiana, coffee and fruits from the tropics,
salt from Turk's Island, fish from Newfound-

[1] From autograph manuscript in the Lincoln Collection of
Charles F. Gunther, Esq., Chicago, Ill.— N. and H.

land, tea from China, and spices from the
Indies. The whale of the Pacific furnishes his
candle-light, he has a diamond ring from Bra-
zil, a gold watch from California, and a Span-
ish cigar from Havana. He not only has a
present supply of all these, and much more; but
thousands of hands are engaged in producing
fresh supplies, and other thousands in bringing
them to him. The iron horse is panting and impatient to carry him everywhere in no time; and
the lightning stands ready harnessed to take and
bring his tidings in a trifle less than no time.
He owns a large part of the world, by right of
possessing it, and all the rest by right of wanting
it, and intending to have it. As Plato had for
the immortality of the soul, so Young America
has "a pleasing hope, a fond desire—a longing
after" territory. He has a great passion—a perfect rage—for the "new"; particularly new men
for office, and the new earth mentioned in the
Revelations, in which, being no more sea, there
must be about three times as much land as in the
present. He is a great friend of humanity; and
his desire for land is not selfish, but merely an
impulse to extend the area of freedom. He is
very anxious to fight for the liberation of enslaved nations and colonies, provided, always,
they have land, and have not any liking for his
interference. As to those who have no land,

and would be glad of help from any quarter, he considers they can afford to wait a few hundred years longer.   In knowledge he is particularly rich.   He knows all that can possibly be known; inclines to believe in spiritual rappings, and is the unquestioned inventor of "Manifest Destiny."   His horror is for all that is old, particularly "Old Fogy"; and if there be anything old which he can endure, it is only old whisky and old tobacco.

If the said Young America really is, as he claims to be, the owner of all present, it must be admitted that he has considerable advantage of Old Fogy.[1]   Take, for instance, the first of all fogies, Father Adam.   There he stood, a very perfect physical man, as poets and painters inform us; but he must have been very ignorant, and simple in his habits.   He had had no sufficient time to learn much by observation, and he had no near neighbors to teach him anything. No part of his breakfast had been brought from the other side of the world; and it is quite probable he had no conception of the world having any other side.   In all these things, it is very

[1] "Young America" was the battle cry of the supporters of Senator Douglas, whose youth has been given as a cause for keeping him from the highest offices.   These enthusiasts exploited this idea through their organ, the "Democratic Review," at the same time calling Cass, Buchanan and other older men "old fogies."   They ardently advocated the Monroe Doctrine, "manifest destiny" and any territorial expansion.

plain, he was no equal of Young America; the most that can be said is, that according to his chance he may have been quite as much of a man as his very self-complacent descendant. Little as was what he knew, let the youngster discard all he has learned from others, and then show, if he can, any advantage on his side. In the way of land and live-stock, Adam was quite in the ascendant. He had dominion over all the earth, and all the living things upon and round about it. The land has been sadly divided out since; but never fret, Young America will re-annex it.

The great difference between Young America and Old Fogy is the result of discoveries, inventions, and improvements. These, in turn, are the result of observation, reflection, and experiment. For instance, it is quite certain that ever since water has been boiled in covered vessels, men have seen the lids of the vessels rise and fall a little, with a sort of fluttering motion, by force of the steam; but so long as this was not specially observed, and reflected, and experimented upon, it came to nothing. At length, however, after many thousand years, some man observes this long-known effect of hot water lifting a pot-lid, and begins a train of reflection upon it. He says, "Why, to be sure, the force that lifts the pot-lid will lift anything else which is no hea-

vier than the pot-lid. And as man has much
hard fighting to do, cannot this hot-water power
be made to help him?" He has become a little
excited on the subject, and he fancies he hears
a voice answering, "Try me." He does try it;
and the observation, reflection, and trial give to
the world the control of that tremendous and
now well-known agent called steam-power.
This is not the actual history in detail, but the
general principle.

But was this first inventor of the application
of steam wiser or more ingenious than those who
had gone before him? Not at all. Had he not
learned much of those, he never would have
succeeded, probably never would have thought
of making the attempt. To be fruitful in invention, it is indispensable to have a habit of
observation and reflection; and this habit our
steam friend acquired, no doubt, from those
who, to him, were old fogies. But for the difference in habit of observation, why did Yan-
kees almost instantly discover gold in California, which had been trodden upon and overlooked by Indians and Mexican greasers for
centuries? Gold-mines are not the only mines
overlooked in the same way. There are more
mines above the earth's surface than below it.
All nature—the whole world, material, moral,
and intellectual—is a mine; and in Adam's day

it was a wholly unexplored mine. Now, it was
the destined work of Adam's race to develop, by
discoveries, inventions, and improvements, the
hidden treasures of this mine. But Adam had
nothing to turn his attention to the work. If he
should do anything in the way of inventions, he
had first to invent the art of invention, the instance, at least, if not the habit, of observation
and reflection. As might be expected, he seems
not to have been a very observing man at first;
for it appears he went about naked a considerable length of time before he ever noticed that
obvious fact. But when he did observe it, the
observation was not lost upon him; for it immediately led to the first of all inventions of which
we have any direct account—the fig-leaf apron.

The inclination to exchange thoughts with one
another is probably an original impulse of our
nature. If I be in pain, I wish to let you know
it, and to ask your sympathy and assistance; and
my pleasurable emotions also I wish to com-
municate to and share with you. But to carry
on such communications, some instrumentality
is indispensable. Accordingly, speech—articulate sounds rattled off from the tongue—was
used by our first parents, and even by Adam
before the creation of Eve. He gave names to
the animals while she was still a bone in his side;
and he broke out quite volubly when she first

stood before him, the best present of his Maker.
From this it would appear that speech was not
an invention of man, but rather the direct gift
of his Creator. But whether divine gift or invention, it is still plain that if a mode of communication had been left to invention, speech
must have been the first, from the superior adap-
tation to the end of the organs of speech over
every other means within the whole range of
nature. Of the organs of speech the tongue is
the principal; and if we shall test it, we shall
find the capacities of the tongue, in the utterance
of articulate sounds, absolutely wonderful. You
can count from one to one hundred quite distinctly in about forty seconds. In doing this
two hundred and eighty-three distinct sounds or
syllables are uttered, being seven to each sound,
and yet there should be enough difference between every two to be easily recognized by the
ear of the hearer. What other signs to represent things could possibly be produced so rapidly? or, even if ready made, could be arranged so
rapidly to express the sense? Motions with the
hands are no adequate substitute. Marks for
the recognition of the eye,—writing,—although
a wonderful auxiliary of speech, is no worthy
substitute for it. In addition to the more slow
and laborious process of getting up a communication in writing, the materials—pen, ink, and

paper—are not always at hand. But one always
has his tongue with him, and the breath of his
life is the ever-ready material with which it
works. Speech, then, by enabling different individuals to interchange thoughts, and thereby
to combine their powers of observation and reflection, greatly facilitates useful discoveries and
inventions. What one observes, and would himself infer nothing from, he tells to another, and
that other at once sees a valuable hint in it. A
result is thus reached which neither alone would
have arrived at. And this reminds me of what
I passed unnoticed before, that the very first
invention was a joint operation, Eve having
shared with Adam the getting up of the apron.
And, indeed, judging from the fact that sewing
has come down to our times as "woman's work,"
it is very probable she took the leading part,—
he, perhaps, doing no more than to stand by and
thread the needle. That proceeding may be
reckoned as the mother of all "sewing-societies,"
and the first and most perfect "World's Fair,"
all inventions and all inventors then in the world
being on the spot.

But speech alone, valuable as it ever has been
and is, has not advanced the condition of the
world much. This is abundantly evident when
we look at the degraded condition of all those
tribes of human creatures who have no consid-

erable additional means of communicating thoughts. Writing, the art of communicating thoughts to the mind through the eye, is the great invention of the world. Great is the astonishing range of analysis and combination which necessarily underlies the most crude and general conception of it—great, very great, in enabling us to converse with the dead, the absent, and the unborn, at all distances of time and space; and great, not only in its direct benefits, but greatest help to all other inventions. Suppose the art, with all conceptions of it, were this day lost to the world, how long, think you, would it be before Young America could get up the letter A with any adequate notion of using it to advantage? The precise period at which writing was invented is not known, but it certainly was as early as the time of Moses; from which we may safely infer that its inventors were very old fogies.

Webster, at the time of writing his dictionary, speaks of the English language as then consisting of seventy or eighty thousand words. If so, the language in which the five books of Moses were written must at that time, now thirty-three or thirty-four hundred years ago, have consisted of at least one quarter as many, or twenty thousand. When we remember that words are sounds merely, we shall conclude that the idea of representing those sounds by marks, so that whoever should at any time after see the marks would understand what sounds they meant, was a bold and ingenious conception, not likely to occur to one man in a million in the run of a thousand years. And when it did occur, a distinct mark for each word, giving twenty thousand different marks first to be learned, and afterward to be remembered, would follow as the second thought, and would present such a difficulty as would lead to the conclusion that the whole thing was impracticable. But the necessity still would exist; and we may readily suppose that the idea was conceived, and lost, and reproduced, and dropped, and taken up again and again, until at last the thought of dividing sounds into parts, and making a mark, not to represent a whole sound, but only a part of one, and then of combining those marks, not very many in number, upon principles of permutation, so as to represent any and all of the whole twenty thousand words, and even any additional number, was somehow conceived and pushed into practice. This was the invention of phonetic writing, as distinguished from the clumsy picture-writing of some of the nations. That it was difficult of conception and execution is apparent, as well by the foregoing reflection, as the fact that so many tribes of men have come down from Adam's time to our own without ever having possessed it. Its utility may be conceived by the reflection that to it we owe everything which distinguishes us from savages. Take it from us, and the Bible, all history, all science, all government, all commerce, and nearly all social intercourse go with it.

The great activity of the tongue in articulating sounds has already been mentioned, and it may be of some passing interest to notice the wonderful power of the eye in conveying ideas to the mind from writing. Take the same example of the numbers from one to one hundred written down, and you can run your eye over the list, and be assured that every number is in it, in about one half the time it would require to pronounce the words with the voice; and not only so, but you can in the same short time determine whether every word is spelled correctly, by which it is evident that every separate letter, amounting to eight hundred and sixty-four, has been recognized and reported to the mind within the incredibly short space of twenty seconds, or one third of a minute.

I have already intimated my opinion that in the world's history certain inventions and discoveries occurred of peculiar value, on account of their great efficiency in facilitating all other inventions and discoveries. Of these were the art of writing and of printing, the discovery of America, and the introduction of patent laws. The date of the first, as already stated, is unknown; but it certainly was as much as fifteen hundred years before the Christian era; the second—printing—came in 1436, or nearly three thousand years after the first. The others followed more rapidly—the discovery of America in 1492, and the first patent laws in 1624. Though not apposite to my present purpose, it is but justice to the fruitfulness of that period to mention two other important events—the Lutheran Reformation in 1517, and, still earlier, the invention of negroes, or of the present mode of using them, in 1434.

But to return to the consideration of printing, it is plain that it is but the other half, and in reality the better half, of writing; and that both together are but the assistants of speech in the communication of thoughts between man and man. When man was possessed of speech alone, the chances of invention, discovery, and improvement were very limited; but by the introduction of each of these they were greatly multiplied. When writing was invented, any important observation likely to lead to a discovery had at least a chance of being written down, and consequently a little chance of never being forgotten, and of being seen and reflected upon by a much greater number of persons; and thereby the chances of a valuable hint being caught proportionately augmented. By this means the observation of a single individual might lead to an important invention years, and even centuries, after he was dead. In one word, by means of writing, the seeds of invention were more permanently preserved and more widely sown. And yet for three thousand years during which printing remained undiscovered after writing was in use, it was only a small portion of the people who could write, or read writing; and consequently the field of invention, though much extended, still continued very limited. At length printing came. It gave ten thousand copies of any written matter quite as cheaply as ten were given before; and consequently a thousand minds were brought into the field were there was but one before. This was a great gain—and history shows a great change corresponding to it—in point of time.

I will venture to consider it the true termination of that period called "the dark ages." Discoveries, inventions, and improvements followed rapidly and have been increasing their rapidity ever since. The effects could not come all at once. It required time to bring them out; and they are still coming. The capacity to read

could not be multiplied as fast as the means of
reading. Spelling-books just began to go into
the hands of the children, but the teachers were
not very numerous or very competent, so that it
is safe to infer they did not advance so speedily
as they do nowadays. It is very probable—almost certain—that the great mass of men at that
time were utterly unconscious that their condition or their minds were capable of improvement. They not only looked upon the educated
few as superior beings, but they supposed themselves to be naturally incapable of rising to
equality. To emancipate the mind from this
false underestimate of itself is the great task
which printing came into the world to perform.
It is difficult for us now and here to conceive
how strong this slavery of the mind was, and
how long it did of necessity take to break its
shackles, and to get a habit of freedom of
thought established. It is, in this connection, a
curious fact that a new country is most favorable
—almost necessary—to the emancipation of
thought, and the consequent advancement of
civilization and the arts.

The human family originated, as is thought,
somewhere in Asia, and have worked their way
principally westward. Just now in civilization and the arts the people of Asia are entirely behind those of Europe; those of the east of

Europe behind those of the west of it; while
we, here, in America, think we discover, and
invent, and improve faster than any of them.
They may think this is arrogance; but they cannot deny that Russia has called on us to show
her how to build steamboats and railroads,
while in the older parts of Asia they scarcely
know that such things as steamboats and railroads exist.   In anciently inhabited countries, the
dust of ages—a real, downright old-fogyism—
seems to settle upon and smother the intellects
and energies of man.   It is in this view that I
have mentioned the discovery of America as
an event greatly favoring and facilitating useful discoveries and inventions.

Next came the patent laws.   These began
in England in 1624, and in this country with
the adoption of our Constitution.   Before then
any man [might] instantly use what another
man had invented, so that the inventor had no
special advantage from his invention.   The patent system changed this, secured to the inventor
for a limited time exclusive use of his inventions, and thereby added the fuel of interest to
the fire of genius in the discovery and produc-
tion of new and useful things.

SPEECH AT CHICAGO ON THE NIGHT OF THE
MUNICIPAL ELECTION, March 1, 1859

I UNDERSTAND that you have to-day
rallied around your principles, and they
have again triumphed in the city of
Chicago. I am exceedingly happy to meet you
under such cheering auspices on this occasion—
the first on which I have appeared before an
audience since the campaign of last year. It is
unsuitable to enter into a lengthy discourse, as
is quite apparent, at a moment like this. I shall
therefore detain you only a very short while.

It gives me peculiar pleasure to find an opportunity under such favorable circumstances to
return my thanks for the gallant support that
the Republicans of the city of Chicago and of
the State gave to the cause in which we were all
engaged in the late momentous struggle in Illinois.

I remember in that canvass but one instance
of dissatisfaction with my course, and I allude
to that now not for the purpose of reviving any
matter of dispute or producing any unpleasant
feeling, but in order to help to get rid of the
point upon which that matter of disagreement

or dissatisfaction arose. I understand that in
some speeches I made I said something, or was
supposed to have said something, that some very
good people, as I really believe them to be, com-
mented upon unfavorably, and said that rather
than support one holding such sentiments as I
had expressed, the real friends of liberty could
afford to wait a while. I don't want to say anything that shall excite unkind feeling, and I
mention this simply to suggest that I am afraid
of the effect of that sort of argument. I do not
doubt that it comes from good men, but I am
afraid of the result upon organized action where
great results are in view, if any of us allow ourselves to seek out minor or separate points, on
which there may be difference of views as to
policy and right, and let them keep us from
uniting in action upon a great principle in a
cause on which we all agree; or are deluded into
the belief that all can be brought to consider
alike and agree upon every minor point before
we unite and press forward in organization, asking the coöperation of all good men in that re-
sistance to the extension of slavery upon which
we all agree. I am afraid that such methods
would result in keeping the friends of liberty
waiting longer than we ought to. I say this for
the purpose of suggesting that we consider
whether it would not be better and wiser, so long

as we all agree that this matter of slavery is a moral, political, and social wrong, and ought to be treated as a wrong, not to let anything minor or subsidiary to that main principle and purpose make us fail to coöperate.

One other thing,—and that again I say in no spirit of unkindness. There was a question amongst Republicans all the time of the canvass of last year, and it has not quite ceased yet, whether it was not the true and better policy for the Republicans to make it their chief object to reëlect Judge Douglas to the Senate of the United States. Now, I differ with those who thought that the true policy, but I have never said an unkind word of any one entertaining that opinion. I believe most of them were as sincerely the friends of our cause as I claim to be myself; yet I thought they were mistaken, and I speak of this now for the purpose of justifying the course that I took and the course of those who supported me. In what I say now there is no unkindness, even toward Judge Douglas. I have believed that in the Republican situation in Illinois, if we, the Republicans of this State, had made Judge Douglas our candidate for the Senate of the United States last year, and had elected him, there would to-day be no Republican party in this Union. I believe that the principles around which we have rallied and organized that party would live; they will live under all circumstances, while we will die. They would reproduce another party in the future. But in the mean time all the labor that has been done to build up the present Republican party would be entirely lost, and perhaps twenty years of time, before we would again have formed around that principle as solid, extensive, and formidable an organization as we have, standing shoulder to shoulder, to-night, in harmony and strength around the Republican banner.

It militates not at all against this view to tell us that the Republicans could make something in the State of New York by electing to Congress John B. Haskin, who occupied a position similar to Judge Douglas; or that they could make something by electing Hickman of Pennsylvania, or Davis of Indiana. I think it likely that they could and do make something by it; but it is false logic to assume that for that reason anything could be gained by us in electing Judge Douglas in Illinois. And for this reason: It is no disparagement to these men, Hickman and Davis, to say that individually they were comparatively small men, and the Republican party could take hold of them, use them, elect them, absorb them, expel them, or do whatever it pleased with them, and the Republican organization be in no wise shaken. But it is not so with

Judge Douglas. Let the Republican party of Illinois dally with Judge Douglas; let them fall in behind him and make him their candidate, and they do not absorb him—he absorbs them. They would come out at the end all Douglas men, claimed by him as having indorsed every one of his doctrines upon the great subject with which the whole nation is engaged at this hour —that the question of negro slavery is simply a question of dollars and cents; that the Almighty has drawn a line across the continent, on one side of which labor—the cultivation of the soil —must always be performed by slaves. It would be claimed that we, like him, do not care whether slavery is voted up or voted down. Had we made him our candidate and given him a great majority, we should never have heard an end of declarations by him that we had indorsed all these dogmas.

You all remember that at the last session of Congress there was a measure introduced in the Senate by Mr. Crittenden which proposed that the pro-slavery Lecompton constitution should be left to a vote to be taken in Kansas, and if it and slavery were adopted, Kansas should be at once admited as a slave State. That same measure was introduced into the House by Mr. Montgomery, and therefore got the name of the Crittenden-Montgomery bill; and in the House of Representatives the Republicans all voted for it under the peculiar circumstances in which they found themselves placed. You may remember also that the New York "Tribune," which was so much in favor of our electing Judge Douglas to the Senate of the United States, has not yet got through the task of defending the Republican party, after that one vote in the House of Representatives, from the charge of having gone over to the doctrine of popular sovereignty. Now, how long would the New York "Tribune" have been in getting rid of the charge that the Republicans had abandoned their principles, if we had taken up Judge Douglas, adopted all his doctrines, and elected him to the Senate, when the single vote upon that one point so confused and embarrassed the position of the Republicans that it has kept them for one entire year arguing against the effect of it?

This much being said on that point, I wish now to add a word that has a bearing on the future. The Republican principle, the profound central truth that slavery is wrong and ought to be dealt with as a wrong,—though we are always to remember the fact of its actual existence amongst us and faithfully observe all the constitutional guarantees,—the unalterable principle never for a moment to be lost sight of, that it is a wrong and ought to be dealt with as such, cannot advance at all upon Judge Douglas's ground; that there is a portion of the country in which slavery must always exist; that he does not care whether it is voted up or voted down, as it is simply a question of dollars and cents. Whenever in any compromise, or arrangement, or combination that may promise some temporary advantage we are led upon that ground, then and there the great living principle upon which we have organized as a party is surrendered. The proposition now in our minds that this thing is wrong being once driven out and surrendered, then the institution of slavery necessarily becomes national.

One or two words more of what I did not think of when I rose. Suppose it is true that the Almighty has drawn a line across this continent, on the south side of which part of the people will hold the rest as slaves; that the Almighty ordered this; that it is right, unchangeably right, that men ought there to be held as slaves; that their fellow-men will always have the right to hold them as slaves. I ask you, this once admitted, how can you believe that it is not right for us, or for them coming here, to hold slaves on this other side of the line? Once we come to acknowledge that it is right, that it is the law of the Eternal Being for slavery to exist on one

side of that line, have we any sure ground to object to slaves being held on the other side? Once
admit the position that a man rightfully holds
another man as property on one side of the line,
and you must, when it suits his convenience to
come to the other side, admit that he has the
same right to hold his property there. Once
admit Judge Douglas's proposition, and we must
all finally give way. Although we may not
bring ourselves to the idea that it is to our interest to have slaves in this Northern country,
we shall soon bring ourselves to admit that while
we may not want them, if any one else does, he
has the moral right to have them. Step by step,
south of the judge's moral climate line in the
States, in the Territories everywhere, and then
in all the States—it is thus that Judge Douglas
would lead us inevitably to the nationalization
of slavery.

Whether by his doctrine of squatter sovereignty, or by the ground taken by him in his recent speeches in Memphis and through the
South,—that wherever the climate makes it the
interest of the inhabitants to encourage slave
property they will pass a slave code,—whether
it is covertly nationalized by congressional legislation, or by Dred Scott decision, or by the
sophistical and misleading doctrine he has last
advanced, the same goal is inevitably reached

by the one or the other device. It is only traveling to the same place by different roads.

It is in this direction lies all the danger that
now exists to the great Republican cause. I
take it that so far as concerns forcibly establishing slavery in the Territories by congressional
legislation, or by virtue of the Dred Scott decision, that day has passed. Our only serious danger is that we shall be led upon this ground of
Judge Douglas, on the delusive assumption that
it is a good way of whipping our opponents,
when in fact it is a way that leads straight to final
surrender. The Republican party should not
dally with Judge Douglas when it knows where
his proposition and his leadership would take
us, nor be disposed to listen to it because it was
best somewhere else to support somebody occupying his ground. That is no just reason why
we ought to go over to Judge Douglas, as we
were called upon to do last year. Never forget
that we have before us this whole matter of the
right or wrong of slavery in this Union, though
the immediate question is as to its spreading out
into new Territories and States.

I do not wish to be misunderstood upon this
subject of slavery in this country. I suppose it
may long exist; and perhaps the best way for it
to come to an end peaceably is for it to exist for
a length of time. But I say that the spread and

strengthening and perpetuation of it is an entirely different proposition. There we should in
every way resist it as a wrong, treating it as a
wrong, with the fixed idea that it must and will
come to an end. If we do not allow ourselves
to be allured from the strict path of our duty by
such a device as shifting our ground and throwing us into the rear of a leader who denies our
first principle, denies that there is an absolute
wrong in the institution of slavery, then the future of the Republican cause is safe, and victory
is assured. You Republicans of Illinois have
deliberately taken your ground; you have heard
the whole subject discussed again and again;
you have stated your faith in platforms laid
down in a State convention and in a national
convention; you have heard and talked over and
considered it until you are now all of opinion
that you are on a ground of unquestionable
right.

All you have to do is to keep the faith, to
remain steadfast to the right, to stand by your
banner. Nothing should lead you to leave your
guns. Stand together, ready, with match in
hand. Allow nothing to turn you to the right
or to the left. Remember how long you have
been in setting out on the true course; how long
you have been in getting your neighbors to understand and believe as you now do. Stand by

your principles, stand by your guns, and victory, complete and permanent, is sure at the last.

LETTER TO W. M. MORRIS

SPRINGFIELD, March 28, 1859.

Dear Sir: Your kind note inviting me to deliver a lecture at Galesburg is received. I regret to say I cannot do so now; I must stick to the courts awhile. I read a sort of lecture to three different audiences during the last month and this; but I did so under circumstances which made it a waste of no time whatever.

Yours very truly,

A. LINCOLN.

LETTER TO H. L. PIERCE AND OTHERS

SPRINGFIELD, ILL., April 6, 1859.

Gentlemen: Your kind note inviting me to attend a festival in Boston, on the 28th instant, in honor of the birthday of Thomas Jefferson, was duly received. My engagements are such that I cannot attend.

Bearing in mind that about seventy years ago two great political parties were first formed in this country, that Thomas Jefferson was the head of one of them and Boston the headquarters of the other, it is both curious and interesting that those supposed to descend politically from the party opposed to Jefferson should now be celebrating his birthday in their own original seat of empire, while those claiming political descent from him have nearly ceased to breathe his name everywhere.

Remembering, too, that the Jefferson party was formed upon its supposed superior devotion to the personal rights of men, holding the rights of property to be secondary only, and greatly inferior, and assuming that the so-called Democracy of to-day are the Jefferson, and their opponents the anti-Jefferson, party, it will be equally interesting to note how completely the two have changed hands as to the principle upon which they were originally supposed to be divided. The Democracy of to-day hold the liberty of one man to be absolutely nothing, when in conflict with another man's right of property; Republicans, on the contrary, are for both the man and the dollar, but in case of conflict the man before the dollar.

I remember being once much amused at seeing two partially intoxicated men engaged in a fight with their great-coats on, which fight, after a long and rather harmless contest, ended in each having fought himself out of his own coat and into that of the other. If the two leading parties of this day are really identical with the two in the days of Jefferson and Adams, they have performed the same feat as the two drunken men.

But, soberly, it is now no child's play to save the principles of Jefferson from total overthrow in this nation. One would state with great confidence that he could convince any sane child that the simpler propositions of Euclid are true; but nevertheless he would fail, utterly, with one who should deny the definitions and axioms. The principles of Jefferson are the definitions and anxioms of free society. And yet they are denied and evaded, with no small show of success. One dashingly calls them "glittering generalities." Another bluntly calls them "self-evident lies." And others insidiously argue that they apply to "superior races." These expressions, differing in form, are identical in object and effect—the supplanting the principles of free government, and restoring those of classification, caste, and legitimacy. They would delight a convocation of crowned heads plotting against the people. They are the vanguard, the miners and sappers of returning despotism. We must repulse them, or they will subjugate us. This is a world of compensation; and he who would be no slave must consent to have no slave. Those who deny freedom to others deserve it not for themselves, and, under a just God, cannot long retain it. All honor to Jefferson—to the

man, who, in the concrete pressure of a struggle
for national independence by a single people,
had the coolness, forecast, and capacity to introduce into a merely revolutionary document an
abstract truth, applicable to all men and all
times, and so to embalm it there that to-day and
in all coming days it shall be a rebuke and a
stumbling-block to the very harbingers of reap-
pearing tyranny and oppression.

Your obedient servant,
A. LINCOLN.

LETTER TO T. J. PICKETT [1]

SPRINGFIELD, April 16, 1859.

My dear Sir: Yours of the 13th is just received. My engagements are such that I cannot at any very early day visit Rock Island to
deliver a lecture, or for any other object. As
to the other matter you kindly mention, I must
in candor say I do not think myself fit for the
presidency. I certainly am flattered and gratified that some partial friends think of me in that
connection; but I really think it best for our

---

[1] Pickett was a newspaper editor and a warm personal friend
of Lincoln, and among the first that were eager to launch a
"presidential boom" for him. Pickett wrote: "I would like
to have a talk with you on political matters, as to the policy
of announcing your name for the Presidency, while you are
in our city. My partner and myself are about addressing the
Republican editors of the State on the subject of a simultaneous
announcement of your name for the Presidency."

cause that no concerted effort, such as you suggest, should be made. Let this be considered
confidential.

Yours very truly,

A. LINCOLN.

LETTER TO M. W. DELAHAY

May 14, 1859.

. . . You will probably adopt resolutions
in the nature of a platform. I think the only
temptation will be to lower the Republican
standard in order to gather recruits. In my
judgment such a step would be a serious mistake,
and open a gap through which more would pass
out than pass in. And this would be the same
whether the letting down should be in deference
to Douglasism or to the Southern opposition element; either would surrender the object of the
Republican organization—the preventing of the
spread and nationalization of slavery. This object surrendered, the organization would go to
pieces. I do not mean by this that no Southern
man must be placed upon our national ticket in
1860. There are many men in the slave States
for any one of whom I could cheerfully vote to
be either President or Vice-President, provided
he would enable me to do so with safety to the
Republican cause, without lowering the Republican standard. This is the indispensable con-

dition of a union with us; it is idle to talk of any other. Any other would be as fruitless to the South as distasteful to the North, the whole ending in common defeat. Let a union be attempted on the basis of ignoring the slavery question, and magnifying other questions which the people are just now not caring about, and it will result in gaining no single electoral vote in the South, and losing every one in the North. . . .

LETTER TO DR. THEODORE CANISIUS

SPRINGFIELD, May 17, 1859.

Dear Sir: Your note asking, in behalf of yourself and other German citizens, whether I am for or against the constitutional provision in regard to naturalized citizens, lately adopted by Massachusetts, and whether I am for or against a fusion of the Republicans, and other opposition elements, for the canvass of 1860, is received.

Massachusetts is a sovereign and independent State; and it is no privilege of mine to scold her for what she does. Still, if from what she has done an inference is sought to be drawn as to what I would do, I may without impropriety speak out. I say, then, that, as I understand the Massachusetts provision, I am against its adoption in Illinois, or in any other place where I have a right to oppose it. Understanding the spirit of our institutions to aim at the elevation of men, I am opposed to whatever tends to degrade them. I have some little notoriety for commiserating the oppressed negro; and I should be strangely inconsistent if I could favor any project for curtailing the existing rights of white men, even though born in different lands, and speaking different languages from myself. As to the matter of fusion, I am for it, if it can be had on Republican grounds; and I am not for it on any other terms. A fusion on any other terms would be as foolish as unprincipled. It would lose the whole North, while the common enemy would still carry the whole South. The question of men is a different one. There are good patriotic men and able statesmen in the South whom I would cheerfully support, if they would now place themselves on Republican ground, but I am against letting down the Republican standard a hair's-breadth.

I have written this hastily, but I believe it answers your questions substantially.

Yours truly,
A. Lincoln.

LETTER TO SCHUYLER COLFAX [1]

SPRINGFIELD, ILL., July 6, 1859.

My dear Sir: I much regret not seeing you while you were here among us. Before learning that you were to be at Jacksonville on the 4th, I had given my word to be at another place. Besides a strong desire to make your personal acquaintance, I was anxious to speak with you on politics a little more fully than I can well do in a letter. My main object in such conversation would be to hedge against divisions in the Republican ranks generally, and particularly for the contest of 1860. The point of danger is the temptation in different localities to "platform" for something which will be popular just there, but which, nevertheless, will be a firebrand elsewhere, and especially in a national convention. As instances, the movement against foreigners in Massachusetts; in New Hampshire, to make obedience to the fugitive-slave law punishable as a crime; in Ohio, to repeal the fugitive-slave

---

[1] Schuyler Colfax, who was vice-president during Grant's first term, was in Congress at the time he received this letter. In replying to Lincoln he agreed that there existed a great majority opposed to slavery, but it was composed of elements almost defying coalition. "How this mass of mind," he wrote, "shall be consolidated into a victorious phalanx in 1860 is the great problem, I think, of our eventful times, and he who could accomplish it is worthier of fame than Napoleon or Victor Emmanuel."

law; and squatter sovereignty, in Kansas. In these things there is explosive enough to blow up half a dozen national conventions, if it gets into them; and what gets very rife outside of conventions is very likely to find its way into them. What is desirable, if possible, is that in every local convocation of Republicans a point should be made to avoid everything which will disturb Republicans elsewhere. Massachusetts Republicans should have looked beyond their noses, and then they could not have failed to see that tilting against foreigners would ruin us in the whole Northwest. New Hampshire and Ohio should forbear tilting against the fugitive-slave law in such a way as to utterly overwhelm us in Illinois with the charge of enmity to the Constitution itself. Kansas, in her confidence that she can be saved to freedom on "squatter sovereignty," ought not to forget that to prevent the spread and nationalization of slavery is a national concern, and must be attended to by the nation.

In a word, in every locality we should look beyond our noses; and at least say nothing on points where it is probable we shall disagree. I write this for your eye only; hoping, however, if you see danger as I think I do, you will do what you can to avert it. Could not suggestions be made to leading men in the State and congressional conventions, and so avoid, to some extent at least, these apples of discord?

Yours very truly,
A. LINCOLN.

LETTER TO JAMES MILLER, TREASURER OF THE STATE OF ILLINOIS.

SPRINGFIELD, ILL., July 11, 1859.

Dear Sir: We suppose you are persistently urged to pay something upon the new McCallister and Stebbins bonds. As friends of yours and of the people, we advise you to pay nothing upon them under any possible circumstances. The holders of them did a great wrong, and are now persisting in it in a way which deserves severe punishment. They know the legislature has again and again refused to fully recognize the old bonds. Seizing upon an act never intended to apply to them, they besieged Governor Bissell more than a year ago to fund the old bonds; he refused. They sought a mandamus upon him from the Supreme Court; the court refused. Again they besieged the governor last winter; he sought to have them go before the legislature; they refused. Still they persisted, and dogged him in his afflicted condition till they got from him what the agent in New York acted upon and issued the new bonds. Now they refuse to surrender them, hoping to force

an acquiescence, for Governor Bissell's sake.
"That cock won't fight," and they may as well
so understand at once. If the news of the surrender of the new bonds does not reach here in
ten days from this date, we shall do what we can
to have them repudiated in toto, finally and forever. If they were less than demons they would
at once relieve Governor Bissell from the pain-
ful position they have dogged him into; and if
they still persist, they shall never see even the
twenty-six cents to the dollar, if we can prevent
it.   Yours very truly,

                      A. LINCOLN,
                      S. T. LOGAN,
                      O. M. HATCH.

LETTER TO SAMUEL GALLOWAY

SPRINGFIELD, ILL., July 27, 1859.

My dear Sir: Your letter in relation to the
claim of Mr. Ambos for the Columbus Machine
Manufacturing Company against Barret and
others is received. This has been a somewhat
disagreeable matter to me. As I remember, you
first wrote me on the general subject, Barret
having a great deal of property, owing a good
dollars, and there was some question about his
taking the machinery. I think you inquired as
to Barret's responsibility; and that I answered
I considered him an honest and honorable man,

having a great deal of property, owing a good many debts, and hard pressed for ready cash. I was a little surprised soon after to learn that they had enlarged the credit to near ten thousand dollars, more or less. They wrote me to take notes and a mortgage, and to hold on to the notes awhile to fix amounts. I inferred the notes and mortgage were both to be held up for a time, and did so; Barret gave a second mortgage on part of the premises which was first recorded, and then I was blamed for not having recorded the other mortgage when first executed. My chief annoyance with the case now is that the parties at Columbus seem to think it is by my neglect that they do not get their money. There is an older mortgage on the real estate mortgaged, though not on the machinery. I got a decree of foreclosure in this present month; but I consented to delay advertising for sale till September, on a reasonable prospect that something will then be paid on a collateral Barret has put in my hands. When we come to sell on the decree, what will we do about the older mortgage? Barret has offered one or two other good notes—that is, notes on good men—if we would take them, *pro tanto,* as payment, but I notified Mr. Ambos, and he declined. My impression is that the whole of the money cannot be got very soon, anyway, but that it all will be ultimately collected, and that it could be got faster by turning in every little parcel we can, than by trying to force it through by the law in a lump. There are no special personal relations between Barret and myself. We are personal friends in a general way—no business transactions between us— not akin, and opposed on politics.

Yours truly,

A. LINCOLN.

LETTER TO SAMUEL GALLOWAY

SPRINGFIELD, ILL., July 28, 1859.

My dear Sir: Your very complimentary, not to say flattering, letter of the 23d inst. is received. Dr. Reynolds had induced me to expect you here; and I was disappointed not a little by your failure to come. And yet I fear you have formed an estimate of me which can scarcely be sustained on a personal acquaintance.

Two things done by the Ohio Republican convention—the repudiation of Judge Swan, and the "plank" for a repeal of the fugitive-slave law—I very much regretted. These two things are of a piece; and they are viewed by many good men, sincerely opposed to slavery, as a struggle against, and in disregard of, the Constitution itself. And it is the very thing that will greatly endanger our cause, if it be not kept out of our national convention. There is another thing our friends are doing which gives me some uneasiness. It is their leaning toward "popular sovereignty." There are three substantial objections to this. First, no party can command respect which sustains this year what it opposed last. Secondly, Douglas (who is the most dangerous enemy of liberty, because the most insidious one) would have little support in the North, and by consequence, no capital to trade on in the South, if it were not for his friends thus magnifying him and his humbug. But lastly, and chiefly, Douglas's popular sovereignty, accepted by the public mind as a just principle, nationalizes slavery, and revives the African slave-trade inevitably. Taking slaves into new Territories, and buying slaves in Africa, are identical things, identical rights or identical wrongs, and the argument which establishes one will establish the other. Try a thousand years for a sound reason why Congress shall not hinder the people of Kansas from having slaves, and when you have found it, it will be an equally good one why Congress should not hinder the people of Georgia from importing slaves from Africa.

As to Governor Chase, I have a kind side for him. He was one of the few distinguished men of the nation who gave us, in Illinois, their sympathy last year. I never saw him, but suppose him to be able and right-minded; but still he may not be the most suitable as a candidate for the presidency.

I must say I do not think myself fit for the presidency. As you propose a correspondence with me, I shall look for your letters anxiously.

I have not met Dr. Reynolds since receiving your letter; but when I shall, I will present your respects as requested.

Yours very truly,
A. LINCOLN.

*LETTER TO HAWKINS TAYLOR

SPRINGFIELD, ILL., September 6, 1859.

My dear Sir: Yours of the 3d is just received. There is some mistake about my expected attendance of the U. S. Court in your city on the 3d Tuesday of this month. I have had no thought of being there. It is bad to be poor. I shall go to the wall for bread and meat, if I neglect my business this year as well as last. It would please me much to see the city, and good people, of Keokuk, but for this year it is little less than an impossibility.

I am constantly receiving invitations which I am compelled to decline. I was pressingly urged to go to Minnesota; and I now have two invitations to go to Ohio. These last are prompted by Douglas going there; and I am really tempted to make a flying trip to Columbus and Cincinnati.

I do hope you will have no serious trouble in Iowa. What thinks Grimes about it? I have not known him to be mistaken about an election in Iowa. Present my respects to Colonel Carter, and any other friends; and believe me,

Yours truly,
A. LINCOLN.

SPEECH AT COLUMBUS, OHIO, September 16, 1859 [1]

FELLOW-CITIZENS of the State of Ohio: I cannot fail to remember that I appear for the first time before an audience in this now great State—an audience that is accustomed to hear such speakers as Corwin, and Chase, and Wade, and many other renowned men; and remembering this, I feel that it will be well for you, as for me, that you should not raise your expectations to that standard to which you would have been justified in raising them had one of these distinguished men appeared before you. You would perhaps be only preparing a disappointment for yourselves, and, as a consequence of your disappointment, mortification to me. I hope, therefore, that you will commence with very moderate expectations; and

[1] Interest in Lincoln increased daily from the close of the joint debates and the senatorial contest in Illinois. Douglas, himself, helped to keep Lincoln before the public by constantly using him as a target while touring the South. The Ohio Democrats called Douglas into their gubernatorial canvass in 1859. The Republicans naturally sought and secured Lincoln as the most capable antagonist. Each of Lincoln's speeches in the Ohio Campaign attracted wide attention. They were made at places where Douglas had but recently preceded him.

perhaps, if you will give me your attention, I shall be able to interest you to a moderate degree.

Appearing here for the first time in my life, I have been somewhat embarrassed for a topic by way of introduction to my speech; but I have been relieved from that embarrassment by an introduction which the "Ohio Statesman" newspaper gave me this morning. In this paper I have read an article in which, among other statements, I find the following:

In debating with Senator Douglas during the memorable contest last fall, Mr. Lincoln declared in favor of negro suffrage, and attempted to defend that vile conception against the Little Giant.

I mention this now, at the opening of my remarks, for the purpose of making three comments upon it. The first I have already announced—it furnished me an introductory topic; the second is to show that the gentleman is mistaken; thirdly, to give him an opportunity to correct it.

In the first place, in regard to this matter being a mistake. I have found that it is not entirely safe, when one is misrepresented under his very nose, to allow the misrepresentation to go uncontradicted. I therefore propose, here at the outset, not only to say that this is a misrepresentation, but to show conclusively that it is so; and you will bear with me while I read a couple of extracts from that very "memorable" debate with Judge Douglas last year, to which this newspaper refers. In the first pitched battle which Senator Douglas and myself had, at the town of Ottawa, I used the language which I will now read. Having been previously reading an extract, I continued as follows:

Now, gentlemen, I don't want to read at any greater length, but this is the true complexion of all I have ever said in regard to the institution of slavery and the black race. This is the whole of it, and anything that argues me into his idea of perfect social and political equality with the negro is but a specious and fantastic arrangement of words, by which a man can prove a horse-chestnut to be a chestnut horse. I will say here, while upon this subject, that I have no purpose either directly or indirectly to interfere with the institution of slavery in the States where it exists. I believe I have no lawful right to do so, and I have no inclination to do so. I have no purpose to introduce political and social equality between the white and the black races. There is a physical difference between the two which, in my judgment, will probably forever forbid their living together upon the footing of perfect equality, and inasmuch as it becomes a necessity that there must be a difference, I, as well as Judge Douglas, am in favor of the race to which I belong having the superior position. I have never said anything to the contrary, but I hold that, notwithstanding all this, there is no reason in the world why the negro is not entitled to all the natural rights enumerated in the Declaration of Independence, the right to life, liberty, and the pursuit of happiness. I hold that he is as much entitled to these as the white man. I agree with Judge Douglas, he is not my equal in many respects — certainly not in color, perhaps not in moral or intellectual endowments. But in the right to eat the bread, without leave of anybody else, which his own hand earns, he is my equal, and the equal of Judge Douglas, and the equal of every living man.

Upon a subsequent occasion, when the reason for making a statement like this recurred, I said:

While I was at the hotel to-day an elderly gentleman called upon me to know whether I was really in favor of producing a perfect equality between the negroes and white people. While I had not proposed to myself on this occasion to say much on that subject, yet as the question was asked me I thought I would occupy perhaps five minutes in saying something in regard to it. I will say, then, that I am not, nor ever have been, in favor of bringing about in any way the social and political equality of the white and the black races — that I am not, nor ever have been, in favor of making voters or jurors of negroes, nor of qualifying them to hold office, nor to intermarry with

white people; and I will say in addition to this, that
there is a physical difference between the white and
the black races, which, I believe, will forever forbid
the two races living together on terms of social and
political equality.   And inasmuch as they cannot so
live, while they do remain together there must be the
position of superior and inferior, and I, as much as
any other man, am in favor of having the superior
position assigned to the white race.   I say upon this
occasion I do not perceive that because the white man
is to have the superior position, the negro should be
denied everything.   I do not understand that because
I do not want a negro woman for a slave, I must
necessarily want her for a wife.   My understanding
is that I can just let her alone.   I am now in my
fiftieth year; and I certainly never have had a black
woman for either a slave or a wife.   So it seems to
me quite possible for us to get along without making
either slaves or wives of negroes.   I will add to this,
that I have never seen to my knowledge a man,
woman, or child who was in favor of producing a
perfect equality, social and political, between negroes
and white men.   I recollect of but one distinguished
instance that I ever heard of so frequently as to be
entirely satisfied of its correctness — and that is the
case of Judge Douglas's old friend, Colonel Richard
M. Johnson.   I will also add to the remarks I have
made (for I am not going to enter at large upon this
subject), that I have never had the least apprehension that I or my friends would marry negroes,
if there was no law to keep them from it; but as

Judge Douglas and his friends seem to be in great apprehension that they might, if there were no law to keep them from it, I give him the most solemn pledge that I will to the very last stand by the law of the State, which forbids the marrying of white people with negroes.

There, my friends, you have briefly what I have, upon former occasions, said upon the subject to which this newspaper, to the extent of its ability, has drawn the public attention. In it you not only perceive, as a probability, that in that contest I did not at any time say I was in favor of negro suffrage; but the absolute proof that twice—once substantially and once express-ly—I declared against it. Having shown you this, there remains but a word of comment upon that newspaper article. It is this: that I presume the editor of that paper is an honest and truth-loving man, and that he will be greatly obliged to me for furnishing him thus early an opportunity to correct the misrepresentation he has made, before it has run so long that malicious people can call him a liar.

The giant himself has been here recently. I have seen a brief report of his speech. If it were otherwise unpleasant to me to introduce the subject of the negro as a topic for discussion, I might be somewhat relieved by the fact that he dealt exclusively in that subject while he was here. I shall, therefore, without much hesitation or diffidence, enter upon this subject.

The American people, on the first day of January, 1854, found the African slave-trade prohibited by a law of Congress. In a majority of the States of this Union, they found African slavery, or any other sort of slavery, prohibited by State constitutions. They also found a law existing, supposed to be valid, by which slavery was excluded from almost all the territory the United States then owned. This was the condition of the country, with reference to the institution of slavery, on the first of January, 1854. A few days after that, a bill was introduced into Congress, which ran through its regular course in the two branches of the national legislature, and finally passed into a law in the month of May, by which the act of Congress prohibiting slavery from going into the Territories of the United States was repealed. In connection with the law itself, and, in fact, in the terms of the law, the then existing prohibition was not only repealed, but there was a declaration of a purpose on the part of Congress never thereafter to exercise any power that they might have, real or supposed, to prohibit the extension or spread of slavery. This was a very great change; for the law thus repealed was of more than thirty years' standing. Following rapidly

upon the heels of this action of Congress, a decision of the Supreme Court is made, by which
it is declared that Congress, if it desires to prohibit the spread of slavery into the Territories,
has no constitutional power to do so. Not only
so, but that decision lays down the principles,
which, if pushed to their logical conclusion,—I
say pushed to their logical conclusion,—would
decide that the constitutions of free States, forbidding slavery, are themselves unconstitutional.
Mark me, I do not say the judges said this, and
let no man say I affirm the judges used these
words; but I only say it is my opinion that what
they did say, if pressed to its logical conclusion,
will inevitably result thus.

Looking at these things, the Republican party, as I understand its principles and policy,
believes that there is great danger of the institution of slavery being spread out and extended,
until it is ultimately made alike lawful in all
the States of this Union; so believing, to prevent that incidental and ultimate consummation
is the original and chief purpose of the Republican organization. I say " chief purpose" of
the Republican organization; for it is certainly
true that if the national house shall fall into the
hands of the Republicans, they will have to attend to all the other matters of national housekeeping as well as this. The chief and real

purpose of the Republican party is eminently conservative. It proposes nothing save and except to restore this government to its original tone in regard to this element of slavery, and there to maintain it, looking for no further change in reference to it than that which the original framers of the government themselves expected and looked forward to.

The chief danger to this purpose of the Republican party is not just now the revival of the African slave-trade, or the passage of a congressional slave-code, or the declaring of a second Dred Scott decision, making slavery lawful in all the States. These are not pressing us just now. They are not quite ready yet. The authors of these measures know that we are too strong for them; but they will be upon us in due time, and we will be grappling with them hand to hand, if they are not now headed off. They are not now the chief danger to the purpose of the Republican organization; but the most imminent danger that now threatens that purpose is that insidious Douglas popular sovereignty. This is the miner and sapper. While it does not propose to revive the African slave-trade, nor to pass a slave-code, nor to make a second Dred Scott decision, it is preparing us for the onslaught and charge of these ultimate enemies when they shall be ready to come on, and the word of command for them to advance shall be given. I say this Douglas popular sovereignty —for there is a broad distinction, as I now understand it, between that article and a genuine popular sovereignty.

I believe there is a genuine popular sovereignty. I think a definition of genuine popular sovereignty, in the abstract, would be about this: That each man shall do precisely as he pleases with himself, and with all those things which exclusively concern him. Applied to government, this principle would be, that a general government shall do all those things which pertain to it, and all the local governments shall do precisely as they please in respect to those matters which exclusively concern them. I understand that this government of the United States, under which we live, is based upon this principle; and I am misunderstood if it is supposed that I have any war to make upon that principle.

Now, what is Judge Douglas's popular sovereignty? It is, as a principle, no other than that if one man chooses to make a slave of another man, neither that other man nor anybody else has a right to object. Applied in government, as he seeks to apply it, it is this: If, in a new Territory into which a few people are beginning to enter for the purpose of making their homes, they choose to either exclude slavery from their limits or to establish it there, however one or the other may affect the persons to be enslaved, or the infinitely greater number of persons who are afterward to inhabit that Territory, or the other members of the families of communities, of which they are but an incipient member, or the general head of the family of States as parent of all—however their action may affect one or the other of these, there is no power or right to interfere. That is Douglas's popular sovereignty applied.

He has a good deal of trouble with popular sovereignty. His explanations explanatory of explanations explained are interminable. The most lengthy and, as I suppose, the most maturely considered of his long series of explanations is his great essay in "Harper's Magazine."[1] I will not attempt to enter on any very thorough investigation of his argument as there made and presented. I will nevertheless occupy a good portion of your time here in drawing your attention to certain points in it. Such of you as may have read this document will have perceived that the judge, early in the document, quotes from two persons as belonging to the Republican party, without naming them, but who can readily be recognized as being Governor Seward, of New York, and myself. It is

[1] "Harper's Magazine" for September, 1859.

true that exactly fifteen months ago this day, I believe, I for the first time expressed a sentiment upon this subject, and in such a manner that it should get into print, that the public might see it beyond the circle of my hearers, and my expression of it at that time is the quotation that Judge Douglas makes. He has not made the quotation with accuracy, but justice to him requires me to say that it is sufficiently accurate not to change its sense.

The sense of that quotation condensed is this —that this slavery element is a durable element of discord among us, and that we shall probably not have perfect peace in this country with it until it either masters the free principle in our government, or is so far mastered by the free principle as for the public mind to rest in the belief that it is going to its end. This sentiment which I now express in this way was, at no great distance of time, perhaps in different language, and in connection with some collateral ideas, expressed by Governor Seward. Judge Douglas has been so much annoyed by the expression of that sentiment that he has constantly, I believe, in almost all his speeches since it was uttered, been referring to it. I find he alluded to it in his speech here, as well as in the copyright essay. I do not now enter upon this for the purpose of making an elaborate argument to show that we were right in the expression of that sentiment. I only ask your attention to this matter for the purpose of making one or two points upon it.

If you will read the copyright essay, you will discover that Judge Douglas himself says a controversy between the American colonies and the government of Great Britain began on the slavery question in 1699, and continued from that time until the Revolution; and, while he did not say so, we all know that it has continued with more or less violence ever since the Revolution.

Then we need not appeal to history, to the declaration of the framers of the government, but we know from Judge Douglas himself that slavery began to be an element of discord among the white people of this country as far back as 1699, or one hundred and sixty years ago, or five generations of men—counting thirty years to a generation. Now it would seem to me that it might have occurred to Judge Douglas, or to anybody who had turned his attention to these facts, that there was something in the nature of that thing, slavery, somewhat durable for mischief and discord.

There is another point I desire to make in regard to this matter before I leave it. From the adoption of the Constitution down to 1820 is the precise period of our history when we had comparative peace upon this question—the precise period of time when we came nearer to having peace about it than any other time of that entire one hundred and sixty years, in which he says it began, or of the eighty years of our own Constitution. Then it would be worth our while to stop and examine into the probable reason of our coming nearer to having peace then than at any other time. This was the precise period of time in which our fathers adopted, and during which they followed, a policy restricting the spread of slavery, and the whole Union was acquiescing in it. The whole country looked forward to the ultimate extinction of the institution. It was when a policy had been adopted and was prevailing, which led all just and right-minded men to suppose that slavery was gradually coming to an end, and that they might be quiet about it, watching it as it expired. I think Judge Douglas might have perceived that too, and, whether he did or not, it is worth the attention of fair-minded men, here and elsewhere, to consider whether that is not the truth of the case. If he had looked at these two facts, that this matter has been an element of discord for one hundred and sixty years among this people, and that the only comparative peace we have had about it was when that policy prevailed in this government, which he now wars upon, he might then, perhaps, have been brought to a more just appreciation of what I said fifteen months ago—that "a house divided against itself cannot stand. I believe this government cannot endure permanently half slave and half free. I do not expect the Union to be dissolved—I do not expect the house to fall; but I do expect it will cease to be divided. It will become all one thing or all the other. Either the opponents of slavery will arrest the further spread of it, and place it where the public mind will rest in the belief that it is in the course of ultimate extinction, or its advocates will push it forward, until it shall become alike lawful in all the States, old as well as new, North as well as South."

That was my sentiment at that time. In connection with it I said, "We are now far into the fifth year since a policy was initiated with the avowed object and confident promise of putting an end to slavery agitation. Under the operation of that policy, that agitation has not only not ceased, but has constantly augmented." I now say to you here that we are advanced still farther into the sixth year since that policy of Judge Douglas—that popular sovereignty of his for quieting the slavery question—was made the national policy. Fifteen months more have been added since I uttered that sentiment, and I call upon you, and all other right-minded men, to say whether those fifteen months have belied or corroborated my words.

While I am here upon this subject, I cannot but express gratitude that the true view of this element of discord among us—as I believe it is —is attracting more and more attention. I do not believe that Governor Seward uttered that sentiment because I had done so before, but because he reflected upon this subject, and saw the truth of it. Nor do I believe, because Governor Seward or I uttered it, that Mr. Hickman, of Pennsylvania, in different language, since that time, has declared his belief in the utter antagonism which exists between the principles of liberty and slavery. You see we are multiplying. Now, while I am speaking of Hickman, let me say, I know but little about him. I have never seen him, and know scarcely anything about the man; but I will say this much about him: Of all the anti-Lecompton Democracy that have been brought to my notice, he alone has the true, genuine ring of the metal. And now, without indorsing anything else he has said, I will ask this audience to give three cheers for Hickman. [The audience responded with three rousing cheers for Hickman.]

Another point in the copyright essay to which

I would ask your attention is rather a feature to be extracted from the whole thing, than from any express declaration of it at any point. It is a general feature of that document, and indeed, of all of Judge Douglas's discussions of this question, that the Territories of the United States and the States of this Union are exactly alike—that there is no difference between them at all—that the Constitution applies to the Territories precisely as it does to the States—and that the United States Government, under the Constitution, may not do in a State what it may not do in a Territory, and what it must do in a State, it must do in a Territory. Gentlemen, is that a true view of the case? It is necessary for this squatter sovereignty; but is it true?

Let us consider. What does it depend upon? It depends altogether upon the proposition that the States must, without the interference of the General Government, do all those things that pertain exclusively to themselves—that are local in their nature, that have no connection with the General Government. After Judge Douglas has established this proposition, which nobody disputes or ever has disputed, he proceeds to assume, without proving it, that slavery is one of those little, unimportant, trivial matters, which are of just about as much consequence as the question would be to me whether my

neighbor should raise horned cattle or plant tobacco; that there is no moral question about it,
but that it is altogether a matter of dollars and
cents; that when a new Territory is opened for
settlement, the first man who goes into it may
plant there a thing which, like the Canada this-
tle, or some other of those pests of the soil, cannot be dug out by the millions of men who will
come thereafter; that it is one of those little
things that is so trivial in its nature that it has
no effect upon anybody save the few men who
first plant upon the soil; that it is not a thing
which in any way affects the family of communities composing these States, nor any way
endangers the General Government. Judge
Douglas ignores altogether the very well-known
fact that we have never had a serious menace
to our political existence, except it sprang from
this thing, which he chooses to regard as only
upon a par with onions and potatoes.

Turn it, and contemplate it in another view.
He says that, according to his popular sovereignty, the General Government may give to
the Territories governors, judges, marshals, sec-
retaries, and all the other chief men to govern
them, but they must not touch upon this other
question. Why? The question of who shall
be governor of a Territory for a year or two, and
pass away, without his track being left upon the

soil, or an act which he did for good or for evil being left behind, is a question of vast national magnitude. It is so much opposed in its nature to locality that the nation itself must decide it; while this other matter of planting slavery upon a soil—a thing which, once planted, cannot be eradicated by the succeeding millions who have as much right there as the first comers, or if eradicated, not without infinite difficulty and a long struggle—he considers the power to prohibit it as one of these little, local, trivial things that the nation ought not to say a word about; that it affects nobody save the few men who are there.

Take these two things and consider them together, present the question of planting a State with the institution of slavery by the side of a question of who shall be governor of Kansas for a year or two, and is there a man here—is there a man on earth—who would not say the governor question is the little one, and the slavery question is the great one? I ask any honest Democrat if the small, the local, and the trivial and temporary question is not, Who shall be governor?—while the durable, the important, and the mischievous one is, Shall this soil be planted with slavery?

This is an idea, I suppose, which has arisen in Judge Douglas's mind from his peculiar structure. I suppose the institution of slavery really looks small to him. He is so put up by nature that a lash upon his back would hurt him, but a lash upon anybody else's back does not hurt him. That is the build of the man, and consequently he looks upon the matter of slavery in this unimportant light.

Judge Douglas ought to remember, when he is endeavoring to force this policy upon the American people, that while he is put up in that way, a good many are not. He ought to remember that there was once in this country a man by the name of Thomas Jefferson, supposed to be a Democrat—a man whose principles and policy are not very prevalent amongst Democrats to-day, it is true; but that man did not take exactly this view of the insignificance of the element of slavery which our friend Judge Douglas does. In contemplation of this thing, we all know he was led to exclaim, "I tremble for my country when I remember that God is just!" We know how he looked upon it when he thus expressed himself. There was danger to this country, danger of the avenging justice of God, in that little unimportant popular-sovereignty question of Judge Douglas. He supposed there was a question of God's eternal justice wrapped up in the enslaving of any race of men, or any man, and that those who did so braved the arm of Jehovah—that when a nation thus dared the Almighty, every friend of that nation had cause to dread his wrath. Choose ye between Jefferson and Douglas as to what is the true view of this element among us.

There is another little difficulty about this matter of treating the Territories and States alike in all things, to which I ask your attention, and I shall leave this branch of the case. If there is no difference between them, why not make the Territories States at once? What is the reason that Kansas was not fit to come into the Union when it was organized into a Territory, in Judge Douglas's view? Can any of you tell any reason why it should not have come into the Union at once?

They are fit, as he thinks, to decide upon the slavery question—the largest and most important with which they could possibly deal; what could they do by coming into the Union that they are not fit to do, according to his view, by staying out of it? Oh, they are not fit to sit in Congress and decide upon the rates of postage, or questions of *ad valorem* or specific duties on foreign goods, or live-oak timber contracts; they are not fit to decide these vastly important matters, which are national in their import, but they are fit, "from the jump," to decide this little negro question. But, gentlemen, the case is too

plain; I occupy too much time on this head, and
I pass on.

Near the close of the copyright essay, the
judge, I think, comes very near kicking his own
fat into the fire. I did not think when I commenced these remarks that I would read from
that article, but I now believe I will:

This exposition of the history of these measures
shows conclusively that the authors of the compromise measures of 1850, and of the Kansas-Nebraska
act of 1854, as well as the members of the Continen-
tal Congress in 1774, and the founders of our system of government subsequent to the Revolution, regarded the people of the Territories and Colonies as
political communities which were entitled to a free
and exclusive power of legislation in their provincial
legislatures, where their representation could alone
be preserved, in all cases of taxation and internal
polity.

When the judge saw that putting in the word
"slavery" would contradict his own history, he
put in what he knew would pass as synonymous
with it—"internal polity." Whenever we find
that in one of his speeches, the substitute is used
in this manner; and I can tell you the reason.
It would be too bald a contradiction to say slavery, but "internal polity" is a general phrase
which would pass in some quarters, and which

he hopes will pass with the reading community, for the same thing.

This right pertains to the people collectively, as a law-abiding and peaceful community, and not to the isolated individuals who may wander upon the public domain in violation of law. It can only be exercised where there are inhabitants sufficient to constitute a government, and capable of performing its various functions and duties, a fact to be ascertained and determined by —

Who do you think? Judge Douglas says, "By Congress."

Whether the number shall be fixed at ten, fifteen, or twenty thousand inhabitants does not affect the principle.

Now I have only a few comments to make. Popular sovereignty, by his own words, does not pertain to the few persons who wander upon the public domain in violation of law. We have his words for that. When it does pertain to them is when they are sufficient to be formed into an organized political community, and he fixes the minimum for that at 10,000, and the maximum at 20,000. Now I would like to know what is to be done with the 9,000? Are they all to be treated, until they are large enough to be organized into a political community, as wanderers upon the public land in violation of law? And if so treated and driven out, at what point of time would there ever be ten thousand? If they were not driven out, but remained there as trespassers upon the public land in violation of the law, can they establish slavery there? No; the judge says popular sovereignty don't pertain to them then. Can they exclude it then? No; popular sovereignty don't pertain to them then. I would like to know, in the case covered by the essay, what condition the people of the Territory are in before they reach the number of ten thousand?

But the main point I wish to ask attention to is that the question as to when they shall have reached a sufficient number to be formed into a regular organized community is to be decided "by Congress." Judge Douglas says so. Well, gentlemen, that is about all we want. No; that is all the Southerners want. That is what all those who are for slavery want. They do not want Congress to prohibit slavery from coming into the new Territories, and they do not want popular sovereignty to hinder it; and as Congress is to say when they are ready to be organized, all that the South has to do is to get Congress to hold off. Let Congress hold off until they are ready to be admitted as a State, and the South has all it wants in taking slavery into and planting it in all the Territories that we now have, or hereafter may have. In a word, the whole thing, at a dash of the pen, is at last put in the power of Congress; for if they do not have this popular sovereignty until Congress organizes them, I ask if it at last does not come from Congress? If, at last, it amounts to anything at all, Congress gives it to them. I submit this rather for your reflection than for comment. After all that is said, at last, by a dash of the pen, everything that has gone before is undone, and he puts the whole question under the control of Congress. After fighting through more than three hours, if you will undertake to read it, he at last places the whole matter under the control of that power which he had been contending against, and arrives at a result directly contrary to what he had been laboring to do. He at last leaves the whole matter to the control of Congress.

There are two main objects, as I understand it, of this "Harper's Magazine" essay. One was to show, if possible, that the men of our Revolutionary times were in favor of his popular sovereignty; and the other was to show that the Dred Scott decision had not entirely squelched out this popular sovereignty. I do not propose, in regard to this argument drawn from the history of former times, to enter into a detailed examination of the historical statements he has made. I have the impression that they are inaccurate in a great many instances; sometimes in positive statement, but very much more inaccurate by the suppression of statements that really belong to the history. But I do not propose to affirm that this is so to any very great extent, or to enter into a very minute examination of his historical statements. I avoid doing so upon this principle—that if it were important for me to pass out of this lot in the least period of time possible, and I came to that fence and saw by a calculation of my own strength and agility that I could clear it at a bound, it would be folly for me to stop and consider whether I could or could not crawl through a crack. So I say of the whole history contained in his essay, where he endeavored to link the men of the Revolution to popular sovereignty. It only requires an effort to leap out of it—a single bound to be entirely successful. If you read it over you will find that he quotes here and there from documents of the Revolutionary times, tending to show that the people of the colonies were desirous of regulating their own concerns in their own way, that the British Government should not interfere; that at one time they struggled with the British Government to be permitted to exclude the African slave-trade;

if not directly, to be permitted to exclude it indirectly by taxation sufficient to discourage and destroy it.   From these and many things of this sort, Judge Douglas argues that they were in favor of the people of our own Territories excluding slavery if they wanted to, or planting it there if they wanted to, doing just as they pleased from the time they settled upon the Territory.   Now, however his history may apply, and whatever of his argument there may be that is sound and accurate or unsound and inaccurate, if we can find out what these men did themselves do upon this very question of slavery in the Territories, does it not end the whole thing? If, after all this labor and effort to show that the men of the Revolution were in favor of his popular sovereignty and his mode of dealing with slavery in the Territories, we can show that these very men took hold of that subject, and dealt with it, we can see for ourselves how they dealt with it.   It is not a matter of argument or inference, but we know what they thought about it.

It is precisely upon that part of the history of the country that one important omission is made by Judge Douglas.   He selects parts of the history of the United States upon the subject of slavery, and treats it as the whole, omitting from his historical sketch the legislation of

Congress in regard to the admission of Missouri, by which the Missouri Compromise was established, and slavery excluded from a country half as large as the present United States. All this is left out of his history, and in no wise alluded to by him, so far as I can remember, save once, when he makes a remark, that upon his principle the Supreme Court was authorized to pronounce a decision that the act called the Missouri Compromise was unconstitutional. All that history has been left out. But this part of the history of the country was not made by the men of the Revolution.

There was another part of our political history made by the very men who were the actors in the Revolution, which has taken the name of the ordinance of '87. Let me bring that history to your attention. In 1784, I believe, this same Mr. Jefferson drew up an ordinance for the government of the country upon which we now stand; or rather a frame or draft of an ordinance for the government of this country, here in Ohio, our neighbors in Indiana, us who live in Illinois, and our neighbors in Wisconsin and Michigan. In that ordinance, drawn up not only for the government of that Territory, but for the Territories south of the Ohio River, Mr. Jefferson expressly provided for the prohibition of slavery. Judge Douglas says, and perhaps he is right, that

that provision was lost from that ordinance. I
believe that is true. When the vote was taken
upon it, a majority of all present in the Congress
of the Confederation voted for it; but there were
so many absentees that those voting for it did not
make the clear majority necessary, and it was
lost. But three years after that the Congress
of the Confederation were together again, and
they adopted a new ordinance for the government of this Northwest Territory, not contem-
plating territory south of the river, for the States
owning that territory had hitherto refrained
from giving it to the General Government;
hence they made the ordinance to apply only to
what the government owned. In that, the provision excluding slavery was inserted and passed
unanimously, or at any rate it passed and became a part of the law of the land. Under that
ordinance we live. First, here, in Ohio, you
were a Territory, then an enabling act
was passed, authorizing you to form a
constitution and State government, provided
it was Republican, and not in conflict
with the ordinance of '87. When you framed
your constitution and presented it for admission,
I think you will find the legislation upon the
subject will show that, "whereas you had formed
a constitution that was Republican, and not in
conflict with the ordinance of '87," therefore

you were admitted upon equal footing with the
original States. The same process in a few years
was gone through with Indiana, and so with
Illinois, and the same substantially with Michigan and Wisconsin.

Not only did that ordinance prevail, but it
was constantly looked to whenever a step was
taken by a new Territory to become a State.
Congress always turned their attention to it, and
in all their movements upon this subject they
traced their course by that ordinance of '87.
When they admitted new States they advised
them of this ordinance as a part of the legislation of the country. They did so because they
had traced the ordinance of '87 throughout the
history of this country. Begin with the men
of the Revolution, and go down for sixty entire
years, and until the last scrap of that Territory
comes into the Union in the form of the State
of Wisconsin, everything was made to conform
to the ordinance of '87, excluding slavery from
that vast extent of country.

I omitted to mention in the right place that
the Constitution of the United States was in
process of being framed when that ordinance
was made by the Congress of the Confederation;
and one of the first acts of Congress itself, under the new Constitution itself, was to give force
to that ordinance by putting power to carry it

out into the hands of new officers under the Constitution, in the place of the old ones, who had been legislated out of existence by the change in the government from the Confederation to the Constitution. Not only so, but I believe Indiana once or twice, if not Ohio, petitioned the General Government for the privilege of suspending that provision and allowing them to have slaves. A report made by Mr. Randolph, of Virginia, himself a slaveholder, was directly against it, and the action was to refuse them the privilege of violating the ordinance of '87.

This period of history, which I have run over briefly, is, I presume, as familiar to most of this assembly as any other part of the history of our country. I suppose that few of my hearers are not as familiar with that part of history as I am, and I only mention it to recall your attention to it at this time. And hence I ask how extraordinary a thing it is that a man who has occupied a position upon the floor of the Senate of the United States, who is now in his third term, and who looks to see the government of this whole country fall into his own hands, pretending to give a truthful and accurate history of the slavery question in this country, should so entirely ignore the whole of that portion of our history —the most important of all. Is it not a most extraordinary spectacle, that a man should stand

up and ask for any confidence in his statements,
who sets out as he does with portions of history,
calling upon the people to believe that it is a
true and fair representation, when the leading
part and controlling feature of the whole history
is carefully suppressed?

But the mere leaving out is not the most remarkable feature of this most remarkable essay.
His proposition is to establish that the leading
men of the Revolution were for his great principle of non-intervention by the government in
the question of slavery in the Territories; while
history shows that they decided in the cases actually brought before them in exactly the contrary way, and he knows it. Not only did they
so decide at that time, but they stuck to it during
sixty years, through thick and thin, as long as
there was one of the Revolutionary heroes upon
the stage of political action. Through their
whole course, from first to last, they clung to
freedom. And now he asks the community to
believe that the men of the Revolution were in
favor of his great principle, when we have the
naked history that they themselves dealt with
this very subject-matter of his principle, and utterly repudiated his principle, acting upon a
precisely contrary ground. It is as impudent
and absurd as if a prosecuting attorney should
stand up before a jury, and ask them to convict

A as the murderer of B, while B was walking alive before them.

I say again, if Judge Douglas asserts that the men of the Revolution acted upon principles by which, to be consistent with themselves, they ought to have adopted his popular sovereignty, then, upon a consideration of his own argument, he had a right to make you believe that they understood the principles of government, but misapplied them—that he has arisen to enlighten the world as to the just application of this principle. He has a right to try to persuade you that he understands their principles better than they did, and therefore he will apply them now, not as they did, but as they ought to have done. He has a right to go before the community, and try to convince them of this; but he has no right to attempt to impose upon any one the belief that these men themselves approved of his great principles. There are two ways of establishing a proposition. One is by trying to demonstrate it upon reason, and the other is, to show that great men in former times have thought so and so, and thus to pass it by the weight of pure authority. Now, if Judge Douglas will demonstrate somehow that this is popular sovereignty —the right of one man to make a slave of another, without any right in that other, or any one else, to object,—demonstrate it as Euclid de-

monstrated propositions,—there is no objection.
But when he comes forward, seeking to carry a
principle by bringing to it the authority of men
who themselves utterly repudiate that principle,
I ask that he shall not be permitted to do it.

I see, in the judge's speech here, a short sentence in these words: "Our fathers, when they
formed this government under which we live,
understood this question just as well and even
better than we do now." This is true; I stick
to that. I will stand by Judge Douglas in that
to the bitter end. And now, Judge Douglas,
come and stand by me, and truthfully show how
they acted, understanding it better than we do.
All I ask of you, Judge Douglas, is to stick to
the proposition that the men of the Revolution
understood this subject better than we do now,
and with that better understanding they acted
better than you are trying to act now.

I wish to say something now in regard to the
Dred Scott decision, as dealt with by Judge
Douglas. In that "memorable debate" between
Judge Douglas and myself, last year, the judge
thought fit to commence a process of catechizing
me, and at Freeport I answered his questions,
and propounded some to him. Among others
propounded to him was one that I have here
now. The substance, as I remember it, is: "Can
the people of a United States Territory, under

the Dred Scott decision, in any lawful way, against the wish of any citizen of the United States, exclude slavery from its limits, prior to the formation of a State constitution?" He answered that they could lawfully exclude slavery from the United States Territories, notwithstanding the Dred Scott decision. There was something about that answer that has probably been a trouble to the judge ever since.

The Dred Scott decision expressly gives every citizen of the United States a right to carry his slaves into the United States Territories. And now there was some inconsistency in saying that the decision was right, and saying, too, that the people of the Territory could lawfully drive slavery out again. When all the trash, the words, the collateral matter, was cleared away from it, —all the chaff was fanned out of it,—it was a bare absurdity; no less than that a thing may be lawfully driven away from where it has a lawful right to be. Clear it of all the verbiage, and that is the naked truth of his proposition— that a thing may be lawfully driven from the place where it has a lawful right to stay. Well, it was because the judge could n't help seeing this that he has had so much trouble with it; and what I want to ask your especial attention to, just now, is to remind you, if you have not noticed the fact, that the judge does not any

longer say that the people can exclude slavery.
He does not say so in the copyright essay; he did
not say so in the speech that he made here; and,
so far as I know, since his reëlection to the Senate, he has never said, as he did at Freeport, that
the people of the Territories can exclude slavery.
He desires that you, who wish the Territories
to remain free, should believe that he stands by
that position, but he does not say it himself. He
escapes, to some extent, the absurd position I
have stated by changing his language entirely.
What he says now is something different in language, and we will consider whether it is not
different in sense too.

It is now that the Dred Scott decision, or
rather the Constitution under that decision, does
not carry slavery into the Territories beyond
the power of the people of the Territories to
control it as other property. He does not say
the people can drive it out, but they can control it as other property. The language is different; we should consider whether the sense
is different. Driving a horse out of this lot
is too plain a proposition to be mistaken about;
it is putting him on the other side of the fence.
Or it might be a sort of exclusion of him from
the lot if you were to kill him and let the
worms devour him; but neither of these things
is the same as "controlling him as other prop-

erty." That would be to feed him, to pamper him, to ride him, to use and abuse him, to make the most money out of him, "as other property"; but, please you, what do the men who are in favor of slavery want more than this? What do they really want, other than that slavery, being in the Territories, shall be controlled as other property?

If they want anything else, I do not comprehend it. I ask your attention to this, first, for the purpose of pointing out the change of ground the judge has made; and, in the second place, the importance of the change—that that change is not such as to give you gentlemen who want his popular sovereignty the power to exclude the institution or drive it out at all. I know the judge sometimes squints at the argument that in controlling it as other property by unfriendly legislation they may control it to death, as you might in the case of a horse, perhaps, feed him so lightly and ride him so much that he would die. But when you come to legislative control, there is something more to be attended to. I have no doubt, myself, that if the Territories should undertake to control slave property as other property—that is, control it in such a way that it would be the most valuable as property, and make it bear its just proportion in the way of burdens as property,—really deal with it as

property,—the Supreme Court of the United
States will say, "God speed you, and amen."
But I undertake to give the opinion, at least,
that if the Territories attempt by any direct legislation to drive the man with his slave out of
the Territory, or to decide that his slave is free
because of his being taken in there, or to
tax him to such an extent that he cannot keep
him there, the Supreme Court will unhesita-
tingly decide all such legislation unconstitutional, as long as that Supreme Court is con-
structed as the Dred Scott Supreme Court is.
The first two things they have already decided,
except that there is a little quibble among lawyers between the words *dicta* and decision.
They have already decided that a negro cannot
be made free by territorial legislation.

What is that Dred Scott decision? Judge
Douglas labors to show that it is one thing,
while I think it is altogether different. It is a
long opinion, but it is all embodied in this short
statement: "The Constitution of the United
States forbids Congress to deprive a man of his
property without due process of law; the right
of property in slaves is distinctly and expressly
affirmed in that Constitution; therefore if Congress shall undertake to say that a man's slave
is no longer his slave when he crosses a certain
line into a Territory, that is depriving him of

his property without due process of law, and is unconstitutional." There is the whole Dred Scott decision. They add that if Congress cannot do so itself, Congress cannot confer any power to do so, and hence any effort by the territorial legislature to do either of these things is absolutely decided against. It is a foregone conclusion by that court.

Now, as to this indirect mode by "unfriendly legislation," all lawyers here will readily understand that such a proposition cannot be tolerated for a moment, because a legislature cannot indirectly do that which it cannot accomplish directly. Then I say any legislation to control this property, as property, for its benefit as property, would be hailed by this Dred Scott Supreme Court, and fully sustained; but any legislation driving slave property out, or destroying it as property, directly or indirectly, will most assuredly by that court be held unconstitutional.

Judge Douglas says that if the Constitution carries slavery into the Territories, beyond the power of the people of the Territories to control it as other property, then it follows logically that every one who swears to support the Constitution of the United States must give that support to that property which it needs. And if the Constitution carries slavery into the Territories beyond the power of the people to control it as other property, then it also carries it into the States, because the Constitution is the supreme law of the land. Now, gentlemen, if it were not for my excessive modesty I would say that I told that very thing to Judge Douglas quite a year ago. This argument is here in print, and if it were not for my modesty, as I said, I might call your attention to it. If you read it, you will find that I not only made that argument, but made it better than he has made it since.

There is, however, this difference. I say now, and said then, there is no sort of question that the Supreme Court has decided that it is the right of the slaveholder to take his slave and hold him in the Territory, and, saying this, Judge Douglas himself admits the conclusion. He says if that is so, this consequence will follow; and because this consequence would follow, his argument is, the decision cannot therefore be that way—"that would spoil my popular sovereignty, and it cannot be possible that this great principle has been squelched out in this extraordinary way. It might be, if it were not for the extraordinary consequences of spoiling my humbug."

Another feature of the judge's argument about the Dred Scott case is an effort to show that that decision deals altogether in declarations of negatives; that the Constitution does not affirm anything as expounded by the Dred Scott decision, but it only declares a want of power, a total absence of power, in reference to the Territories. It seems to be his purpose to make the whole of that decision to result in a mere negative declaration of a want of power in Congress to do anything in relation to this matter in the Territories. I know the opinion of the judges states that there is a total absence of power; but that is, unfortunately, not all it states; for the judges add that the right of property in a slave is distinctly and expressly affirmed in the Constitution. It does not stop at saying that the right of property in a slave is recognized in the Constitution, is declared to exist somewhere in the Constitution, but says it is affirmed in the Constitution. Its language is equivalent to saying that it is embodied and so woven into that instrument that it cannot be detached without breaking the Constitution itself, —in a word, it is a part of the Constitution.

Douglas is singularly unfortunate in his effort to make out that decision to be altogether negative, when the express language at the vital part is that this is distinctly affirmed in the Constitution. I think myself, and I repeat it here, that this decision does not merely carry slavery into the Territories, but by its logical conclusion it carries it into the States in which we live. One provision of that Constitution is, that it shall be the supreme law of the land,—I do not quote the language,—any constitution or law of any State to the contrary notwithstanding. This Dred Scott decision says that the right of property in a slave is affirmed in that Constitution which is the supreme law of the land, any State constitution or law notwithstanding. Then I say that to destroy a thing which is distinctly affirmed and supported by the supreme law of the land, even by a State constitution or law, is a violation of that supreme law, and there is no escape from it. In my judgment there is no avoiding that result, save that the American people shall see that State constitutions are better construed than our Constitution is construed in that decision. They must take care that it is more faithfully and truly carried out than it is there expounded.

I must hasten to a conclusion. Near the beginning of my remarks I said that this insidious Douglas popular sovereignty is the measure that now threatens the purpose of the Republican party to prevent slavery from being nationalized in the United States. I propose to ask your attention for a little while to some propositions in affirmance of that statement. Take it just as it stands, and apply it as a principle; extend and apply that principle elsewhere, and consider where it will lead you. I now put this proposition, that Judge Douglas's popular sovereignty applied will reopen the African slave-trade; and I will demonstrate it by any variety of ways in which you can turn the subject or look at it.

The judge says that the people of the Territories have the right, by his principle, to have slaves if they want them. Then I say that the people in Georgia have the right to buy slaves in Africa if they want them, and I defy any man on earth to show any distinction between the two things—to show that the one is either more wicked or more unlawful; to show, on original principles, that one is better or worse than the other; or to show by the Constitution that one differs a whit from the other. He will tell me, doubtless, that there is no constitutional provision against people taking slaves into the new Territories, and I tell him that there is equally no constitutional provision against buying slaves in Africa. He will tell you that a people in the exercise of popular sovereignty ought to do as they please about that thing, and have slaves if they want them; and I tell you that the people of Georgia are as much entitled to popular sovereignty, and to buy slaves in Africa, if they

want them, as the people of the Territory are
to have slaves if they want them. I ask any man,
dealing honestly with himself, to point out a
distinction.

I have recently seen a letter of Judge Douglas's, in which, without stating that to be the
object, he doubtless endeavors to make a distinction between the two. He says he is unalterably
opposed to the repeal of the laws against the
African slave-trade. And why? He then
seeks to give a reason that would not apply to
his popular sovereignty in the Territories.
What is that reason? "The abolition of the
African slave-trade is a compromise of the Constitution." I deny it. There is no truth in the
proposition that the abolition of the African
slave-trade is a compromise of the Constitution.
No man can put his finger on anything in the
Constitution, or on the line of history, which
shows it. It is a mere barren assertion, made
simply for the purpose of getting up a distinction between the revival of the African slave-
trade and his "great principle."

At the time the Constitution of the United
States was adopted it was expected that the
slave-trade would be abolished. I should assert, and insist upon that, if Judge Douglas denied it. But I know that it was equally expected that slavery would be excluded from the

Territories, and I can show by history that in regard to these two things public opinion was exactly alike, while in regard to positive action, there was more done in the ordinance of '87 to resist the spread of slavery than was ever done to abolish the foreign slave-trade. Lest I be misunderstood, I say again that at the time of the formation of the Constitution, public expectation was that the slave-trade would be abolished, but no more so than that the spread of slavery in the Territories should be restrained. They stand alike, except that in the ordinance of '87 there was a mark left by public opinion, showing that it was more committed against the spread of slavery in the Territories than against the foreign slave-trade.

Compromise! What word of compromise was there about it? Why, the public sense was then in favor of the abolition of the slave-trade; but there was at the time a very great commercial interest involved in it, and extensive capital in that branch of trade. There were doubtless the incipient stages of improvement in the South in the way of farming, dependent on the slave-trade, and they made a proposition to Congress to abolish the trade after allowing it twenty years, a sufficient time for the capital and commerce engaged in it to be transferred to other channels. They made no provision that it should be abolished in twenty years; I do not doubt that they expected it would be; but they made no bargain about it. The public sentiment left no doubt in the minds of any that it would be done away. I repeat, there is nothing in the history of those times in favor of that matter being a compromise of the Constitution. It was the public expectation at the time, manifested in a thousand ways, that the spread of slavery should also be restricted.

Then I say if this principle is established, that there is no wrong in slavery, and whoever wants it has a right to have it; that it is a matter of dollars and cents; a sort of question as to how they shall deal with brutes; that between us and the negro here there is no sort of question, but that at the South the question is between the negro and the crocodile; that it is a mere matter of policy; that there is a perfect right, according to interest, to do just as you please— when this is done, where this doctrine prevails, the miners and sappers will have formed public opinion for the slave-trade. They will be ready for Jeff Davis and Stephens, and other leaders of that company, to sound the bugle for the revival of the slave-trade, for the second Dred Scott decision, for the flood of slavery to be poured over the free States, while we shall be here tied down and helpless, and run over like sheep.

It is to be a part and parcel of this same idea to say to men who want to adhere to the Democratic party, who have always belonged to that party, and are only looking about for some excuse to stick to it, but nevertheless hate slavery, that Douglas's popular sovereignty is as good a way as any to oppose slavery. They allow themselves to be persuaded easily, in accordance with their previous dispositions, into this belief, that it is about as good a way of opposing slavery as any, and we can do that without straining our old party ties or breaking up old political associations. We can do so without being called negro-worshippers. We can do that without being subjected to the gibes and sneers that are so readily thrown out in place of argument where no argument can be found. So let us stick to this popular sovereignty—this insidious popular sovereignty. Now let me call your attention to one thing that has really happened, which shows this gradual and steady debauching of public opinion, this course of preparation for the revival of the slave-trade, for the territorial slave-code, and the new Dred Scott decision that is to carry slavery into the free States. Did you ever, five years ago, hear of anybody in the world saying that the negro had no share in the Declaration of National Independence; that it did not mean negroes at all, and when "all men" were spoken of negroes were not included?

I am satisfied that five years ago that proposition was not put upon paper by any living being anywhere. I have been unable at any time to find a man in an audience who would declare that he had ever known anybody saying so five years ago. But last year there was not a "Douglas popular sovereignty" man in Illinois who did not say it. Is there one in Ohio but declares his firm belief that the Declaration of Independence did not mean negroes at all? I do not know how this is; I have not been here much; but I presume you are very much alike everywhere. Then I suppose that all now express the belief that the Declaration of Independence never did mean negroes. I call upon one of them to say that he said it five years ago.

If you think that now, and did not think it then, the next thing that strikes me is to remark that there has been a change wrought in you, and a very significant change it is, being no less than changing the negro, in your estimation, from the rank of a man to that of a brute. They are taking him down, and placing him, when spoken of, among reptiles and crocodiles, as Judge Douglas himself expresses it.

Is not this change wrought in your minds a very important change? Public opinion in this country is everything. In a nation like ours this popular sovereignty and squatter sovereignty have already wrought a change in the public mind to the extent I have stated. There is no man in this crowd who can contradict it.

Now, if you are opposed to slavery honestly, as much as anybody, I ask you to note that fact, and the like of which is to follow, to be plastered on, layer after layer, until very soon you are prepared to deal with the negro everywhere as with the brute. If public sentiment has not been debauched already to this point, a new turn of the screw in that direction is all that is wanting; and this is constantly being done by the teachers of this insidious popular sovereignty. You need but one or two turns further until your minds, now ripening under these teachings, will be ready for all these things, and you will receive and support, or submit to, the slave-trade revived with all its horrors, a slave-code enforced in our Territories, and a new Dred Scott decision to bring slavery up into the very heart of the free North.   This, I must say, is but carrying out those words prophetically spoken by Mr. Clay many, many years ago,—I believe more than thirty years,—when he told an audience that if they would repress all tendencies

to liberty and ultimate emancipation, they must
go back to the era of our independence and muz-
zle the cannon which thundered its annual joy-
ous return on the Fourth of July; they must
blow out the moral lights around us; they must
penetrate the human soul, and eradicate the love
of liberty; but until they did these things, and
others eloquently enumerated by him, they could
not repress all tendencies to ultimate emancipation.

I ask attention to the fact that in a preëminent
degree these popular sovereigns are at this work:
blowing out the moral lights around us; teaching
that the negro is no longer a man, but a brute;
that the Declaration has nothing to do with him;
that he ranks with the crocodile and the reptile;
that man, with body and soul, is a matter of dollars and cents. I suggest to this portion of the
Ohio Republicans, or Democrats, if there be any
present, the serious consideration of this fact,
that there is now going on among you a steady
process of debauching public opinion on this
subject. With this, my friends, I bid you adieu.

SPEECH AT CINCINNATI, OHIO, September 17, 1859

MY FELLOW-CITIZENS of the State of Ohio: This is the first time in my life that I have appeared before an audience in so great a city as this. I therefore—though I am no longer a young man—make this appearance under some degree of embarrassment. But I have found that when one is embarrassed, usually the shortest way to get through with it is to quit talking or thinking about it, and go at something else.

I understand that you have had recently with you my very distinguished friend, Judge Douglas, of Illinois, and I understand, without having had an opportunity (not greatly sought, to be sure) of seeing a report of the speech that he made here, that he did me the honor to mention my humble name. I suppose that he did so for the purpose of making some objection to some sentiment at some time expressed by me. I should expect, it is true, that Judge Douglas had reminded you, or informed you, if you had never before heard it, that I had once in my life declared it as my opinion that this govern-

Old State House, Springfield, Ills.

Where Lincoln had his office during his first Presidential campaign.

ment cannot "endure permanently half slave and half free; that a house divided against itself cannot stand," and, as I had expressed it, I did not expect the house to fall; that I did not expect the Union to be dissolved, but that I did expect it would cease to be divided; that it would become all one thing or all the other; that either the opposition of slavery will arrest the further spread of it, and place it where the public mind would rest in the belief that it was in the course of ultimate extinction, or the friends of slavery will push it forward until it becomes alike lawful in all the States, old or new, free as well as slave. I did, fifteen months ago, express that opinion, and upon many occasions Judge Douglas has denounced it, and has greatly, intentionally or unintentionally, misrepresented my purpose in the expression of that opinion.

I presume, without having seen a report of his speech, that he did so here. I presume that he alluded also to that opinion in different language, having been expressed at a subsequent time by Governor Seward, of New York, and that he took the two in a lump and denounced them; that he tried to point out that there was something couched in this opinion which led to the making of an entire uniformity of the local institutions of the various States of the Union, in utter disregard of the different States, which in their nature would seem to require a variety of institutions, and a variety of laws conforming to the differences in the nature of the different States.

Not only so; I presume he insisted that this was a declaration of war between the free and slave States—that it was the sounding to the onset of continual war between the different States, the slave and free States.

This charge, in this form, was made by Judge Douglas on, I believe, the 9th of July, 1858, in Chicago, in my hearing. On the next evening I made some reply to it. I informed him that many of the inferences he drew from that expression of mine were altogether foreign to any purpose entertained by me, and in so far as he should ascribe these inferences to me, as my purpose, he was entirely mistaken; and in so far as he might argue that whatever might be my purpose, actions, conforming to my views, would lead to these results, he might argue and establish if he could; but, so far as purposes were concerned, he was totally mistaken as to me.

When I made that reply to him, I told him, on the question of declaring war between the different States of the Union, that I had not said I did not expect any peace upon this question until slavery was exterminated; that I had only said I expected peace when that institution was

put where the public mind should rest in the
belief that it was in course of ultimate extinction; that I believed, from the organization of
our government until a very recent period of
time, the institution had been placed and continued upon such a basis; that we had comparative peace upon that question through a portion
of that period of time, only because the public
mind rested in that belief in regard to it, and
that when we returned to that position in relation to that matter, I supposed we should again
have peace as we previously had. I assured
him, as I now assure you, that I neither then had,
nor have, nor ever had, any purpose in any way
of interfering with the institution of slavery
where it exists. I believe we have no power,
under the Constitution of the United States, or
rather under the form of government under
which we live, to interfere with the institution
of slavery, or any other of the institutions of
our sister States, be they free or slave States. I
declared then, and I now re-declare, that I have
as little inclination to interfere with the institution of slavery where it now exists, through
the instrumentality of the General Government,
or any other instrumentality, as I believe we
have no power to do so. I accidentally used
this expression: I had no purpose of entering
into the slave States to disturb the institution of

slavery. So, upon the first occasion that Judge Douglas got an opportunity to reply to me, he passed by the whole body of what I had said upon that subject, and seized upon the particular expression of mine, that I had no purpose of entering into the slave States to disturb the institution of slavery. "Oh, no," said he; "he [Lincoln] won't enter into the slave States to disturb the institution of slavery; he is too prudent a man to do such a thing as that; he only means that he will go on to the line between the free and slave States, and shoot over at them. This is all he means to do. He means to do them all the harm he can, to disturb them all he can, in such a way as to keep his own hide in perfect safety."

Well, now, I did not think, at that time, that that was either a very dignified or very logical argument; but so it was, and I had to get along with it as well as I could.

It has occurred to me here to-night that if I ever do shoot over the line at the people on the other side of the line, into the slave State, and propose to do so keeping my skin safe, that I have now about the best chance I shall ever have. I should not wonder if there are some Kentuckians about this audience; we are close to Kentucky; and whether that be so or not, we are on elevated ground, and by speaking distinctly I should not wonder if some of the Kentuckians would hear me on the other side of the river. For that reason I propose to address a portion of what I have to say to the Kentuckians.

I say, then, in the first place, to the Kentuckians, that I am what they call, as I understand it, a "Black Republican." I think slavery is wrong, morally and politically. I desire that it should be no further spread in these United States, and I should not object if it should gradually terminate in the whole Union. While I say this for myself, I say to you Kentuckians that I understand you differ radically with me upon this proposition; that you believe slavery is a good thing; that slavery is right; that it ought to be extended and perpetuated in this Union. Now, there being this broad difference between us, I do not pretend, in addressing myself to you Kentuckians, to attempt proselyting you; that would be a vain effort. I do not enter upon it. I only propose to try to show you that you ought to nominate for the next presidency, at Charleston, my distinguished friend, Judge Douglas. In all that there is no real difference between you and him; I understand he is as sincerely for you, and more wisely for you, than you are for yourselves. I will try to demonstrate that proposition. Understand now, I say that I believe he is as sincerely for you, and more wisely for you, than you are for yourselves.

What do you want more than anything else to make successful your views of slavery—to advance the outspread of it, and to secure and perpetuate the nationality of it? What do you want more than anything else? What is needed absolutely? What is indispensable to you? Why, if I may be allowed to answer the question, it is to retain a hold upon the North—it is to retain support and strength from the free States. If you can get this support and strength from the free States, you can succeed. If you do not get this support and this strength from the free States, you are in the minority, and you are beaten at once.

If that proposition be admitted,—and it is undeniable,—then the next thing I say to you is, that Douglas of all the men in this nation is the only man that affords you any hold upon the free States; that no other man can give you any strength in the free States. This being so, if you doubt the other branch of the proposition, whether he is for you,—whether he is really for you, as I have expressed it,—I propose asking your attention for a while to a few facts.

The issue between you and me, understand, is that I think slavery is wrong, and ought not to be outspread, and you think it is right, and ought to be extended and perpetuated. I now proceed to try to show to you that Douglas is as sincerely for you, and more wisely for you, than you are for yourselves.

In the first place, we know that in a government like this, a government of the people, where the voice of all the men of the country, substantially, enters into the administration of the government, what lies at the bottom of all of it is public opinion. I lay down the proposition that Judge Douglas is not only the man that promises you in advance a hold upon the North, and support in the North, but that he constantly molds public opinion to your ends; that in every possible way he can, he molds the public opinion of the North to your ends; and if there are a few things in which he seems to be against you,—a few things which he says that appear to be against you, and a few that he forbears to say which you would like to have him say, you ought to remember that the saying of the one, or the forbearing to say the other, would lose his hold upon the North, and, by consequence, would lose his capacity to serve you.

Upon this subject of molding public opinion, I call your attention to the fact—for a well-established fact it is—that the judge never says your institution of slavery is wrong; he never says it is right, to be sure, but he never says it is wrong. There is not a public man in the United States, I believe, with the exception of Senator Douglas, who has not, at some time in his life, declared his opinion whether the thing is right or wrong; but Senator Douglas never declares it is wrong. He leaves himself at perfect liberty to do all in your favor which he would be hindered from doing if he were to declare the thing to be wrong. On the contrary, he takes all the chances that he has for inveigling the sentiment of the North, opposed to slavery, into your support, by never saying it is right. This you ought to set down to his credit. You ought to give him full credit for this much, little though it be in comparison to the whole which he does for you.

Some other things I will ask your attention to. He said upon the floor of the United States Senate, and he has repeated it, as I understand, a great many times, that he does not care whether slavery is "voted up or voted down." This again shows you, or ought to show you, if you would reason upon it, that he does not believe it to be wrong; for a man may say, when he sees nothing wrong in a thing, that he does not care whether it be voted up or voted down; but no man can logically say that he cares not whether a thing goes up or goes down which appears to him to be wrong. You therefore have a demonstration in this, that to Judge Douglas's mind your favorite institution, which you desire to have spread out and made perpetual, is no wrong.

Another thing he tells you, in a speech made at Memphis, in Tennessee, shortly after the canvass in Illinois, last year. He there distinctly told the people that there was a "line drawn by the Almighty across this continent, on the one side of which the soil must always be cultivated by slaves"; that he did not pretend to know exactly where that line was, but that there was such a line. I want to ask your attention to that proposition again—that there is one portion of this continent where the Almighty has designed the soil shall always be cultivated by slaves; that its being cultivated by slaves at that place is right; that it has the direct sympathy and authority of the Almighty. Whenever you can get these Northern audiences to adopt the opinion that slavery is right on the other side of the Ohio; whenever you can get them, in pursuance of Douglas's views, to adopt that sentiment, they will very readily make the other argument, which is perfectly logical, that that which is right on that side of the Ohio cannot be wrong on this, and that if you have that property on that side of the Ohio, under the seal and stamp

of the Almighty, when by any means it escapes
over here, it is wrong to have constitutions and
laws "to devil" you about it. So Douglas is
molding the public opinion of the North, first
to say that the thing is right in your State over
the Ohio River, and hence to say that that which
is right there is not wrong here, and that all laws
and constitutions here, recognizing it as being
wrong, are themselves wrong, and ought to be
repealed and abrogated. He will tell you, men
of Ohio, that if you choose here to have laws
against slavery, it is in conformity to the idea
that your climate is not suited to it; that your
climate is not suited to slave labor, and therefore you have constitutions and laws against it.

Let us attend to that argument for a little
while, and see if it be sound. You do not raise
sugar-cane (except the new-fashioned sugar-
cane, and you won't raise that long), but they
do raise it in Louisiana. You don't raise it in
Ohio because you can't raise it profitably, because the climate don't suit it. They do raise
it in Louisiana because there it is profitable.
Now Douglas will tell you that is precisely the
slavery question; that they do have slaves there
because they are profitable, and you don't have
them here because they are not profitable. If
that is so, then it leads to dealing with the one
precisely as with the other. Is there, then, any-

thing in the constitution or laws of Ohio against raising sugar-cane?   Have you found it necessary to put any such provision in your law? Surely not!   No man desires to raise sugar-cane in Ohio; but if any man did desire to do so, you would say it was a tyrannical law that forbids his doing so; and whenever you shall agree with Douglas, whenever your minds are brought to adopt his argument, as surely you will have reached the conclusion that although slavery is not profitable in Ohio, if any man want it, it is wrong to him not to let him have it.

In this matter Judge Douglas is preparing the public mind for you of Kentucky, to make perpetual that good thing in your estimation, about which you and I differ.

In this connection let me ask your attention to another thing.   I believe it is safe to assert that, five years ago, no living man had expressed the opinion that the negro had no share in the Declaration of Independence.   Let me state that again: Five years ago no living man had expressed the opinion that the negro had no share in the Declaration of Independence.   If there is in this large audience any man who ever knew of that opinion being put upon paper as much as five years ago, I will be obliged to him now, or at a subsequent time, to show it.

If that be true, I wish you then to note the

next fact—that within the space of five years
Senator Douglas, in the argument of this question, has got his entire party, so far as I know,
without exception, to join in saying that the negro has no share in the Declaration of Independence. If there be now in all these United
States one Douglas man that does not say this,
I have been unable upon any occasion to scare
him up. Now, if none of you said this five years
ago, and all of you say it now, that is a matter
that you Kentuckians ought to note. That is a
vast change in the Northern public sentiment
upon that question.

Of what tendency is that change? The tendency of that change is to bring the public mind
to the conclusion that when men are spoken of,
the negro is not meant; that when negroes are
spoken of, brutes alone are contemplated. That
change in public sentiment has already degraded
the black man, in the estimation of Douglas and
his followers, from the condition of a man of
some sort, and assigned him to the condition of
a brute. Now you Kentuckians ought to give
Douglas credit for this. That is the largest
possible stride that can be made in regard to the
perpetuation of your good thing of slavery.

In Kentucky, perhaps,—in many of the slave
States certainly,—you are trying to establish the
rightfulness of slavery by reference to the Bible.

You are trying to show that slavery existed in the Bible times by divine ordinance. Now Douglas is wiser than you for your own benefit, upon that subject. Douglas knows that whenever you establish that slavery was right by the Bible, it will occur that that slavery was the slavery of the white man,—of men without reference to color,—and he knows very well that you may entertain that idea in Kentucky as much as you please, but you will never win any Northern support upon it. He makes a wiser argument for you; he makes the argument that the slavery of the black man, the slavery of the man who has a skin of a different color from your own, is right. He thereby brings to your support Northern voters who could not for a moment be brought by your own argument of the Bible-right of slavery. Will you not give him credit for that? Will you not say that in this matter he is more wisely for you than you are for yourselves?

Now, having established with his entire party this doctrine,—having been entirely successful in that branch of his efforts in your behalf,—he is ready for another.

At this same meeting at Memphis, he declared that in all contests between the negro and the white man, he was for the white man, but that in all questions between the negro and the croco-

dile he was for the negro. He did not make
that declaration accidentally at Memphis. He
made it a great many times in the canvass in
Illinois last year (though I don't know that it
was reported in any of his speeches there; but
he frequently made it). I believe he repeated
it at Columbus, and I should not wonder if he
repeated it here. It is, then, a deliberate way of
expressing himself upon that subject. It is a
matter of mature deliberation with him thus to
express himself upon that point of his case. It
therefore requires some deliberate attention.

The first inference seems to be that if you do
not enslave the negro you are wronging the white
man in some way or other; and that whoever is opposed to the negro being enslaved is,
in some way or other, against the white man.
Is not that a falsehood? If there was a necessary conflict between the white man and the
negro, I should be for the white man as much
as Judge Douglas; but I say there is no such
necessary conflict. I say that there is room
enough for us all to be free, and that it not only
does not wrong the white man that the negro
should be free, but it positively wrongs the mass
of the white men that the negro should be enslaved; that the mass of white men are really in-
jured by the effects of slave-labor in the vicinity
of the fields of their own labor.

hear him try it. If any man can show how the people of Kansas have a better right to slaves because they want them, than the people of Georgia have to buy them in Africa, I want him to do it. I think it cannot be done. If it is "popular sovereignty" for the people to have slaves because they want them, it is popular sovereignty for them to buy them in Africa, because they desire to do so.

I know that Douglas has recently made a little effort—not seeming to notice that he had a different theory—has made an effort to get rid of that. He has written a letter, addressed to somebody, I believe, who resides in Iowa, declaring his opposition to the repeal of the laws that prohibit the African slave-trade. He bases his opposition to such repeal upon the ground that these laws are themselves one of the compromises of the Constitution of the United States. Now it would be very interesting to see Judge Douglas, or any of his friends, turn to the Constitution of the United States and point out that compromise, to show where there is any compromise in the Constitution, or provision in the Constitution, expressed or implied, by which the administrators of that Constitution are under any obligation to repeal the African slave-trade. I know, or at least I think I know, that the framers of that Constitution did expect that the

African slave-trade would be abolished at the end of twenty years, to which time their prohibition against its being abolished extended. I think there is abundant contemporaneous history to show that the framers of the Constitution expected it to be abolished. But while they so expected, they gave nothing for that expectation, and they put no provision in the Constitution requiring it should be so abolished. The migration or importation of such persons as the States shall see fit to admit shall not be prohibited, but a certain tax might be levied upon such importation. But what was to be done after that time? The Constitution is as silent about that as it is silent, personally, about myself. There is absolutely nothing in it about that subject—there is only the expectation of the framers of the Constitution that the slave-trade would be abolished at the end of that time, and they expected it would be abolished, owing to public sentiment, before that time, and they put that provision in, in order that it should not be abolished before that time, for reasons which I suppose they thought to be sound ones, but which I will not now try to enumerate before you.

But while they expected the slave-trade would be abolished at that time, they expected that the spread of slavery into the new Territories should also be restricted. It is as easy to prove

that the framers of the Constitution of the
United States expected that slavery should be
prohibited from extending into the new Territories, as it is to prove that it was expected that
the slave-trade should be abolished. Both these
things were expected. One was no more expected than the other, and one was no more a
compromise of the Constitution than the other.
There was nothing said in the Constitution in
regard to the spread of slavery into the Territories. I grant that, but there was something
very important said about it by the same generation of men in the adoption of the old ordinance
of '87, through the influence of which you here
in Ohio, our neighbors in Indiana, we in Illinois, our neighbors in Michigan and Wisconsin, are happy, prosperous, teeming millions of
free men. That generation of men, though not
to the full extent members of the convention
that framed the Constitution, were to some extent members of that convention, holding seats
at the same time in one body and the other, so
that if there was any compromise on either of
these subjects, the strong evidence is that that
compromise was in favor of the restriction of
slavery from the new Territories.

But Douglas says that he is unalterably opposed to the repeal of those laws; because, in his
view, it is a compromise of the Constitution.

You Kentuckians, no doubt, are somewhat of-
fended with that! You ought not to be! You
ought to be patient! You ought to know that if
he said less than that, he would lose the power
of "lugging" the Northern States to your support. Really, what you would push him to do
would take from him his entire power to serve
you. And you ought to remember how long,
by precedent, Judge Douglas holds himself
obliged to stick by compromises. You ought
to remember that by the time you yourselves
think you are ready to inaugurate measures for
the revival of the African slave-trade, that sufficient time will have arrived, by precedent, for
Judge Douglas to break through that compromise. He says now nothing more strong than
he said in 1849 when he declared in favor of the
Missouri Compromise—that precisely four
years and a quarter after he declared that compromise to be a sacred thing, which "no ruthless
hand would ever dare to touch," he, himself,
brought forward the measure ruthlessly to destroy it. By a mere calculation of time it will
only be four years more until he is ready to take
back his profession about the sacredness of the
compromise abolishing the slave-trade. Precisely as soon as you are ready to have his services in that direction, by fair calculation, you
may be sure of having them.

But you remember and set down to Judge Douglas's debt, or discredit, that he, last year, said the people of Territories can, in spite of the Dred Scott decision, exclude your slaves from those Territories; that he declared by "unfriendly legislation" the extension of your property into the new Territories may be cut off in the teeth of that decision of the Supreme Court of the United States.

He assumed that position at Freeport, on the 27th of August, 1858. He said that the people of the Territories can exclude slavery, in so many words. You ought, however, to bear in mind that he has never said it since. You may hunt in every speech that he has since made, and he has never used that expression once. He has never seemed to notice that he is stating his views differently from what he did then; but by some sort of accident, he has always really stated it differently. He has always since then declared that "the Constitution does not carry slavery into the Territories of the United States beyond the power of the people legally to control it, as other property." Now there is a difference in the language used upon that former occasion and in this latter day. There may or may not be a difference in the meaning, but it is worth while considering whether there is not also a difference in meaning.

What is it to exclude? Why, it is to drive it out. It is in some way to put it out of the Territory. It is to force it across the line, or change its character, so that as property it is out of existence. But what is the controlling of it "as other property"? Is controlling it as other property the same thing as destroying it, or driving it away? I should think not. I should think the controlling of it as other property would be just about what you in Kentucky should want. I understand the controlling of property means the controlling of it for the benefit of the owner of it. While I have no doubt the Supreme Court of the United States would say "God speed" to any of the territorial legislatures that should thus control slave property, they would sing quite a different tune if by the pretense of controlling it they were to undertake to pass laws which virtually excluded it, and that upon a very well known principle to all lawyers, that what a legislature cannot directly do, it cannot do by indirection; that as the legislature has not the power to drive slaves out, they have no power by indirection, by tax, or by imposing burdens in any way on that property, to effect the same end, and that any attempt to do so would be held by the Dred Scott court unconstitutional.

Douglas is not willing to stand by his first

proposition that they can exclude it, because we have seen that that proposition amounts to nothing more nor less than the naked absurdity that you may lawfully drive out that which has a lawful right to remain. He admitted at first that the slave might be lawfully taken into the Territories under the Constitution of the United States, and yet asserted that he might be lawfully driven out. That being the proposition, it is the absurdity I have stated. He is not willing to stand in the face of that direct, naked, and impudent absurdity; he has, therefore, modified his language into that of being "controlled as other property."

The Kentuckians don't like this in Douglas! I will tell you where it will go. He now swears by the court. He was once a leading man in Illinois to break down a court because it had made a decision he did not like. But he now not only swears by the court, the courts having got to working for you, but he denounces all men that do not swear by the courts as unpatriotic, as bad citizens. When one of these acts of unfriendly legislation shall impose such heavy burdens as to, in effect, destroy property in slaves in a Territory, and show plainly enough that there can be no mistake in the purpose of the legislature to make them so burdensome, this same Supreme Court will decide that

law to be unconstitutional, and he will be ready
to say for your benefit, "I swear by the court; I
give it up"; and while that is going on he has
been getting all his men to swear by the courts,
and to give it up with him. In this again he
serves you faithfully, and, as I say, more wisely
than you serve yourselves.

Again, I have alluded in the beginning of
these remarks to the fact that Judge Douglas
has made great complaint of my having expressed the opinion that this government "cannot endure permanently half slave and half
free." He has complained of Seward for using
different language, and declaring that there is
an "irrepressible conflict" between the principles of free and slave labor. [A voice: "He
says it is not original with Seward. That is
original with Lincoln."] I will attend to that
immediately, sir. Since that time, Hickman, of
Pennsylvania, expressed the same sentiment.
He has never denounced Mr. Hickman. Why?
There is a little chance, notwithstanding that
opinion in the mouth of Hickman, that he may
yet be a Douglas man. That is the difference.
It is not unpatriotic to hold that opinion, if a
man is a Douglas man.

But neither I, nor Seward, nor Hickman is
entitled to the enviable or unenviable distinction
of having first expressed that idea. That same

idea was expressed by the Richmond "Enquirer" in Virginia, in 1856, quite two years before it was expressed by the first of us. And while Douglas was pluming himself that in his conflict with my humble self, last year, he had "squelched out" that fatal heresy, as he delighted to call it, and had suggested that if he only had had a chance to be in New York and meet Seward he would have "squelched" it there also, it never occurred to him to breathe a word against Pryor. I don't think that you can discover that Douglas ever talked of going to Virginia to "squelch" out that idea there. No. More than that. That same Roger A. Pryor was brought to Washington City and made the editor of the *par excellence* Douglas paper after making use of that expression, which, in us, is so unpatriotic and heretical. From all this my Kentucky friends may see that this opinion is heretical in his view only when it is expressed by men suspected of a desire that the country shall all become free, and not when expressed by those fairly known to entertain the desire that the whole country shall become slave. When expressed by that class of men, it is in no wise offensive to him. In this again, my friends of Kentucky, you have Judge Douglas with you.

There is another reason why you Southern people ought to nominate Douglas at your convention at Charleston. That reason is the wonderful capacity of the man; the power he has of doing what would seem to be impossible. Let me call your attention to one of these apparently impossible things.

Douglas had three or four very distinguished men, of the most extreme antislavery views of any men in the Republican party, expressing their desire for his reëlection to the Senate last year. That would, of itself, have seemed to be a little wonderful, but that wonder is heightened when we see that Wise, of Virginia, a man exactly opposed to them, a man who believes in the divine right of slavery, was also expressing his desire that Douglas should be reëlected; that another man that may be said to be kindred to Wise, Mr. Breckinridge, the Vice-President, and of your own State, was also agreeing with the antislavery men in the North that Douglas ought to be reëlected. Still, to heighten the wonder, a senator from Kentucky, whom I have always loved with an affection as tender and endearing as I have ever loved any man, who was opposed to the antislavery men for reasons which seemed sufficient to him, and equally opposed to Wise and Breckinridge, was writing letters into Illinois to secure the reëlection of Douglas. Now that all these conflicting elements should be brought, while at daggers' points with one another, to support him, is a feat that is worthy for you to note and consider. It is quite probable that each of these classes of men thought, by the reëlection of Douglas, their peculiar views would gain something; it is probable that the antislavery men thought their views would gain something; that Wise and Breckinridge thought so too, as regards their opinions; that Mr. Crittenden thought that his views would gain something, although he was opposed to both these other men. It is probable that each and all of them thought that they were using Douglas, and it is yet an unsolved problem whether he was not using them all. If he was, then it is for you to consider whether that power to perform wonders is one for you lightly to throw away.

There is one other thing that I will say to you in this relation. It is but my opinion; I give it to you without a fee. It is my opinion that it is for you to take him or be defeated; and that if you do take him you may be beaten. You will surely be beaten if you do not take him. We, the Republicans and others forming the opposition of the country, intend to "stand by our guns," to be patient and firm, and in the long run to beat you whether you take him or not. We know that before we fairly beat you, we have to beat you both together. We know

that "you are all of a feather," and that we have
to beat you all together, and we expect to do it.
We don't intend to be very impatient about it.
We mean to be as deliberate and calm about it
as it is possible to be, but as firm and resolved
as it is possible for men to be. When we do as
we say, beat you, you perhaps want to know
what we will do with you.

I will tell you, so far as I am authorized to
speak for the opposition, what we mean to do
with you. We mean to treat you, as near as
we possibly can, as Washington, Jefferson, and
Madison treated you. We mean to leave you
alone, and in no way to interfere with your institution; to abide by all and every compromise
of the Constitution, and, in a word, coming back
to the original proposition, to treat you, so far
as degenerated men (if we have degenerated)
may, according to the example of those noble
fathers—Washington, Jefferson, and Madison.
We mean to remember that you are as good as
we; that there is no difference between us other
than the difference of circumstances. We mean
to recognize and bear in mind always that you
have as good hearts in your bosoms as other people, or as we claim to have, and treat you accordingly. We mean to marry your girls when
we have a chance—the white ones, I mean, and

I have the honor to inform you that I once did have a chance in that way.

I have told you what we mean to do. I want to know, now, when that thing takes place, what do you mean to do? I often hear it intimated that you mean to divide the Union whenever a Republican or anything like it is elected President of the United States. [A voice: "That is so."] "That is so," one of them says; I wonder if he is a Kentuckian? [A voice: "He is a Douglas man."] Well, then, I want to know what you are going to do with your half of it? Are you going to split the Ohio down through, and push your half off a piece? Or are you going to keep it right alongside of us outrageous fellows? Or are you going to build up a wall some way between your country and ours, by which that movable property of yours can't come over here any more, to the danger of your losing it? Do you think you can better yourselves on that subject by leaving us here under no obligation whatever to return those specimens of your movable property that come hither? You have divided the Union because we would not do right with you, as you think, upon that subject; when we cease to be under obligations to do anything for you, how much better off do you think you will be? Will you make war upon us and kill us all? Why,

gentlemen, I think you are as gallant and as
brave men as live; that you can fight as bravely
in a good cause, man for man, as any other people living; that you have shown yourselves capable of this upon various occasions; but man
for man, you are not better than we are, and
there are not so many of you as there are of us.
You will never make much of a hand at whipping us. If we were fewer in numbers than
you, I think that you could whip us; if we were
equal it would likely be a drawn battle; but being inferior in numbers, you will make nothing
by attempting to master us.

But perhaps I have addressed myself as long,
or longer, to the Kentuckians than I ought to
have done, inasmuch as I have said that whatever course you take, we intend in the end to
beat you. I propose to address a few remarks
to our friends, by way of discussing with them
the best means of keeping that promise that I
have in good faith made.

It may appear a little episodical for me to
mention the topic of which I shall speak now.
It is a favorite proposition of Douglas's that
the interference of the General Government,
through the ordinance of '87, or through any
other act of the General Government, never has
made, nor ever can make, a free State; that the
ordinance of '87 did not make free States of

Ohio, Indiana, or Illinois; that these States are free upon his "great principle" of popular sovereignty, because the people of those several States have chosen to make them so. At Columbus, and probably here, he undertook to compliment the people that they themselves had made the State of Ohio free, and that the ordinance of '87 was not entitled in any degree to divide the honor with him. I have no doubt that the people of the State of Ohio did make her free according to their own will and judgment; but let the facts be remembered.

In 1802, I believe, it was you who made your first constitution, with the clause prohibiting slavery, and you did it, I suppose, very nearly unanimously; but you should bear in mind that you—speaking of you as one people—that you did so unembarrassed by the actual presence of the institution amongst you; that you made it a free State, not with the embarrassment upon you of already having among you many slaves, which, if they had been here, and you had sought to make a free State, you would not know what to do with. If they had been among you, embarrassing difficulties, most probably, would have induced you to tolerate a slave Constitution instead of a free one; as, indeed, these very difficulties have constrained every people on this continent who have adopted slavery.

Pray, what was it that made you free? What kept you free? Did you not find your country free when you came to decide that Ohio should be a free State? It is important to inquire by what reason you found it so. Let us take an illustration between the States of Ohio and Kentucky. Kentucky is separated by this river Ohio, not a mile wide. A portion of Kentucky by reason of the course of the Ohio, is further north than this portion of Ohio in which we now stand. Kentucky is entirely covered with slavery—Ohio is entirely free from it. What made that difference? Was it climate? No! A portion of Kentucky was further north than this portion of Ohio. Was it soil? No! There is nothing in the soil of the one more favorable to slave-labor than the other. It was not climate or soil that caused one side of the line to be entirely covered with slavery and the other side free of it. What was it? Study over it. Tell us, if you can, in all the range of conjecture, if there be anything you can conceive of that made that difference, other than that there was no law of any sort keeping it out of Kentucky, while the ordinance of '87 kept it out of Ohio. If there is any other reason than this, I confess that it is wholly beyond my power to conceive of it. This, then, I offer to combat

the idea that that ordinance has never made any
State free.

I don't stop at this illustration. I come to
the State of Indiana; and what I have said as
between Kentucky and Ohio, I repeat as between
Indiana and Kentucky; it is equally applicable.
One additional argument is applicable also to
Indiana. In her territorial condition she more
than once petitioned Congress to abrogate the
ordinance entirely, or at least so far as to suspend
its operation for a time, in order that they should
exercise the "popular sovereignty" of having
slaves if they wanted them. The men then controlling the General Government, imitating the
men of the Revolution, refused Indiana that
privilege. And so we have the evidence that
Indiana supposed she could have slaves, if it
were not for that ordinance; that she besought
Congress to put that barrier out of the way; that
Congress refused to do so, and it all ended at
last in Indiana being a free State. Tell me not
then that the ordinance of '87 had nothing to do
with making Indiana a free State, when we find
some men chafing against and only restrained
by that barrier.

Come down again to our State of Illinois.
The great Northwest Territory, including Ohio,
Indiana, Illinois, Michigan, and Wisconsin,
was acquired first, I believe, by the British gov-

ernment, in part, at least, from the French. Before the establishment of our independence, it became a part of Virginia, enabling Virginia afterward to transfer it to the General Government. There were French settlements in what is now Illinois, and at the same time there were French settlements in what is now Missouri—in the tract of country that was not purchased till about 1803. In these French settlements negro slavery had existed for many years —perhaps more than a hundred, if not as much as two hundred, years—at Kaskaskia, in Illinois, and at St. Genevieve, or Cape Girardeau, perhaps, in Missouri. The number of slaves was not very great, but there was about the same number in each place. They were there when we acquired the Territory. There was no effort made to break up the relation of master and slave, and even the ordinance of '87 was not so enforced as to destroy that slavery in Illinois; nor did the ordinance apply to Missouri at all.

What I want to ask your attention to, at this point, is that Illinois and Missouri came into the Union about the same time, Illinois in the latter part of 1818, and Missouri, after a struggle, I believe, some time in 1820. They had been filling up with American people about the same period of time, their progress enabling them to

come into the Union about the same. At the
end of that ten years, in which they had been so
preparing (for it was about that period of
time), the number of slaves in Illinois had actually decreased; while in Missouri, beginning
with very few, at the end of that ten years there
were about ten thousand. This being so, and it
being remembered that Missouri and Illinois
are, to a certain extent, in the same parallel of
latitude,—that the northern half of Missouri
and the southern half of Illinois are in the same
parallel of latitude,—so that climate would
have the same effect upon one as upon the other;
and that in the soil there is no material difference so far as bears upon the question of slavery
being settled upon one or the other; there being
none of those natural causes to produce a difference in filling them, and yet there being a broad
difference in their filling up, we are led again
to inquire what was the cause of that difference.

It is most natural to say that in Missouri
there was no law to keep that country from filling up with slaves, while in Illinois there was
the ordinance of '87. The ordinance being
there, slavery decreased during that ten years—
the ordinance not being in the other, it increased
from a few to ten thousand. Can anybody doubt
the reason of the difference?

I think all these facts most abundantly prove

that my friend Judge Douglas's proposition, that the ordinance of '87, or the national restriction of slavery, never had a tendency to make a free State, is a fallacy—a proposition without the shadow or substance of truth about it.

Douglas sometimes says that all the States (and it is part of that same proposition I have been discussing) that have become free, have become so upon his "great principle"; that the State of Illinois itself came into the Union as a slave State, and that the people, upon the "great principle" of popular sovereignty, have since made it a free State. Allow me but a little while to state to you what facts there are to justify him in saying that Illinois came into the Union as a slave State.

I have mentioned to you that there were a few old French slaves there. They numbered, I think, one or two hundred. Besides that, there had been a territorial law for indenturing black persons. Under that law, in violation of the ordinance of '87, but without any enforcement of the ordinance to overthrow the system, there had been a small number of slaves introduced as indentured persons. Owing to this, the clause for the prohibition of slavery was slightly modified. Instead of running like yours, that neither slavery nor involuntary servitude, except for crime, of which the party shall

have been duly convicted, should exist in the
State, they said that neither slavery nor involuntary servitude should thereafter be introduced, and that the children of indentured servants should be born free; and nothing was said
about the few old French slaves. Out of this
fact, that the clause for prohibiting slavery was
modified because of the actual presence of it,
Douglas asserts again and again that Illinois
came into the Union as a slave State. How far
the facts sustain the conclusion that he draws,
it is for intelligent and impartial men to decide. I leave it with you, with these remarks,
worthy of being remembered, that that little
thing, those few indentured servants being there,
was of itself sufficient to modify a constitution
made by a people ardently desiring to have a
free constitution; showing the power of the actual presence of the institution of slavery to prevent any people, however anxious to make a
free State from making it perfectly so. I have
been detaining you longer perhaps than I ought
to do.

I am in some doubt whether to introduce
another topic upon which I could talk awhile.
[Cries of "Go on," and "Give us it."] It is
this then—Douglas's popular sovereignty, as a
principle, is simply this: If one man chooses
to make a slave of another man, neither that man

nor anybody else has a right to object. Apply
it to government, as he seeks to apply it, and it
is this: If, in a new Territory, into which a few
people are beginning to enter for the purpose
of making their homes, they choose to either
exclude slavery from their limits, or to establish
it there, however one or the other may affect
the persons to be enslaved, or the infinitely
greater number of persons who are afterward to
inhabit that Territory, or the other members of
the family of communities, of which they are
but an incipient member, or the general head
of the family of States as parent of all—however
their action may affect one or the other of these,
there is no power or right to interfere. That is
Douglas's popular sovereignty applied. Now
I think that there is a real popular sovereignty
in the world. I think a definition of popular
sovereignty, in the abstract, would be about this
—that each man shall do precisely as he pleases
with himself, and with all those things which
exclusively concern him. Applied in government, this principle would be, that a general
government shall do all those things which pertain to it, and all the local governments shall do
precisely as they please in respect to those matters which exclusively concern them.

Douglas looks upon slavery as so insignificant
that the people must decide that question for

themselves, and yet they are not fit to decide who shall be their governor, judge, or secretary, or who shall be any of their officers. These are vast national matters, in his estimation; but the little matter in his estimation is that of planting slavery there. That is purely of local interest, which nobody should be allowed to say a word about.

Labor is the great source from which nearly all, if not all, human comforts and necessities are drawn. There is a difference in opinion about the elements of labor in society. Some men assume that there is a necessary connection between capital and labor, and that connection draws within it the whole of the labor of the community. They assume that nobody works unless capital excites them to work. They begin next to consider what is the best way. They say there are but two ways—one is to hire men and to allure them to labor by their consent; the other is to buy the men and drive them to it, and that is slavery. Having assumed that, they proceed to discuss the question of whether the laborers themselves are better off in the condition of slaves or of hired laborers, and they usually decide that they are better off in the condition of slaves.

In the first place, I say that the whole thing is a mistake. That there is a certain relation between capital and labor, I admit. That it does exist, and rightfully exists, I think is true. That men who are industrious and sober and honest in the pursuit of their own interests should after a while accumulate capital, and after that should be allowed to enjoy it in peace, and also if they should choose, when they have accumulated it, to use it to save themselves from actual labor, and hire other people to labor for them, is right. In doing so, they do not wrong the man they employ, for they find men who have not their own land to work upon, or shops to work in, and who are benefited by working for others—hired laborers, receiving their capital for it. Thus a few men that own capital hire a few others, and these establish the relation of capital and labor rightfully—a relation of which I make no complaint. But I insist that that relation, after all, does not embrace more than one eighth of the labor of the country.

[The speaker proceeded to argue that the hired laborer, with his ability to become an employer, must have every precedence over him who labors under the inducement of force. He continued:]

I have taken upon myself, in the name of some of you, to say that we expect upon these principles to ultimately beat them. In order to do so, I think we want and must have a national policy

in regard to the institution of slavery that ac-
knowledges and deals with that institution as
being wrong. Whoever desires the prevention
of the spread of slavery and the nationalization
of that institution, yields all when he yields to
any policy that either recognizes slavery as being right, or as being an indifferent thing.
Nothing will make you successful but setting
up a policy which shall treat the thing as being
wrong. When I say this, I do not mean to say
that this General Government is charged with
the duty of redressing or preventing all the
wrongs in the world; but I do think that it is
charged with preventing and redressing all
wrongs which are wrongs to itself. This government is expressly charged with the duty of providing for the general welfare. We believe that
the spreading out and perpetuity of the institution of slavery impairs the general welfare. We
believe—nay, we know—that that is the only
thing that has ever threatened the perpetuity
of the Union itself. The only thing which has
ever menaced the destruction of the government
under which we live, is this very thing. To repress this thing, we think, is providing for the
general welfare. Our friends in Kentucky differ from us. We need not make our argument
for them; but we who think it is wrong in all its
relations, or in some of them at least, must de-

cide as to our own actions, and our own course, upon our own judgment.

I say that we must not interfere with the institution of slavery in the States where it exists, because the Constitution forbids it, and the general welfare does not require us to do so. We must not withhold an efficient fugitive-slave law, because the Constitution requires us, as I understand it, not to withhold such a law. But we must prevent the outspreading of the institution, because neither the Constitution nor general welfare requires us to extend it. We must prevent the revival of the African slave-trade, and the enacting by Congress of a territorial slave-code. We must prevent each of these things being done by either congresses or courts. The people of these United States are the rightful masters of both congresses and courts, not to overthrow the Constitution, but to overthrow the men who pervert the Constitution.

To do these things we must employ instrumentalities. We must hold conventions; we must adopt platforms, if we conform to ordinary custom; we must nominate candidates; and we must carry elections. In all these things, I think that we ought to keep in view our real purpose, and in none do anything that stands adverse to our purpose. If we shall adopt a platform that fails to recognize or express our purpose, or elect a man that declares himself inimical to our purpose, we not only take nothing by our success, but we tacitly admit that we act upon no other principle than a desire to have "the loaves and fishes," by which, in the end, our apparent success is really an injury to us.

I know that it is very desirable with me, as with everybody else, that all the elements of the Opposition shall unite in the next presidential election, and in all future time. I am anxious that that should be, but there are things seriously to be considered in relation to that matter. If the terms can be arranged, I am in favor of the union. But suppose we shall take up some man, and put him upon one end or the other of the ticket, who declares himself against us in regard to the prevention of the spread of slavery, who turns up his nose and says he is tired of hearing anything more about it, who is more against us than against the enemy—what will be the issue? Why, he will get no slave States after all—he has tried that already until being beat is the rule for him. If we nominate him upon that ground, he will not carry a slave State, and not only so, but that portion of our men who are high strung upon the principle we really fight for will not go for him, and he won't get a single electoral vote anywhere, except, perhaps, in the State of Maryland. There is no use in saying to us that we are stubborn and obstinate because we won't do some such thing as this. We cannot do it. We cannot get our men to vote it. I speak by the card, that we cannot give the State of Illinois in such case by fifty thousand. We would be flatter down than the "Negro Democracy" themselves have the heart to wish to see us.

After saying this much, let me say a little on the other side. There are plenty of men in the slave States that are altogether good enough for me to be either President or Vice-President, provided they will profess their sympathy with our purpose, and will place themselves on such ground that our men, upon principle, can vote for them. There are scores of them—good men in their character for intelligence, and talent, and integrity. If such an one will place himself upon the right ground, I am for his occupying one place upon the next Republican or Opposition ticket. I will heartily go for him. But unless he does so place himself, I think it is a matter of perfect nonsense to attempt to bring about a union upon any other basis; that if a union be made, the elements will scatter so that there can be no success for such a ticket, nor anything like success. The good old maxims of the Bible are applicable, and truly applicable, to human affairs, and in this, as in other things, we may say here that he who is not for us is against us; he who gathereth not with us scattereth. I should be glad to have some of the many good, and able, and noble men of the South to place themselves where we can confer upon them the high honor of an election upon one or the other end of our ticket. It would do my soul good to do that thing. It would enable us to teach them that, inasmuch as we select one of their own number to carry out our principles, we are free from the charge that we mean more than we say.

But, my friends, I have detained you much longer than I expected to do. I believe I may allow myself the compliment to say that you have stayed and heard me with great patience, for which I return you my most sincere thanks.

ANNUAL ADDRESS BEFORE THE WISCONSIN
STATE AGRICULTURAL SOCIETY, AT MILWAU-
KEE, WISCONSIN, September 30, 1859

MEMBERS of the Agricultural Society
and Citizens of Wisconsin: Agricultural fairs are becoming an institution of the country. They are useful in more
ways than one. They bring us together, and
thereby make us better acquainted and better
friends than we otherwise would be. From
the first appearance of man upon the earth down
to very recent times, the words "stranger" and
"enemy" were quite or almost synonymous.
Long after civilized nations had defined rob-
bery and murder as high crimes, and had af-
fixed severe punishments to them, when practised among and upon their own people respectively, it was deemed no offense, but even
meritorious, to rob and murder and enslave
strangers, whether as nations or as individuals.
Even yet, this has not totally disappeared.
The man of the highest moral cultivation, in
spite of all which abstract principle can do,
likes him whom he does know much better
than him whom he does not know. To correct

evils, great and small, which spring from want of sympathy, and from positive enmity among strangers, as nations or as individuals, is one of the highest functions of civilization. To this end our agricultural fairs contribute in no small degree. They render more pleasant, and more strong and more durable, the bond of social and political union among us. Again, if, as Pope declares, "happiness is our being's end and aim," our fairs contribute much to that end and aim, as occasions of recreation, as holidays. Constituted as man is, he has positive need of occasional recreation, and whatever can give him this associated with virtue and advantage, and free from vice and disadvantage, is a positive good. Such recreation our fairs afford. They are a present pleasure, to be followed by no pain as a consequence; they are a present pleasure, making the future more pleasant.

But the chief use of agricultural fairs is to aid in improving the great calling of agriculture in all its departments and minute divisions; to make mutual exchange of agricultural discovery, information, and knowledge; so that, at the end, all may know everything which may have been known to but one or to but few, at the beginning; to bring together especially all which is supposed to be not generally known because of recent discovery or invention.

And not only to bring together and to impart all which has been accidentally discovered and invented upon ordinary motive, but by exciting emulation for premiums, and for the pride and honor of success,—of triumph, in some sort,— to stimulate that discovery and invention into extraordinary activity.   In this these fairs are kindred to the patent clause in the Constitution of the United States, and to the department and practical system based upon that clause.

One feature, I believe, of every fair is a regular address.   The Agricultural Society of the young, prosperous, and soon to be great State of Wisconsin has done me the high honor of selecting me to make that address upon this occasion —an honor for which I make my profound and grateful acknowledgment.

I presume I am not expected to employ the time assigned me in the mere flattery of the farmers as a class.   My opinion of them is that, in proportion to numbers, they are neither better nor worse than other people.   In the nature of things they are more numerous than any other class; and I believe there really are more attempts at flattering them than any other, the reason for which I cannot perceive, unless it be that they can cast more votes than any other.   On reflection, I am not quite sure that there is not cause of suspicion against you in selecting me, in some sort a politician and in no sort a farmer, to address you.

But farmers being the most numerous class, it follows that their interest is the largest interest. It also follows that that interest is most worthy of all to be cherished and cultivated — that if there be inevitable conflict between that interest and any other, that other should yield.

Again, I suppose it is not expected of me to impart to you much specific information on agriculture. You have no reason to believe, and do not believe, that I possess it; if that were what you seek in this address, any one of your own number or class would be more able to furnish it. You, perhaps, do expect me to give some general interest to the occasion, and to make some general suggestions on practical matters. I shall attempt nothing more. And in such suggestions by me, quite likely very little will be new to you, and a large part of the rest will be possibly already known to be erroneous.

My first suggestion is an inquiry as to the effect of greater thoroughness in all the departments of agriculture than now prevails in the Northwest — perhaps I might say in America. To speak entirely within bounds, it is known that fifty bushels of wheat, or one hundred bushels of Indian corn, can be produced from an acre. Less than a year ago I saw it stated that a man, by extraordinary care and labor, had produced of wheat what was equal to two hundred bushels from an acre. But take fifty of wheat, and one hundred of corn, to be the possibility, and compare it with the actual crops of the country. Many years ago I saw it stated, in a patent-office report, that eighteen bushels was the average crop throughout the United States; and this year an intelligent farmer of Illinois assures me that he did not believe the land harvested in that State this season had yielded more than an average of eight bushels to the acre; much was cut, and then abandoned as not worth threshing, and much was abandoned as not worth cutting. As to Indian corn, and indeed, most other crops, the case has not been much better. For the last four years I do not believe the ground planted with corn in Illinois has produced an average of twenty bushels to the acre. It is true that heretofore we have had better crops with no better cultivation, but I believe it is also true that the soil has never been pushed up to one half of its capacity.

What would be the effect upon the farming interest to push the soil up to something near its full capacity? Unquestionably it will take more labor to produce fifty bushels from an acre than it will to produce ten bushels from the same acre; but will it take more labor to produce fifty bushels from one acre than from five? Unquestionably thorough cultivation will require more labor to the acre; but will it require more to the bushel? If it should require just as much to the bushel, there are some probable, and several certain, advantages in favor of the thorough practice. It is probable it would develop those unknown causes which of late years have cut down our crops below their former average. It is almost certain, I think, that by deeper plowing, analysis of the soils, experiments with manures and varieties of seeds, observance of seasons, and the like, these causes would be discovered and remedied. It is certain that thorough cultivation would spare half, or more than half, the cost of land, simply because the same product would be got from half, or from less than half, the quantity of land. This proposition is self-evident, and can be made no plainer by repetitions or illustrations. The cost of land is a great item, even in new countries, and it constantly grows greater and greater, in comparison with other items, as the country grows older.

It also would spare the making and maintaining of inclosures for the same, whether these inclosures should be hedges, ditches, or fences. This again is a heavy item — heavy at first, and heavy in its continual demand for repairs. I remember once being greatly astonished by an apparently authentic exhibition of the proportion the cost of an inclosure bears to all the other expenses of the farmer, though I cannot remember exactly what that proportion was. Any farmer, if he will, can ascertain it in his own case for himself.

Again, a great amount of locomotion is spared by thorough cultivation. Take fifty bushels of wheat ready for harvest, standing upon a single acre, and it can be harvested in any of the known ways with less than half the labor which would be required if it were spread over five acres. This would be true if cut by the old hand-sickle; true, to a greater extent, if by the scythe and cradle; and to a still greater extent, if by the machines now in use. These machines are chiefly valuable as a means of substituting animal-power for the power of men in this branch of farm-work. In the highest degree of perfection yet reached in applying the horse-power to harvesting, fully nine-tenths of the power is expended by the animal in carrying himself and dragging the machine over the field, leaving certainly not more than one-tenth to be applied directly to the only end of the whole operation — the gathering in of the grain, and clipping of the straw. When grain is very thin on the ground, it is always more or less intermingled with weeds, chess, and the like, and a large part of the power is expended in cutting these. It is plain that when the crop is very thick upon the ground, a larger proportion of the power is directly applied to gathering in and cutting it; and the smaller to that which is totally useless as an end. And what I have said of harvesting is true in a greater or less degree of mowing, plowing, gathering in of crops generally, and indeed of almost all farm-work.

The effect of thorough cultivation upon the farmer's own mind, and in reaction through his mind back upon his business, is perhaps quite equal to any other of its effects. Every man is proud of what he does well, and no man is proud to that he does not well. With the former his heart is in his work, and he will do twice as much of it with less fatigue; the latter he performs a little imperfectly, looks at it in disgust, turns from it, and imagines himself exceedingly tired—the little he has done comes to nothing for want of finishing.

The man who produces a good full crop will scarcely ever let any part of it go to waste; he will keep up the inclosure about it, and allow neither man nor beast to trespass upon it; he will gather it in due season, and store it in perfect security. Thus he labors with satisfaction, and saves himself the whole fruit of his labor. The other, starting with no purpose for a full crop, labors less, and with less satisfaction, allows his fences to fall, and cattle to trespass, gathers not in due season, or not at all. Thus the labor he has performed is wasted away, little by little, till in the end he derives scarcely anything from it.

The ambition for broad acres leads to poor farming, even with men of energy. I scarcely ever knew a mammoth farm to sustain itself, much less to return a profit upon the outlay. I have more than once known a man to spend a respectable fortune upon one, fail, and leave it, and then some man of modest aim get a small fraction of the ground, and makes a good living upon it. Mammoth farms are like tools or weapons which are too heavy to be handled; ere long they are thrown aside at a great loss.

The successful application of steam-power to farm-work is a desideratum—especially a steam-plow. It is not enough that a machine operated by steam will really plow. To be successful, it must, all things considered, plow better than can be done with animal-power. It must do all the work as well, and cheaper; or more rapidly, so as to get through more perfectly in season; or in some way afford an advantage over plowing with animals, else it is no success. I have never seen a machine intended for a steam-plow. Much praise and admiration are bestowed upon some of them, and they may be, for aught I know, already successful; but I have not perceived the demonstration of it. I have thought a good deal, in an abstract way, about a steam-plow. That one which shall be so contrived as to apply the larger proportion of its power to the cutting and turning of the soil, and the smallest, to the moving itself over the field, will be the best one. A very small stationary-engine would draw a large gang of plows through the ground from a short distance to itself; but when it is not stationary, but has to move along like a horse, dragging the plows after it, it must have additional power to carry itself; and the difficulty grows by what is intended to overcome it; for what adds power also adds size and weight to the machine, thus increasing again the demand for power.

Suppose you construct the machine so as to cut a succession of short furrows, say a rod in length, transversely to the course the machine is locomoting, something like the shuttle in weaving. In such case the whole machine would move north only the width of a furrow, while in length the furrow would be a rod from east to west. In such case a very large proportion of the power would be applied to the actual plowing. But in this, too, there would be difficulty, which would be the getting of the plow into and out of the ground, at the end of all these short furrows.

I believe, however, ingenious men will, if they have not already, overcome the difficulty I have suggested. But there is still another, about which I am less sanguine. It is the supply of fuel, and especially water, to make steam. Such supply is clearly practicable; but can the expense of it be borne? Steamboats live upon the water, and find their fuel at stated places. Steam-mills and other stationary steam-machinery have their stationary supplies of fuel and water. Railroad locomotives have their regular wood and water stations. But the steam plow is less fortunate. It does not live upon the water, and if it be once at a water-station, it will work away from it, and when it gets away cannot return without leaving its work, at a great expense of its time and strength. It will occur that a wagon-and-horse team might be employed to supply it with fuel and water; but this, too, is expensive; and the question recurs, "Can the expense be borne?" When this is added to all other expenses, will not plowing cost more than in the old way?

It is to be hoped that the steam-plow will be finally successful, and if it shall be, "thorough cultivation"—putting the soil to the top of its capacity, producing the largest crop possible from a given quantity of ground—will be most favorable for it. Doing a large amount of work upon a small quantity of ground, it will be as nearly as possible stationary while working, and as free as possible from locomotion, thus expending its strength as much as possible upon its work, and as little as possible in traveling. Our thanks, and something more substantial than thanks, are due to every man engaged in the effort to produce a successful steam-plow. Even the unsuccessful will bring something to light which, in the hands of others, will contribute to the final success. I have not pointed out difficulties in order to discourage, but in order that, being seen, they may be the more readily overcome.

The world is agreed that labor is the source from which human wants are mainly supplied. There is no dispute upon this point. From this point, however, men immediately diverge. Much disputation is maintained as to the best way of applying and controlling the labor element. By some it is assumed that labor is available only in connection with capital—that nobody labors, unless somebody else owning capital, somehow, by the use of it, induces him to do it. Having assumed this, they proceed to consider whether it is best that capital shall hire laborers, and thus induce them to work by their own consent, or buy them, and drive them to it, without their consent. Having proceeded so far, they naturally conclude that all laborers are naturally either hired laborers or slaves. They further assume that whoever is once a hired laborer, is fatally fixed in that condition for life; and thence again, that his condition is as bad as, or worse than,\ that of a slave. This is the "mud-sill" theory. But another class of reasoners hold the opinion that there is no such relation between capital and labor as assumed; that there is no such thing as a free man being fatally fixed for life in the condition of a hired laborer; that both these assumptions are false, and all inferences from them groundless. They hold that labor is prior to, and independent of, capital; that, in fact, capital is the fruit of labor, and could never have existed if labor had not first existed; that labor can exist without capital, but that capital could never have existed without labor. Hence they hold that labor is the superior—greatly the superior—of capital.

They do not deny that there is, and probably always will be, a relation between labor and capital. The error, as they hold, is in assuming that the whole labor of the world exists within that relation. A few men own capital; and that few avoid labor themselves, and with their capital hire or buy another few to labor for them. A large majority belong to neither class—neither work for others, nor have others working for them. Even in all our slave States except South Carolina, a majority of the whole people of all colors are neither slaves nor masters. In these free States, a large majority are neither hirers nor hired. Men, with their families—wives, sons and daughters—work for themselves, on their farms, in their houses, and in their shops, taking the whole product to themselves, and asking no favors of capital on the one hand, nor of hirelings or slaves on the other. It is not forgotten that a considerable number of persons mingle their own labor with capital—that is, labor with their own hands and also buy slaves or hire free men to labor for them; but this is only a mixed, and not a distinct, class. No principle stated is disturbed by the existence of this mixed class. Again, as has already been said, the opponents of the "mud-sill" theory insist that there is not, of necessity, any such thing as the free hired laborer being fixed to that condition for life. There is demonstration for saying this. Many independent men in this assembly doubtless a few years ago were hired laborers. And their case is almost, if not quite, the general rule.

The prudent, penniless beginner in the world

labors for wages awhile, saves a surplus with
which to buy tools or land for himself, then labors on his own account another while, and at
length hires another new beginner to help him.
This, say its advocates, is free labor—the just,
and generous, and prosperous system, which
opens the way for all, gives hope to all, and
energy, and progress, and improvement of condition to all. If any continue through life
in the condition of the hired laborer, it is not
the fault of the system, but because of either a
dependent nature which prefers it, or improvi-
dence, folly, or singular misfortune. I have
said this much about the elements of labor generally, as introductory to the consideration of
a new phase which that element is in process of
assuming. The old general rule was that educated people did not perform manual labor.
They managed to eat their bread, leaving the
toil of producing it to the uneducated. This
was not an insupportable evil to the working
bees, so long as the class of drones remained
very small. But now, especially in these free
States, nearly all are educated—quite too nearly
all to leave the labor of the uneducated in any
wise adequate to the support of the whole. It
follows from this that henceforth educated people must labor. Otherwise, education itself
would become a positive and intolerable evil.

No country can sustain in idleness more than a small percentage of its numbers. The great majority must labor at something productive. From these premises the problem springs, "How can labor and education be the most satisfactorily combined?"

By the "mud-sill" theory it is assumed that labor and education are incompatible, and any practical combination of them impossible. According to that theory, a blind horse upon a tread-mill is a perfect illustration of what a laborer should be—all the better for being blind, that he could not kick understandingly. According to that theory, the education of laborers is not only useless but pernicious and dangerous. In fact, it is, in some sort, deemed a misfortune that laborers should have heads at all. Those same heads are regarded as explosive materials, only to be safely kept in damp places, as far as possible from that peculiar sort of fire which ignites them. A Yankee who could invent a strong-handed man without a head would receive the everlasting gratitude of the "mud-sill" advocates.

But free labor says, "No." Free labor argues that as the Author of man makes every individual with one head and one pairs of hands, it was probably intended that heads and hands should coöperate as friends, and that that par-

ticular head should direct and control that pair
of hands.   As each man has one mouth to be
fed, and one pair of hands to furnish food, it
was probably intended that that particular pair
of hands should feed that particular mouth—
that each head is the natural guardian, director,
and protector of the hands and mouth insepa-
rably connected with it; and that being so, every
head should be cultivated and improved by
whatever will add to its capacity for performing its charge.   In one word, free labor insists
on universal education.

I have so far stated the opposite theories of
"mud-sill" and "free labor," without declaring
any preference of my own between them.   On
an occasion like this, I ought not to declare any,
I suppose, however, I shall not be mistaken in
assuming as a fact that the people of Wisconsin prefer free labor, with its natural compan-
ion, education.

This leads to the further reflection that no
other human occupation opens so wide a field
for the profitable and agreeable combination of
labor with cultivated thought, as agriculture.
I know nothing so pleasant to the mind as the
discovery of anything that is at once new and
valuable—nothing that so lightens and sweetens
toil as the hopeful pursuit of such discovery.
And how vast and how varied a field is agricul-

ture for such discovery! The mind, already trained to thought in the country school, or higher school, cannot fail to find there an exhaustless source of enjoyment. Every blade of grass is a study; and to produce two where there was but one is both a profit and a pleasure. And not grass alone, but soils, seeds, and seasons— hedges, ditches, and fences—draining, droughts, and irrigation—plowing, hoeing, and harrowing—reaping, mowing, and threshing—saving crops, pests of crops, diseases of crops, and what will prevent or cure them—implements, utensils, and machines, their relative merits, and how to improve them—hogs, horses, and cattle —sheep, goats, and poultry—trees, shrubs, fruits, plants, and flowers—the thousand things of which these are specimens—each a world of study within itself.

In all this, book-learning is available. A capacity and taste for reading gives access to whatever has already been discovered by others. It is the key, or one of the keys, to the already solved problems. And not only so: it gives a relish and facility for successfully pursuing the unsolved ones. The rudiments of science are available, and highly available. Some knowledge of botany assists in dealing with the vegetable world—with all growing crops. Chemistry assists in the analysis of soils, selection and application of manures, and in numerous other ways. The mechanical branches of natural philosophy are ready help in almost everything, but especially in reference to implements and machinery.

The thought recurs that education—cultivated thought—can best be combined with agricultural labor, or any labor, on the principle of thorough work; that careless, half performed, slovenly work makes no place for such combination; and thorough work, again, renders sufficient the smallest quantity of ground to each man; and this, again, conforms to what must occur in a world less inclined to wars and more devoted to the arts of peace than heretofore. Population must increase rapidly, more rapidly than in former times, and ere long the most valuable of all arts will be the art of deriving a comfortable subsistence from the smallest area of soil. No community whose every member possesses this art, can ever be the victim of oppression in any of its forms. Such community will be alike independent of crowned kings, money kings, and land kings.

But, according to your program, the awarding of premiums awaits the closing of this address. Considering the deep interest necessarily pertaining to that performance, it would be no wonder if I am already heard with some impatience. I will detain you but a moment longer. Some of you will be successful, and such will need but little philosophy to take them home in cheerful spirits; others will be disappointed, and will be in a less happy mood. To such let it be said, "Lay it not too much to heart." Let them adopt the maxim, "Better luck next time," and then by renewed exertion make that better luck for themselves.

And by the successful and unsuccessful let it be remembered that while occasions like the present bring their sober and durable benefits, the exultations and mortifications of them are but temporary; that the victor will soon be vanquished if he relax in his exertion; and that the vanquished this year may be victor the next, in spite of all competition.

It is said an Eastern monarch once charged his wise men to invent him a sentence to be ever in view, and which should be true and appropriate in all times and situations. They presented him the words, "And this, too, shall pass away." How much it expresses! How chastening in the hour of pride! How consoling in the depths of affliction! "And this, too, shall pass away." And yet, let us hope, it is not quite true. Let us hope, rather, that by the best cultivation of the physical world beneath and around us, and the best intellectual and moral world within us, we shall secure an individual, social, and political prosperity and happiness, whose course shall be onward and upward, and which, while the earth endures, shall not pass away.

LETTER TO DR. EDWARD WALLACE

CLINTON, October 11, 1859.

My dear Sir: I am here just now attending court. Yesterday, before I left Springfield, your brother, Dr. William S. Wallace, showed me a letter of yours, in which you kindly mention my name, inquire for my tariff views, and suggest the propriety of my writing a letter upon the subject. I was an old Henry Clay-Tariff-Whig. In old times I made more speeches on that subject than any other.

I have not since changed my views. I believe yet, if we could have a moderate, carefully adjusted protective tariff, so far acquiesced in as not to be a perpetual subject of political strife, squabbles, changes, and uncertainties, it would be better for us. Still it is my opinion that just now the revival of that question will not advance the cause itself, or the man who revives it.

I have not thought much on the subject recently, but my general impression is that the necessity for a protective tariff will ere long force its old opponents to take it up; and then its old friends can join in and establish it on a more firm and durable basis. We, the Old Whigs, have been entirely beaten out of the tariff question, and we shall not be able to reëstablish the policy until the absence of it shall have demonstrated the necessity for it in the minds of men heretofore opposed to it. With this view, I should prefer to not now write a public letter on the subject. I therefore wish this to be considered confidential. I shall be very glad to receive a letter from you.

Yours truly,
A. Lincoln.

LETTER TO W. E. FRAZER

SPRINGFIELD, ILLINOIS, November 1, 1859.

Dear Sir: Yours of the 24th ult. was forwarded to me from Chicago. It certainly is important to secure Pennsylvania for the Republicans in the next presidential contest, and not unimportant to also secure Illinois. As to the ticket you name, I shall be heartily for it after it shall have been fairly nominated by a Republican national convention; and I cannot be committed to it before. For my single self, I have enlisted for the permanent success of the Republican cause; and for this object I shall labor faithfully in the ranks, unless, as I think not probable, the judgment of the party shall assign me a different position. If the Republicans of the great State of Pennsylvania shall present Mr. Cameron as their candidate for the presidency, such an indorsement for his fitness for the place could scarcely be deemed insufficient. Still, as I would not like the public to know, so I would not like myself to know, I had entered a combination with any man to the prejudice of all others whose friends respectively may consider them preferable.

Yours truly,
A. LINCOLN.

*LETTER TO DR. ————

SPRINGFIELD, November 2, 1859.

Dear Doctor: Your business makes it convenient for you to do a good deal in the way of getting all our friends to the polls next Tuesday. Please do it. We begin to hope we can elect Palmer. He is a good man, and deserves to be elected, both for his own, and the Cause's sake.   Yours truly,

A. LINCOLN.

LETTER TO JAMES A. BRIGGS

DANVILLE, ILLINOIS, November 13, 1859.

Dear Sir: Yours of the 1st, closing with my proposition for compromise, was duly received.

I will be on hand, and in due time notify you of the exact day. I believe, after all, I shall make a political speech of it. You have no objection? I would like to know in advance whether I am also to speak or lecture in New York. Very, very glad your election went right.

Yours truly,
A. LINCOLN.

SPEECHES IN KANSAS, December 1-5, 1859 [1]

Introduction.

PURPOSE of the Republican organization.—The Republican party believe
there is danger that slavery will be further extended, and ultimately made national in
the United States; and to prevent this incidental
and final consummation, is the purpose of this
organization.

Chief danger to that purpose.—A congressional slave code for the Territories, and the revival of the African trade, and a second Dred
Scott decision, are not just now the chief danger to our purpose.   These will press us in due
time, but they are not quite ready yet—they
know that, as yet, we are too strong for them.
The insidious Douglas popular sovereignty,

[1] In response to invitations from Republicans of the then
Territory, Mr. Lincoln made a visit to Kansas in December,
1859, and made speeches at Elwood (opposite St. Joseph, Mo.),
at Troy, Doniphan, Atchison, and Leavenworth, Kansas. Among
his papers were a number of disconnected sheets of autograph
manuscript, which contained internal evidence that they were
portions of the addresses made by him on these occasions.
Though the fragments seem to belong to different addresses,
the topics treated in them justify their presentation in the order
here arranged, as the general line of argument followed by him.
— N. and H.

which prepares the way for this ultimate danger, it is which just now constitutes our chief
danger.

Popular Sovereignty.—I say Douglas popular sovereignty; for there is a broad distinction
between real popular sovereignty and Douglas
popular sovereignty. That the nation shall
control what concerns it; that a State, or any
minor political community, shall control what
exclusively concerns it; and that an individual
shall control what exclusively concerns him,—
is a real popular sovereignty, which no Republican opposes.

But this is not Douglas popular sovereignty.
Douglas popular sovereignty, as a matter of
principle, simply is: " If one man would enslave another, neither that other nor any third
man has a right to object."

Douglas popular sovereignty, as he practically applies it, is: "If any organized political
community, however new and small, would enslave men or forbid their being enslaved within
its own territorial limits; however the doing
the one or the other may affect the men sought
to be enslaved, or the vastly superior number
of men who are afterward to come within those
limits, or the family of communities of which
it is but a member, or the head of that family,
as the present and common guardian of the

whole—however any or all these are to be affected, neither any nor all may interfere."

This is Douglas popular sovereignty. He has great difficulty with it. His speeches and letters and essays and explanations explanatory of explanations explained upon it, are legion. The most lengthy, and as I suppose the most maturely considered, is that recently published in "Harper's Magazine." It has two leading objects: the first, to appropriate the authority and reverence due the great and good men of the Revolution to his popular sovereignty; and, secondly, to show that the Dred Scott decision has not entirely squelched his popular sovereignty.

Before considering these mains objects, I wish to consider a few minor points of the copyright essay.

Last year Governor Seward and myself, at different times and occasions, expressed the opinion that slavery is a durable element of discord, and that we shall not have peace with it until it either masters or is mastered by the free principle. This gave great offense to Judge Douglas, and his denunciations of it, and absurd inferences from it, have never ceased. Almost at the very beginning of the copyright essay he quotes the language respectively of Seward and myself—not quite accurately, but substantially, in my case—upon this point, and repeats his absurd and extravagant inference. For lack of time I omit much which I might say here with propriety, and content myself with two remarks only upon this point. The first is, that inasmuch as Douglas in this very essay tells us slavery agitation began in this country in 1699, and has not yet ceased; has lasted through a hundred and sixty years, through ten entire generations of men,—it might have occurred to even him that slavery in its tendency to agitation and discord has something slightly durable about it. The second remark is that Judge Douglas might have noted, if he would, while he was diving so deeply into history, the historical fact that the only comparative peace we have had with slavery during that hundred and sixty years was in the period from the Revolution to 1820, precisely the period through which we were closing out the African slave-trade, abolishing slavery in several of the States, and restraining the spread of it into new ones by the ordinance of '87, precisely the period in which the public mind had reason to rest, and did rest, in the belief that slavery was in course of ultimate extinction.

Another point, which for the present I shall touch only hastily, is Judge Douglas's assumption that the States and Territories differ only in the fact that the States are in the Union, and the Territories are not in it. But if this be the only difference, why not instantly bring the Territories in? Why keep them out? Do you say they are unfitted for it? What unfits them? Especially what unfits them for any duty in the Union, after they are fit, if they choose, to plant the soil they sparsely inhabit with slavery, beyond the power of their millions of successors to eradicate it, and to the durable discord of the Union? What function of sovereignty, out of the Union or in it, is so portentous as this? What function of government requires such perfect maturity, in numbers and everything else, among those who exercise it? It is a concealed assumption of Douglas's popular sovereignty that slavery is a little, harmless, indifferent thing, having no wrong in it, and no power for mischief about it. If all men looked upon it as he does, his policy in regard to it might do. But neither all, nor half the world, so look upon it.

Near the close of the essay in "Harper's Magazine" Douglas tells us that his popular sovereignty pertains to a people only after they are regularly organized into a political community; and that Congress in its discretion must decide when they are fit in point of numbers to be so organized. Now I should like for him to point out in the Constitution any clause conferring that discretion upon Congress, which, when pointed out, will not be equally a power in Congress to govern them, in its discretion, till they are admitted as a State. Will he try? He intimates that before the exercise of that discretion, their number must be ten, fifteen, or twenty thousand. Well, what is to be done for them, or with them, or by them, before they number ten thousand? If any one of them desires to have slaves, is any other one bound to help him or at liberty to hinder him? Is it his plan that any time before they reach the required numbers, those who are on hand shall be driven out as trespassers? If so, it will probably be a good while before a sufficient number to organize will get in.

But plainly enough this conceding to Congress the discretion as to when a community shall be organized, is a total surrender of his popular sovereignty. He says himself it does not pertain to a people until they are organized; and that when they shall be organized is in the discretion of Congress. Suppose Congress shall choose to not organize them until they are numerous enough to come into the Union as a State. By his own rule, his popular sovereignty is derived from Congress, and cannot be exercised by the people till Congress chooses to confer it. After toiling through nineteen mortal pages of "Harper," to show that Congress cannot keep the people of a new country from excluding slavery, in a single closing paragraph he makes the whole thing depend on Congress at last. And should Congress refuse to organize, how will that affect the question of planting slavery in a new country? If individuals choose to plant it, the people cannot prevent them, for they are not yet clothed with popular sovereignty. If it be said that it cannot be planted, in fact, without protective law, that assertion is already falsified by history; for it was originally planted on this continent without protective law.

And, by the way, it is probable that no act of territorial organization could be passed by the present Senate; and almost certainly not by both the Senate and House of Representatives. If an act declared the right of Congress to exclude slavery, the Republicans would vote for it, and both wings of the Democracy against it. If it denied the power to either exclude or protect it, the Douglasites would vote for it, and both the Republicans and slave-coders against it. If it denied the power to exclude, and asserted the power to protect, the slave-coders would vote for it, and the Republicans and Douglasites against it.

You are now a part of a people of a Territory, but that Territory is soon to be a State of the Union. Both in your individual and collective capacities, you have the same interest in the past, the present, and the future of the United States as any other portion of the people. Most of you came from the States, and all of you soon will be citizens of the common Union. What I shall now address to you will have neither greater nor less application to you than to any other people of the Union.

You are gathered to-day as a Republican convention—Republican in the party sense, and, as we hope, in the true, original sense of the word republican.

I assume that Republicans throughout the nation believe they are right, and are earnest and determined in their cause.

Let them then keep constantly in view that the chief object of their organization is to prevent the spread and nationalization of slavery. With this ever distinctly before us, we can always better see at what point our cause is most in danger.

We are, as I think, in the present temper or state of public sentiment, in no danger from the open advocates of a congressional slave code for the Territories, and of the revival of the African slave-trade. As yet we are strong enough

to meet and master any combination openly
formed on those grounds.   It is only the insidious position of Douglas that endangers our
cause.   That position is simply an ambuscade.
By entering into contest with our open enemies,
we are to be lured into his train; and then, having lost our own organization and arms, we are
to be turned over to those same open enemies.

Douglas's position leads to the nationalization of slavery as surely as does that of Jeff
Davis and Mason of Virginia.   The two positions are but slightly different roads to the same
place—with this difference, that the nationalization of slavery can be reached by Douglas's
route, and never can be by the other.

I have said that in our present moral tone
and temper we are strong enough for our open
enemies, and so we are.   But the chief effect
of Douglasism is to change that tone and temper.   Men who support the measures of a political leader do, almost of necessity, adopt the
reasoning and sentiments the leader advances in
support of them.   The reasoning and sentiments
advanced by Douglas in support of his policy
as to slavery all spring from the view that
slavery is not wrong.   In the first place, he
never says it is wrong.   He says he does
not care whether it shall be voted down or
voted up.   He says whoever wants slavery

has a right to have it. He says the question whether people will have it or not is simply a question of dollars and cents. He says the Almighty has drawn a line across the continent, on one side of which the soil must be cultivated by slave labor.

Now let the people of the free States adopt these sentiments, and they will be unable to see a single reason for maintaining their prohibitions of slavery in their own States. "What! do you mean to say that anything in these sentiments requires us to believe it will be the interest of Northern States to have slavery?" No. But I do mean to say that although it is not the interest of Northern States to grow cotton, none of them have, or need, any law against it; and it would be tyranny to deprive any one man of the privilege to grow cotton in Illinois. There are many individual men in all the free States who desire to have slaves; and if you admit that slavery is not wrong, it is also but tyranny to deny them the privilege. It is no just function of government to prohibit what is not wrong.

Again, if slavery is right—ordained by the Almighty—on one side of a line dividing sister States of a common Union, then it is positively wrong to harass and bedevil the owners of it with constitutions and laws and prohibitions of

it on the other side of the line.   In short, there
is no justification for prohibiting slavery anywhere, save only in the assumption that slavery
is wrong; and whenever the sentiment that slavery is wrong shall give way in the North, all
legal prohibitions of it will also give way.

If it be insisted that men may support Douglas's measures without adopting his sentiments,
let it be tested by what is actually passing before us.   You can even now find no Douglas
man who will disavow any one of these sentiments; and none but will actually indorse them
if pressed to the point.

Five years ago no living man had placed on
record, nor, as I believe, verbally expressed, a
denial that negroes have a share in the Declaration of Independence.   Two or three years
since, Douglas began to deny it; and now every
Douglas man in the nation denies it.

To the same effect is the absurdity compound-
ed of support to the Dred Scott decision, and
legislation unfriendly to slavery by the Territories—the absurdity which asserts that a
thing may be lawfully driven from a place, at
which place it has a lawful right to remain.
That absurd position will not be long maintained by any one.   The Dred Scott half of
it will soon master the other half.   The process
will probably be about this: some territorial

legislature will adopt unfriendly legislation; the Supreme Court will decide that legislation to be unconstitutional, and then the advocates of the present compound absurdity will acquiesce in the decision. The only effect of that position now is to prepare its advocates for such acquiescence when the time comes. Like wood for ox-bows, they are merely being soaked in it preparatory to the bending. The advocates of a slave code are not now strong enough to master us; and they never will be, unless recruits enough to make them so be tolled in through the gap of Douglasism. Douglas, on the sly, is affecting more for them than all their open advocates. He has reason to be provoked that they will not understand him, and recognize him as their best friend. He cannot be more plain, without being so plain as to lure no one into their trap—so plain as to lose his power to serve them profitably. Take other instances. Last year both Governor Seward and myself expressed the belief that this government cannot endure permanently half slave and half free. This gave great offense to Douglas, and after the fall election in Illinois he became quite rampant upon it. At Chicago, St. Louis, Memphis and New Orleans, he denounced it as a "fatal heresy." With great pride he claimed that he had crushed it in Illinois, and modestly regretted that he could not have been in New York to crush it there too. How the heresy is fatal to anything, or what the thing is to which it is fatal, he has never paused to tell us. At all events, it is a fatal heresy in his view when expressed by a Northern man. Not so when expressed by men of the South. In 1856, Roger A. Pryor, editor of the Richmond "Enquirer," expressed the same belief in that paper, quite two years before it was expressed by either Seward or me. But Douglas perceived no " heresy " in him—talked not of going to Virginia to crush it out; nay, more, he now has that same Mr. Pryor at Washington, editing the "States" newspaper as his especial organ.

This brings us to see that in Douglas's view this opinion is a "fatal heresy" when expressed by men wishing to have the nation all free, and it is no heresy at all when expressed by men wishing to have it all slave. Douglas has cause to complain that the South will not note this and give him credit for it.

At Memphis Douglas told his audience that he was for the negro against the crocodile, but for the white man against the negro. This was not a sudden thought hastily thrown off at Memphis. He said the same thing many times in Illinois last summer and autumn, though I am not sure it was reported then.

It is a carefully formed illustration of the estimate he places upon the negro and the manner he would have him dealt with.   It is a sort of proposition in proportion.   "As the negro is to the crocodile, so the white man is to the negro."   As the negro ought to treat the crocodile as a beast, so the white man ought to treat the negro as a beast.   Gentlemen of the South, is not that satisfactory?   Will you give Douglas no credit for impressing that sentiment on the Northern mind for your benefit?   Why, you should magnify him to the utmost, in order that he may impress it the more deeply, broadly, and surely.

A hope is often expressed that all the elements of opposition to the so-called Democracy may unite in the next presidential election; and to favor this it is suggested that at least one candidate on the opposition national ticket must be resident in the slave States.   I strongly sympathize with this hope; and the particular suggestion presents no difficulty to me.   There are very many men in the slave States who as men and statesmen and patriots are quite acceptable to me for either President or Vice-President. But there is a difficulty of another sort; and I think it most prudent for us to face that difficulty at once.   Will those good men of the South occupy any ground upon which we of

the free States can vote for them?   There is the
rub.   They seem to labor under a huge mistake
in regard to us.   They say they are tired of slavery agitation.   We think the slaves, and free
white laboring-men too, have more reason to be
tired of slavery than masters have to be tired of
agitation about it.   In Kentucky a Democratic
candidate for Congress takes ground against a
congressional slave-code for the Territories,
whereupon his opponent, in full hope to unite
with Republicans in 1860, takes ground in favor
of such slave-code.   Such hope, under such circumstances, is delusion gross as insanity itself.
Rational men can only entertain it in the strange
belief that Republicans are not in earnest for
their principles; that they are really devoted to
no principle of their own, but are ready for, and
anxious to jump to, any position not occupied by
the Democracy.   This mistake must be dispelled.
For the sake of their principles, in forming their
party, they broke and sacrificed the strongest
mere party ties and advantages which can exist.
Republicans believe that slavery is wrong; and
they insist, and will continue to insist, upon a
national policy which recognizes it and deals
with it as a wrong.   There can be no letting down
about this.   Simultaneously with such letting
down the Republican organization would go to
pieces, and half its elements would go in a dif-

ferent direction, leaving an easy victory to the
common enemy. No ingenuity of political trad-
ing could possibly hold it together. About this
there is no joke, and can be no trifling. Understanding this, that Republicanism can never mix
with territorial slave-codes becomes self-evident.

In this contest mere men are nothing. We
could come down to Douglas quite as well as to
any other man standing with him, and better
than to any other standing below or beyond him.
The simple problem is: will any good and
capable man of the South allow the Republicans to elect him on their own platform? If
such man can be found, I believe the thing can
be done. It can be done in no other way.

What do we gain, say some, by such a union?
Certainly not everything; but still something,
and quite all that we for our lives can possibly
give. In yielding a share of the high honors and
offices to you, you gain the assurance that ours
is not a mere struggle to secure those honors and
offices for one section. You gain the assurance
that we mean no more than we say in our platforms, else we would not intrust you to execute
them. You gain the assurance that we intend no
invasion of your rights or your honor, else we
would not make one of you the executor of the
laws and commander of the army and navy.

As a matter of mere partizan policy, there is

no reason for and much against any letting down of the Republican party in order to form a union with the Southern opposition. By no possibility can a union ticket secure a simple electoral vote in the South, unless the Republican platform be so far let down as to lose every electoral vote in the North; and even at that, not a single vote would be secured in the South, unless by bare possibility those of Maryland. There is no successful basis of union but for some good Southern man to allow us of the North to elect him square on our platform. Plainly it is that or nothing.

The St. Louis "Intelligencer" is out in favor of a good man for President, to be run without a platform. Well, I am not wedded to the formal written platform system; but a thousand to one the editor is not himself in favor of his plan, except with the qualification that he and his sort are to select and name the "good man." To bring him to the test, is he willing to take Seward without a platform? Oh, no; Seward's antecedents exclude him, say you. Well, is your good man without antecedents? If he is, how shall the nation know that he is a good man? The sum of the matter is that, in the absence of formal written platforms, the antecedents of candidates become their platforms. On just such platforms all our earlier and better Presidents were elected, but this by no means facilitates a union of men who differ in principles.

Nor do I believe we can ever advance our principles by supporting men who oppose our principles. Last year, as you know, we Republicans in Illinois were advised by numerous and respectable outsiders to reëlect Douglas to the Senate by our votes. I never questioned the motives of such advisers, nor the devotion to the Republican cause of such as professed to be Republicans. But I never for a moment thought of following the advice, and have never yet regretted that we did not follow it. True, Douglas is back in the Senate in spite of us; but we are clear of him and his principles, and we are uncrippled and ready to fight both him and them straight along till they shall be finally "closed out." Had we followed the advice, there would now be no Republican party in Illinois, and none to speak of anywhere else. The whole thing would now be floundering along after Douglas upon the Dred Scott and crocodile theory. It would have been the grandest "haul" for slavery ever yet made. Our principles would still live, and ere long would produce a party; but we should have lost all our past labor and twenty years of time by the folly.

Take an illustration. About a year ago all the Republicans in Congress voted for what was

called the Crittenden-Montgomery bill; and
forthwith Douglas claimed, and still claims,
that they were all committed to his "gur-reat
pur-rinciple." And Republicans have been so
far embarrassed by the claim that they have ever
since been protesting that they were not so committed, and trying to explain why. Some of the
very newspapers which advised Douglas's return
to the Senate by Republican votes have been
largely and continuously engaged in these protests
and explanations. For such let us state a question in the rule of three. If voting for the Crittenden-Montgomery bill entangle the Republicans with Douglas's dogmas for one year, how
long would voting for Douglas himself so entangle them?

It is nothing to the contrary that Republicans
gained something by electing Haskins, Hickman, and Davis. They were comparatively
small men. I mean no disrespect; they may have
large merit; but Republicans can dally with
them, and absorb or expel them at pleasure. If
they dally with Douglas, he absorbs them.

We want, and must have, a national policy
as to slavery which deals with it as being a
wrong. Whoever would prevent slavery becoming national and perpetual yields all when
he yields to a policy which treats it either as
being right, or as being a matter of indifference.

We admit that the United States General Government is not charged with the duty of redressing or preventing all the wrongs in the world. But the government rightfully may, and subject to the Constitution ought to, redress and prevent all wrongs which are wrongs to the nation itself.

It is expressly charged with the duty of providing for the general welfare. We think slavery impairs and endangers the general welfare. Those who do not think this are not of us, and we cannot agree with them. We must shape our own course by our own judgment.

We must not disturb slavery in the States where it exists, because the Constitution and the peace of the country both forbid us. We must not withhold an efficient fugitive-slave law, because the Constitution demands it.

But we must, by a national policy, prevent the spread of slavery into new Territories, or free States, because the Constitution does not forbid us, and the general welfare does demand such prevention. We must prevent the revival of the African slave-trade, because the Constitution does not forbid us, and the general welfare does require the prevention. We must prevent these things being done by either congresses or courts. The people—the people—are the rightful masters of both congresses and courts,—not to overthrow the Constitution, but to overthrow the men who pervert it.

To effect our main object we have to employ auxiliary means. We must hold conventions, adopt platforms, select candidates, and carry elections. At every step we must be true to the main purpose.

If we adopt a platform falling short of our principle, or elect a man rejecting our principle, we not only take nothing affirmative by our success, but we draw upon us the positive embarrassment of seeming ourselves to have abandoned our principle.

That our principle, however baffled or delayed, will finally triumph, I do not permit myself to doubt. Men will pass away—die, die politically and naturally; but the principle will live, and live forever. Organizations rallied around that principle may, by their own dereliction, go to pieces, thereby losing all their time and labor; but the principle will remain, and will reproduce another, and another, till the final triumph will come.

But to bring it soon, we must save our labor already performed—our organization, which has cost us so much time and toil to create. We must keep our principle constantly in view, and never be false to it.

And as to men for leaders, we must remember

that " He that is not for us is against us; and he that gathereth not with us scattereth."

LETTER TO N. B. JUDD

SPRINGFIELD, December 9, 1859.

My dear Sir: I have just reached home from Kansas and found your long letter of the 1st inst. It has a tone of blame toward myself which I think is not quite just; but I will not stand upon that, but will consider a day or two, and put something in the best shape I can, and send it to you. A great difficulty is that they make no distinct charge against you which I can contradict. You did vote for Trumbull against me; and, although I think, and have said a thousand times, that was no injustice to me, I cannot change the fact, nor compel people to cease speaking of it. Ever since that matter occurred, I have constantly labored, as I believe you know, to have all recollection of it dropped.

The vague charge that you played me false last year I believe to be false and outrageous; but it seems I can make no impression by expressing that belief. I made a special job of trying to impress that upon Baker, Bridges, and Wilson here last winter. They all well know that I believe no such charge against you. But they chose to insist that they know better about it than I do.

As to the charge of your intriguing for Trumbull against me, I believe as little of that as any other charge. If Trumbull and I were candidates for the same office, you would have a right to prefer him, and I should not blame you for it; but all my acquaintance with you induces me to believe you would not pretend to be for me while really for him. But I do not understand Trumbull and myself to be rivals. You know I am pledged to not enter a struggle with him for the seat in the Senate now occupied by him; and yet I would rather have a full term in the Senate than in the presidency.

Your friend as ever,

A. LINCOLN.

P. S.—I omitted to say that I have, in no single instance, permitted a charge such as alluded to above to go uncontradicted when made in my presence. A. L.

LETTER TO N. B. JUDD

SPRINGFIELD, December 14, 1859.

Dear Judd: Herewith is the letter of our old Whig friends, and my answer, sent as you requested. I showed both to Dubois, and he feared the clause about leave to publish, in the answer, would not be quite satisfactory to you. I hope it will be satisfactory, as I would rather not seem to come before the public as a volun-

teer; still if, after considering this, you still
deem it important, you may substitute the in-
closed slip by pasting it down over the original
clause.

I find some of our friends here attach more
consequence to getting the national convention
into our State than I did, or do. Some of them
made me promise to say so to you. As to the
time, it must certainly be after the Charleston
fandango; and I think, within bounds of reason,
the later the better.

As to that matter about the committee, in relation to appointing delegates by general convention, or by districts, I shall attend to it as well
as I know how, which, God knows, will not be
very well. Write me if you can find anything
to write. Yours as ever,

A. LINCOLN.

[Inclosure.]

LETTER TO MESSRS. GEORGE W. DOLE, G. S.
HUBBARD, AND W. H. BROWN

SPRINGFIELD, ILLINOIS, December 14, 1859.

Gentlemen: Your letter of the 12th instant
is received. To your question: "In the election
of senator in 1854 [1855 you mean], when Mr.
Trumbull was the successful candidate, was
there any unfairness in the conduct of Mr. Judd
toward you, or anything blamable on his part?"

I answer, I have never believed, and do not now believe, that on that occasion there was any unfairness in the conduct of Mr. Judd toward me, or anything blamable on his part. Without deception, he preferred Judge Trumbull to myself, which was his clear right, morally as well as legally.

To your question: "During the canvass of last year, did he do his whole duty toward you and the Republican party?" I answer, I have always believed, and now believe that during that canvass he did his whole duty toward me and the Republican party.

To your question: "Do you know of anything unfair in his conduct toward yourself in any way?" I answer, I neither know nor suspect anything unfair in his conduct toward myself in any way.

I take pleasure in adding that of all the avowed friends I had in the canvass of last year, I do not suspect a single one of having acted treacherously to me, or to our cause; and that there is not one of them in whose honor and integrity I have more confidence to-day than in that of Mr. Judd.

You can use your discretion as to whether you make this public.

Yours very truly,

A. LINCOLN.

LETTER TO G. M. PARSONS AND OTHERS

SPRINGFIELD, ILLINOIS, December 19, 1859.

Gentlemen: Your letter of the 7th instant, accompanied by a similar one from the governor-elect, the Republican State officers, and the Republican members of the State Board of Equalization of Ohio, both requesting of me, for publication in permanent form, copies of the political debates between Senator Douglas and myself last year, has been received. With my grateful acknowledgments to both you and them for the very flattering terms in which the request is communicated, I transmit you the copies. The copies I send you are as reported and printed by the respective friends of Senator Douglas and myself, at the time—that is, his by his friends, and mine by mine. It would be an unwarrantable liberty for us to change a word or a letter in his, and the changes I have made in mine, you perceive, are verbal only, and very few in number. I wish the reprint to be precisely as the copies I send, without any comment whatever.

Yours very truly,

A. LINCOLN.

LETTER TO J. W. FELL

SPRINGFIELD, December 20, 1859.

My dear Sir: Herewith is a little sketch, as you requested. There is not much of it, for the reason, I suppose, that there is not much of me. If anything be made out of it, I wish it to be modest, and not to go beyond the material. If it were thought necessary to incorporate anything from any of my speeches, I suppose there would be no objection. Of course it must not appear to have been written by myself.

Yours very truly,

A. LINCOLN.

I was born February 12, 1809, in Hardin County, Kentucky. My parents were both born in Virginia, of undistinguished families—second families, perhaps I should say. My mother, who died in my tenth year, was of a family of the name of Hanks, some of whom now reside in Adams, and others in Macon County, Illinois. My paternal grandfather, Abraham Lincoln, emigrated from Rockingham County, Virginia, to Kentucky about 1781 or 1782, where a year or two later he was killed by the Indians, not in battle, but by stealth, when he was laboring to open a farm in the forest. His ancestors, who were Quakers, went to Virginia from Berks County, Pennsylvania. An effort to identify them with the New England family of the same name ended in nothing more definite than a similarity of Christian names in both families, such as Enoch, Levi, Mordecai, Solomon, Abraham, and the like.

My father, at the death of his father, was but six years of age, and he grew up literally without education. He removed from Kentucky to what is now Spencer County, Indiana, in my eighth year. We reached our new home about the time the State came into the Union. It was a wild region, with many bears and other wild animals still in the woods. There I grew up. There were some schools, so called, but no qualification was ever required of a teacher beyond "readin,' writin', and cipherin' " to the rule of three. If a straggler supposed to understand Latin happen to sojourn in the neighborhood, he was looked upon as a wizard. There was absolutely nothing to excite ambition for education. Of course, when I came of age I did not know much. Still, somehow, I could read, write, and cipher to the rule of three, but that was all. I have not been to school since. The little advance I now have upon this store of education, I have picked up from time to time under the pressure of necessity.

I was raised to farm work, which I continued

till I was twenty-two. At twenty-one I came to Illinois, Macon County. Then I got to New Salem, at that time in Sangamon, now in Menard County, where I remained a year as a sort of clerk in a store. Then came the Black Hawk war; and I was elected a captain of volunteers, a success which gave me more pleasure than any I have had since. I went the campaign, was elated, ran for the legislature the same year (1832), and was beaten—the only time I ever have been beaten by the people. The next and three succeeding biennial elections I was elected to the legislature. I was not a candidate afterward. During this legislative period I had studied law, and removed to Springfield to practise it. In 1846 I was once elected to the lower House of Congress. Was not a candidate for reëlection. From 1849 to 1854, both inclusive, practised law more assiduously than ever before. Always a Whig in politics; and generally on the Whig electoral tickets, making active canvasses. I was losing interest in politics when the repeal of the Missouri compromise aroused me again. What I have done since then is pretty well known.

If any personal description of me is thought desirable, it may be said I am, in height, six feet four inches, nearly; lean in flesh, weighing on an average one hundred and eighty pounds;

dark complexion, with coarse black hair and gray eyes. No other marks or brands recollected. Yours truly,

A. LINCOLN.

LETTER TO J. W. SHEAHAN

SPRINGFIELD, January 24, 1860.

Dear Sir: Yours of the 21st, requesting copies of my speeches now in progress of publication in Ohio, is received. I have no such copies now at my control, having sent the only set I ever had to Ohio. Mr. George M. Parsons has taken an active part among those who have the matter in charge in Ohio; and I understand Messrs. Follett, Foster & Co. are to be the publishers. I make no objection to any satisfactory arrangement you may make with Mr. Parsons and the publishers; and if it will facilitate you, you are at liberty to show them this note.

You labor under a mistake somewhat injurious to me, if you suppose I have revised the speeches in any just sense of the word. I only made some small verbal corrections, mostly such as an intelligent reader would make for himself, not feeling justified to do more when publishing the speeches along with those of Senator Douglas, his and mine being mutually answers and replies to one another. Yours truly,

A. LINCOLN.

LETTER TO N. B. JUDD

SPRINGFIELD, February 5, 1860.

My dear Sir: Your two letters were duly received. Whether Mr. Storrs shall come to Illinois and assist in our approaching campaign, is a question of dollars and cents. Can we pay him? If we can, that is the sole question. I consider his services very valuable.

A day or so before you wrote about Mr. Herndon, Dubois told me that he (Herndon) had been talking to William Jayne in the way you indicate. At first sight afterward, I mentioned it to him; he rather denied the charge, and I did not press him about the past, but got his solemn pledge to say nothing of the sort in the future. I had done this before I received your letter. I impressed upon him as well as I could, first, that such [*sic*] was untrue and unjust to you; and, second, that I would be held responsible for what he said. Let this be private.

Some folks are pretty bitter toward me about the Dole, Hubbard, and Brown letter.

Yours as ever,

A. LINCOLN.

LETTER TO N. B. JUDD

SPRINGFIELD, February 9, 1860.

Dear Sir: I am not in a position where it would hurt much for me to not be nominated on

the national ticket; but I am where it would
hurt some for me to not get the Illinois delegates. What I expected when I wrote the letter
to Messrs. Dole and others is now happening.
Your discomfited assailants are most bitter
against me; and they will, for revenge upon me,
lay to the Bates egg in the South, and to the
Seward egg in the North, and go far toward
squeezing me out in the middle with nothing.
Can you not help me a little in this matter in
your end of the vineyard? I mean this to be
private.   Yours as ever,

A. LINCOLN.

LETTER TO J. M. LUCAS.

SPRINGFIELD, February 9, 1860.

My dear Sir: Your late letter, suggesting,
among other things, that I might aid your election as postmaster, by writing to Mr. Burlin-
game, was duly received the day the Speaker
was elected; so that I had no hope a letter of
mine could reach Mr. B. before your case would
be decided, as it turned out in fact it could not.
We are all much gratified here to see you are
elected. We consider you our peculiar friend
at court.

I shall be glad to receive a letter from you at
any time you can find leisure to write one.

Yours very truly, A. LINCOLN.

*LETTER TO MR. WHITE.

SPRINGFIELD, February 13, 1860.

Friend White: Your kind note, inclosing the letter of Mr. Billinghurst is just received. It so happens that I am engaged to be at Brooklyn, on the evening of the 27th, so that, of course, I cannot be in Wisconsin on the 28th, and I have so written Mr. B.

Thank you for your anticipations of the future for me, as well as for your many past kindnesses.   Your friend as ever,

A. LINCOLN.

Abraham Lincoln

*Reproduced from a copy in possession of Judge
Daniel Fish of an Original Photograph taken
in 1860, and owned by Mrs. Cyrus Aldrich.*

ADDRESS AT COOPER INSTITUTE, NEW YORK, February 27, 1860.[1]

MR. PRESIDENT AND FELLOW-CITIZENS OF NEW YORK: The facts with which I shall deal this evening are mainly old and familiar; nor is there anything new in the general use I shall make of them. If there shall be any novelty, it will be in the mode of presenting the facts, and the inferences and observations following that presentation. In his speech last autumn at Columbus, Ohio, as reported in the "New-York Times," Senator Douglas said:

[1] Originally Lincoln had been invited to lecture in Plymouth Church, Brooklyn, but financial or other difficulties arose and the engagement was taken over by "The Young Men's Central Republican Union" of New York City, which had determined upon a series of political addresses. It was not until he reached New York that Lincoln became fully aware of the change. The audience he faced in Cooper Institute was made up of the culture and wealth of the great metropolis. Horace Greeley and David Dudley Field escorted Lincoln to the platform and William Cullen Bryant introduced him. The speech he delivered is now acknowledged one of the greatest efforts of his life, and won instant recognition for him in the East. It is supposed to have been largely instrumental in securing his nomination for the Presidency.

Our fathers, when they framed the government under which we live, understood this question just as well, and even better, than we do now.

I fully indorse this, and I adopt it as a text for this discourse. I so adopt it because it furnishes a precise and an agreed starting-point for a discussion between Republicans and that wing of the Democracy headed by Senator Douglas. It simply leaves the inquiry: What was the understanding those fathers had of the question mentioned?

What is the frame of government under which we live? The answer must be, "The Constitution of the United States." That Constitution consists of the original, framed in 1787, and under which the present government first went into operation, and twelve subsequently framed amendments, the first ten of which were framed in 1789.

Who were our fathers that framed the Constitution? I suppose the "thirty-nine" who signed the original instrument may be fairly called our fathers who framed that part of the present government. It is almost exactly true to say they framed it, and it is altogether true to say they fairly represented the opinion and sentiment of the whole nation at that time. Their names, being familiar to nearly all,

and accessible to quite all, need not now be repeated.

I take these "thirty-nine," for the present, as
being "our fathers who framed the government
under which we live." What is the question
which, according to the text, those fathers understood "just as well, and even better, than we
do now"?

It is this: Does the proper division of local
from Federal authority, or anything in the Constitution, forbid our Federal Government to
control as to slavery in our Federal Territories?

Upon this, Senator Douglas holds the affirmative, and Republicans the negative. This affirmation and denial form an issue; and this issue
—this question—is precisely what the text declares our fathers understood "better than we."
Let us now inquire whether the "thirty-nine,"
or any of them, ever acted upon this question;
and if they did, how they acted upon it—how
they expressed that better understanding. In
1784, three years before the Constitution, the
United States then owning the Northwestern
Territory, and no other, the Congress of the
Confederation had before them the question of
prohibiting slavery in that Territory; and four
of the "thirty-nine" who afterward framed the
Constitution were in that Congress, and voted on
that question. Of these, Roger Sherman,

Thomas Mifflin, and Hugh Williamson voted for the prohibition, thus showing that, in their understanding, no line dividing local from Federal authority, nor anything else, properly forbade the Federal Government to control as to slavery in Federal territory. The other of the four, James McHenry, voted against the prohibition, showing that for some cause he thought it improper to vote for it.

In 1787, still before the Constitution, but while the convention was in session framing it, and while the Northwestern Territory still was the only Territory owned by the United States, the same question of prohibiting slavery in the Territory again came before the Congress of the Confederation; and two more of the "thirty-nine" who afterward signed the Constitution were in that Congress, and voted on the question. They were William Blount and William Few; and they both voted for the prohibition—thus showing that in their understanding no line dividing local from Federal authority, nor anything else, properly forbade the Federal Government to control as to slavery in Federal territory. This time the prohibition became a law, being part of what is now well known as the ordinance of '87.

The question of Federal control of slavery in the Territories seems not to have been directly before the convention which framed the original Constitution; and hence it is not recorded that the "thirty-nine," or any of them, while engaged on that instrument, expressed any opinion on that precise question.

In 1789, by the first Congress which sat under the Constitution, an act was passed to enforce the ordinance of '87, including the prohibition of slavery in the Northwestern Territory. The bill for this act was reported by one of the "thirty-nine"—Thomas Fitzsimmons, then a member of the House of Representatives from Pennsylvania. It went through all its stages without a word of opposition, and finally passed both branches without ayes and nays, which is equivalent to a unanimous passage. In this Congress there were sixteen of the thirty-nine fathers who framed the original Constitution. They were John Langdon, Nicholas Gilman, Wm. S. Johnson, Roger Sherman, Robert Morris, Thos. Fitzsimmons, William Few, Abraham Baldwin, Rufus King, William Paterson, George Clymer, Richard Bassett, George Read, Pierce Butler, Daniel Carroll and James Madison.

This shows that, in their understanding, no line dividing local from Federal authority, nor anything in the Constitution, properly forbade Congress to prohibit slavery in the Federal territory; else both their fidelity to correct principle, and their oath to support the Constitution, would have constrained them to oppose the prohibition.

Again, George Washington, another of the "thirty-nine," was then President of the United States and as such approved and signed the bill, thus completing its validity as a law, and thus showing that, in his understanding, no line dividing local from Federal authority, nor anything in the Constitution, forbade the Federal Government to control as to slavery in Federal territory.

No great while after the adoption of the original Constitution, North Carolina ceded to the Federal Government the country now constituting the State of Tennessee; and a few years later Georgia ceded that which now constitutes the States of Mississippi and Alabama. In both deeds of cession it was made a condition by the ceding States that the Federal Government should not prohibit slavery in the ceded country. Besides this, slavery was then actually in the ceded country. Under these circumstances, Congress, on taking charge of these countries, did not absolutely prohibit slavery within them. But they did interfere with it—take control of it—even there, to a certain extent. In 1798 Congress organized the Territory of Mississippi. In the act of organization they prohibited the bringing of slaves into the Territory from any place without the United States, by fine, and giving freedom to slaves so brought. This act passed both branches of Congress without yeas and nays. In that Congress were three of the "thirty-nine" who framed the original Constitution. They were John Langdon, George Read, and Abraham Baldwin. They all probably voted for it. Certainly they would have placed their opposition to it upon record if, in their understanding, any line dividing local from Federal authority, or anything in the Constitution, properly forbade the Federal Government to control as to slavery in Federal territory.

In 1803 the Federal Government purchased the Louisiana country. Our former territorial acquisitions came from certain of our own States; but this Louisiana country was acquired from a foreign nation. In 1804 Congress gave a territorial organization to that part of it which now constitutes the State of Louisiana. New Orleans, lying within that part, was an old and comparatively large city. There were other considerable towns and settlements, and slavery was extensively and thoroughly intermingled with the people. Congress did not, in the Territorial Act, prohibit slavery; but they did interfere with it—take control of it—in a more marked and extensive way than they did in the case of Mississippi. The substance of the provision therein made in relation to slaves was:

1st. That no slave should be imported into the Territory from foreign parts.

2d. That no slave should be carried into it who had been imported into the United States since the first day of May, 1798.

3d. That no slave should be carried into it, except by the owner, and for his own use as a settler; the penalty in all the cases being a fine upon the violator of the law, and freedom to the slave.

This act also was passed without ayes or nays. In the Congress which passed it there were two of the "thirty-nine." They were Abraham Baldwin and Jonathan Dayton. As stated in the case of Mississippi, it is probable they both voted for it. They would not have allowed it to pass without recording their opposition to it if, in their understanding, it violated either the line properly dividing local from Federal authority, or any provision of the Constitution.

In 1819–20 came and passed the Missouri question. Many votes were taken, by yeas and nays, in both branches of Congress, upon the various phases of the general question. Two of the "thirty-nine"—Rufus King and Charles Pinckney—were members of that Congress. Mr. King steadily voted for slavery prohibition and against all compromises, while Mr. Pinckney as steadily voted against slavery prohibition and against all compromises. By this, Mr. King showed that, in his understanding, no line dividing local from Federal authority, nor anything in the Constitution, was violated by Congress prohibiting slavery in Federal territory; while Mr. Pinckney, by his votes, showed that, in his understanding, there was some sufficient reason for opposing such prohibition in that case.

The cases I have mentioned are the only acts of the "thirty-nine," or of any of them, upon the direct issue, which I have been able to discover.

To enumerate the persons who thus acted as being four in 1784, two in 1787, seventeen in 1789, three in 1798, two in 1804, and two in 1819–20, there would be thirty of them. But this would be counting John Langdon, Roger Sherman, William Few, Rufus King, and George Read each twice, and Abraham Baldwin three times. The true number of those of the "thirty-nine" whom I have shown to have acted upon the question which, by the text, they understood better than we, is twenty-three, leaving sixteen not shown to have acted upon it in any way.

Here, then, we have twenty-three out of our thirty-nine fathers "who framed the government under which we live," who have, upon their official responsibility and their corporal oaths, acted upon the very question which the text affirms they "understood just as well, and even better, than we do now"; and twenty-one of them—a clear majority of the whole "thirty-nine"—so acting upon it as to make them guilty of gross political impropriety and wilful perjury if, in their understanding, any proper division between local and Federal authority, or anything in the Constitution they had made themselves, and sworn to support, forbade the Federal Government to control as to slavery in the Federal Territories. Thus the twenty-one acted; and, as actions speak louder than words, so actions under such responsibility speak still louder.

Two of the twenty-three voted against congressional prohibition of slavery in the Federal Territories, in the instances in which they acted upon the question. But for what reasons they so voted is not known. They may have done so because they thought a proper division of local from Federal authority, or some provision or principle of the Constitution, stood in the way; or they may, without any such question, have voted against the prohibition on what appeared to them to be sufficient grounds of expediency. No one who has sworn to support the Constitution can conscientiously vote for what he understands to be an unconstitutional

measure, however expedient he may think it;
but one may and ought to vote against a
measure which he deems constitutional if,
at the same time, he deems it inexpedient. It,
therefore, would be unsafe to set down even the
two who voted against the prohibition as having
done so because, in their understanding, any
proper division of local from Federal authority,
or anything in the Constitution, forbade the
Federal Government to control as to slavery in
Federal territory.

The remaining sixteen of the "thirty-nine," so
far as I have discovered, have left no record of
their understanding upon the direct question of
Federal control of slavery in the Federal Territories. But there is much reason to believe that
their understanding upon that question would
not have appeared different from that of their
twenty-three compeers, had it been manifested
at all.

For the purpose of adhering rigidly to the
text, I have purposely omitted whatever understanding may have been manifested by any person, however distinguished, other than the
thirty-nine fathers who framed the original Constitution; and, for the same reason, I have also
omitted whatever understanding may have been
manifested by any of the "thirty-nine" even on
any other phase of the general question of slav-

ery. If we should look into their acts and declarations on those other phases, as the foreign slave-trade, and the morality and policy of slavery generally, it would appear to us that on the direct question of Federal control of slavery in Federal Territories, the sixteen, if they had acted at all, would probably have acted just as the twenty-three did. Among that sixteen were several of the most noted antislavery men of those times,—as Dr. Franklin, Alexander Hamilton, and Gouverneur Morris,—while there was not one now known to have been otherwise, unless it may be John Rutledge, of South Carolina.

The sum of the whole is that of our thirty-nine fathers who framed the original Constitution, twenty-one—a clear majority of the whole—certainly understood that no proper division of local from Federal authority, nor any part of the Constitution, forbade the Federal Government to control slavery in the Federal Territories; while all the rest had probably the same understanding. Such, unquestionably, was the understanding of our fathers who framed the original Constitution; and the text affirms that they understood the question "better than we."

But, so far, I have been considering the understanding of the question manifested by the framers of the original Constitution. In and

by the original instrument, a mode was provided
for amending it; and, as I have already stated,
the present frame of "the government under
which we live" consists of that original, and
twelve amendatory articles framed and adopted since. Those who now insist that Federal
control of slavery in Federal Territories violates the Constitution, point us to the provisions
which they suppose it thus violates; and, as I
understand, they all fix upon provisions in these
amendatory articles, and not in the original instrument. The Supreme Court, in the Dred
Scott case, plant themselves upon the Fifth
Amendment, which provides that no person
shall be deprived of "life, liberty, or property
without due process of law"; while Senator
Douglas and his peculiar adherents plant themselves upon the Tenth Amendment, providing
that "the powers not delegated to the United
States by the Constitution" "are reserved to the
States respectively, or to the people."

Now, it so happens that these amendments
were framed by the first Congress which sat under the Constitution—the identical Congress
which passed the act, already mentioned, enforcing the prohibition of slavery in the Northwestern Territory. Not only was it the same
Congress, but they were the identical, same individual men who, at the same session, and at

the same time within the session, had under
consideration, and in progress toward maturity,
these constitutional amendments, and this act
prohibiting slavery in all the territory the nation then owned. The constitutional amendments were introduced before, and passed after,
the act enforcing the ordinance of '87; so that,
during the whole pendency of the act to enforce the ordinance, the constitutional amendments were also pending.

The seventy-six members of that Congress, including sixteen of the framers of the original
Constitution, as before stated, were preëminent-
ly our fathers who framed that part of "the
government under which we live" which is now
claimed as forbidding the Federal Government
to control slavery in the Federal Territories.

Is it not a little presumptuous in any one at
this day to affirm that the two things which that
Congress deliberately framed, and carried to
maturity at the same time, are absolutely inconsistent with each other? And does not such
affirmation become impudently absurd when
coupled with the other affirmation, from the
same mouth, that those who did the two things
alleged to be inconsistent, understood whether
they really were inconsistent better than we—
better than he who affirms that they are inconsistent?

It is surely safe to assume that the thirty-nine framers of the original Constitution, and the seventy-six members of the Congress which framed the amendments thereto, taken together, do certainly include those who may be fairly called "our fathers who framed the government under which we live." And so assuming, I defy any man to show that any one of them ever, in his whole life, declared that, in his understanding, any proper division of local from Federal authority, or any part of the Constitution, forbade the Federal Government to control as to slavery in the Federal Territories. I go a step further. I defy any one to show that any living man in the whole world ever did, prior to the beginning of the present century (and I might almost say prior to the beginning of the last half of the present century), declare that, in his understanding, any proper division of local from Federal authority, or any part of the Constitution, forbade the Federal Government to control as to slavery in the Federal Territories. To those who now so declare I give not only "our fathers who framed the government under which we live," but with them all other living men within the century in which it was framed, among whom to search, and they shall not be able to find the evidence of a single man agreeing with them.

Now, and here, let me guard a little against being misunderstood. I do not mean to say we are bound to follow implicitly in whatever our fathers did. To do so would be to discard all the lights of current experience—to reject all progress, all improvement. What I do say is that if we would supplant the opinions and policy of our fathers in any case, we should do so upon evidence so conclusive, and argument so clear, that even their great authority, fairly considered and weighed, cannot stand; and most surely not in a case whereof we ourselves declare they understood the question better than we.

If any man at this day sincerely believes that a proper division of local from Federal authority, or any part of the Constitution, forbids the Federal Government to control as to slavery in the Federal Territories, he is right to say so, and to enforce his position by all truthful evidence and fair argument which he can. But he has no right to mislead others, who have less access to history, and less leisure to study it, into the false belief that "our fathers who framed the government under which we live" were of the same opinion—thus substituting falsehood and deception for truthful evidence and fair argument. If any man at this day sincerely believes "our fathers who framed the government under which we live" used and applied principles, in other cases, which ought to have led them to understand that a proper division of local from Federal authority, or some part of the Constitution, forbids the Federal Government to control as to slavery in the Federal Territories, he is right to say so. But he should, at the same time, brave the responsibility of declaring that, in his opinion, he understands their principles better than they did themselves; and especially should he not shirk that responsibility by asserting that they "understood the question just as well, and even better, than we do now."

But enough! Let all who believe that "our fathers who framed the government under which we live understood this question just as well, and even better, than we do now," speak as they spoke, and act as they acted upon it. This is all Republicans ask—all Republicans desire—in relation to slavery. As those fathers marked it, so let it be again marked, as an evil not to be extended, but to be tolerated and protected only because of and so far as its actual presence among us makes that toleration and protection a necessity. Let all the guaranties those fathers gave it be not grudgingly, but fully and fairly, maintained. For this Republicans contend, and with this, so far as I know or believe, they will be content.

And now, if they would listen,—as I suppose they will not,—I would address a few words to the Southern people.

I would say to them: You consider yourselves a reasonable and a just people; and I consider that in the general qualities of reason and justice you are not inferior to any other people. Still, when you speak of us Republicans, you do so only to denounce us as reptiles, or, at the best, as no better than outlaws. You will grant a hearing to pirates or murderers, but nothing like it to "Black Republicans." In all your contentions with one another, each of you deems an unconditional condemnation of "Black Republicanism" as the first thing to be attended to. Indeed, such condemnation of us seems to be an indispensable prerequisite—license, so to speak —among you to be admitted or permitted to speak at all. Now can you or not be prevailed upon to pause and to consider whether this is quite just to us, or even to yourselves? Bring forward your charges and specifications, and then be patient long enough to hear us deny or justify.

You say we are sectional. We deny it. That makes an issue; and the burden of proof is upon you. You produce your proof; and what is it? Why, that our party has no existence in your section—gets no votes in your section. The fact is

substantially true; but does it prove the issue?
If it does, then in case we should, without change
of principle, begin to get votes in your section,
we should thereby cease to be sectional. You
cannot escape this conclusion; and yet, are you
willing to abide by it? If you are, you will
probably soon find that we have ceased to be
sectional, for we shall get votes in your section
this very year. You will then begin to discover,
as the truth plainly is, that your proof does not
touch the issue. The fact that we get no votes in
your section is a fact of your making, and not of
ours. And if there be fault in that fact, that
fault is primarily yours, and remains so until you
show that we repel you by some wrong principle
or practice. If we do repel you by any wrong
principle or practice, the fault is ours; but this
brings you to where you ought to have started
—to a discussion of the right or wrong of our
principle. If our principle, put in practice,
would wrong your section for the benefit of ours,
or for any other object, then our principle, and
we with it, are sectional, and are justly opposed
and denounced as such. Meet us, then, on the
question of whether our principle, put in practice, would wrong your section; and so meet us
as if it were possible that something may be said
on our side. Do you accept the challenge? No!
Then you really believe that the principle which

"our fathers who framed the government under which we live" thought so clearly right as to adopt it, and indorse it again and again, upon their official oaths, is in fact so clearly wrong as to demand your condemnation without a moment's consideration.

Some of you delight to flaunt in our faces the warning against sectional parties given by Washington in his Farewell Address. Less than eight years before Washington gave that warning, he had, as President of the United States, approved and signed an act of Congress enforcing the prohibition of slavery in the North-western Territory, which act embodied the policy of the government upon that subject up to and at the very moment he penned that warning; and about one year after he penned it, he wrote Lafayette that he considered that prohibition a wise measure, expressing in the same connection his hope that we should at some time have a confederacy of free States.

Bearing this in mind, and seeing that sectionalism has since arisen upon this same subject, is that warning a weapon in your hands against us, or in our hands against you? Could Washington himself speak, would he cast the blame of that sectionalism upon us, who sustain his policy, or upon you, who repudiate it? We respect that warning of Washington, and we commend it to you, together with his example pointing to the right application of it.

But you say you are conservative—eminently conservative—while we are revolutionary, destructive, or something of the sort. What is conservatism? Is it not adherence to the old and tried, against the new and untried? We stick to, contend for, the identical old policy on the point in controversy which was adopted by "our fathers who framed the government under which we live"; while you with one accord reject, and scout, and spit upon that old policy, and insist upon substituting something new. True, you disagree among yourselves as to what that substitute shall be. You are divided on new propositions and plans, but you are unanimous in rejecting and denouncing the old policy of the fathers. Some of you are for reviving the foreign slave-trade; some for a congressional slave code for the Territories; some for Congress forbidding the Territories to prohibit slavery within their limits; some for maintaining slavery in the Territories through the judiciary; some for the "gur-reat pur-rinciple" that "if one man would enslave another, no third man should object," fantastically called "popular sovereignty"; but never a man among you is in favor of Federal prohibition of slavery in Federal Territories, according to the practice of "our fathers who

framed the government under which we live."
Not one of all your various plans can show a
precedent or an advocate in the century within
which our government originated. Consider,
then, whether your claim of conservatism for
yourselves, and your charge of destructiveness
against us, are based on the most clear and
stable foundations.

Again, you say we have made the slavery
question more prominent than it formerly was.
We deny it. We admit that it is more prominent, but we deny that we made it so. It was not
we, but you, who discarded the old policy of the
fathers. We resisted, and still resist, your in-
novation; and thence comes the greater promi-
nence of the question. Would you have that
question reduced to its former proportions? Go
back to that old policy. What has been will be
again, under the same conditions. If you would
have the peace of the old times, readopt the
precepts and policy of the old times.

You charge that we stir up insurrections
among your slaves. We deny it; and what is
your proof? Harper's Ferry! John Brown!!
John Brown was no Republican; and you have
failed to implicate a single Republican in his
Harper's Ferry enterprise. If any member of
our party is guilty in that matter, you know it,
or you do not know it. If you do know it, you

are inexcusable for not designating the man and proving the fact. If you do not know it, you are inexcusable for asserting it, and especially for persisting in the assertion after you have tried and failed to make the proof. You need not be told that persisting in a charge which one does not know to be true, is simply malicious slander.

Some of you admit that no Republican designedly aided or encouraged the Harper's Ferry affair, but still insist that our doctrines and declarations necessarily lead to such results. We do not believe it. We know we hold no doctrine, and make no declaration, which were not held to and made by "our fathers who framed the government under which we live." You never dealt fairly by us in relation to this affair. When it occurred, some important State elections were near at hand, and you were in evident glee with the belief that, by charging the blame upon us, you could get an advantage of us in those elections. The elections came, and your expectations were not quite fulfilled. Every Republican man knew that, as to himself at least, your charge was a slander, and he was not much inclined by it to cast his vote in your favor. Republican doctrines and declarations are accompanied with a continual protest against any interference whatever with your slaves, or with you about your slaves. Surely, this does not encourage them to revolt. True, we do, in common with "our fathers who framed the government under which we live," declare our belief that slavery is wrong; but the slaves do not hear us declare even this. For anything we say or do, the slaves would scarcely know there is a Republican party. I believe they would not, in fact, generally know it but for your misrepresentations of us in their hearing. In your political contests among yourselves, each faction charges the other with sympathy with Black Republicanism; and then, to give point to the charge, defines Black Republicanism to simply be insurrection, blood, and thunder among the slaves.

Slave insurrections are no more common now than they were before the Republican party was organized. What induced the Southampton insurrection, twenty-eight years ago, in which at least three times as many lives were lost as at Harper's Ferry? You can scarcely stretch your very elastic fancy to the conclusion that Southampton was "got up by Black Republicanism." In the present state of things in the United States, I do not think a general, or even a very extensive, slave insurrection is possible. The indispensable concert of action cannot be attained. The slaves have no means of rapid communication; nor can incendiary free-men, black or white, supply it. The explosive materials are everywhere in parcels; but there neither are, nor can be supplied, the indispensable connecting trains.

Much is said by Southern people about the affection of slaves for their masters and mistresses; and a part of it, at least, is true. A plot for an uprising could scarcely be devised and communicated to twenty individuals before some one of them, to save the life of a favorite master or mistress, would divulge it. This is the rule; and the slave revolution in Hayti was not an exception to it, but a case occurring under peculiar circumstances. The gunpowder plot of British history, though not connected with slaves, was more in point. In that case, only about twenty were admitted to the secret; and yet one of them, in his anxiety to save a friend, betrayed the plot to that friend, and, by consequence, averted the calamity. Occasional poisonings from the kitchen, and open or stealthy assassinations in the field, and local revolts extending to a score or so, will continue to occur as the natural results of slavery; but no general insurrection of slaves, as I think, can happen in this country for a long time. Whoever much fears, or much hopes, for such an event, will be alike disappointed.

In the language of Mr. Jefferson, uttered many years ago, "It is still in our power to direct the process of emancipation and deportation peaceably, and in such slow degrees, as that the evil will wear off insensibly; and their places be, *pari passu,* filled up by free white laborers. If, on the contrary, it is left to force itself on, human nature must shudder at the prospect held up."

Mr. Jefferson did not mean to say, nor do I, that the power of emancipation is in the Federal Government. He spoke of Virginia; and, as to the power of emancipation, I speak of the slaveholding States only. The Federal Government, however, as we insist, has the power of restraining the extension of the institution—the power to insure that a slave insurrection shall never occur on any American soil which is now free from slavery.

John Brown's effort was peculiar. It was not a slave insurrection. It was an attempt by white men to get up a revolt among slaves, in which the slaves refused to participate. In fact, it was so absurd that the slaves, with all their ignorance, saw plainly enough it could not succeed. That affair, in its philosophy, corresponds with the many attempts, related in history, at the assassination of kings and emperors. An enthusiast broods over the oppression of a people till he fancies himself commissioned by Heaven to liberate them. He ventures the attempt, which ends in little else than his own execution. Orsini's attempt on Louis Napoleon, and John Brown's attempt at Harper's Ferry, were, in their philosophy, precisely the same. The eagerness to cast blame on old England in the one case, and on New England in the other, does not disprove the sameness of the two things.

And how much would it avail you, if you could, by the use of John Brown, Helper's Book, and the like, break up the Republican organization? Human action can be modified to some extent, but human nature cannot be changed. There is a judgment and a feeling against slavery in this nation, which cast at least a million and a half of votes. You cannot destroy that judgment and feeling—that senti-ment—by breaking up the political organiza-tion which rallies around it. You can scarcely scatter and disperse an army which has been formed into order in the face of your heaviest fire; but if you could, how much would you gain by forcing the sentiment which created it out of the peaceful channel of the ballot-box into some other channel? What would that other channel probably be? Would the number of John Browns be lessened or enlarged by the operation?

But you will break up the Union rather than submit to a denial of your constitutional rights.

That has a somewhat reckless sound; but it would be palliated, if not fully justified, were we proposing, by the mere force of numbers, to deprive you of some right plainly written down in the Constitution. But we are proposing no such thing.

When you make these declarations you have a specific and well-understood allusion to an assumed constitutional right of yours to take slaves into the Federal Territories, and to hold them there as property. But no such right is specifically written in the Constitution. That instrument is literally silent about any such right. We, on the contrary, deny that such a right has any existence in the Constitution, even by implication.

Your purpose, then, plainly stated, is that you will destroy the government, unless you be allowed to construe and force the Constitution as you please, on all points in dispute between you and us. You will rule or ruin in all events.

This, plainly stated, is your language. Perhaps you will say the Supreme Court has decided the disputed constitutional question in your favor. Not quite so. But waiving the lawyer's distinction between dictum and decision, the court has decided the question for you in a sort of way. The court has substantially said, it is your constitutional right to take slaves into the Federal Territories, and to hold them there as property. When I say the decision was made in a sort of way, I mean it was made in a divided court, by a bare majority of the judges, and they not quite agreeing with one another in the reasons for making it; that it is so made as that its avowed supporters disagree with one another about its meaning, and that it was mainly based upon a mistaken statement of fact— the statement in the opinion that "the right of property in a slave is distinctly and expressly affirmed in the Constitution."

An inspection of the Constitution will show that the right of property in a slave is not "distinctly and expressly affirmed" in it. Bear in mind, the judges do not pledge their judicial opinion that such right is impliedly affirmed in the Constitution; but they pledge their veracity that it is "distinctly and expressly" affirmed there—"distinctly," that is, not mingled with anything else—"expressly," that is, in words meaning just that, without the aid of any inference, and susceptible of no other meaning.

If they had only pledged their judicial opinion that such right is affirmed in the instrument by implication, it would be open to others to show that neither the word "slave" nor "slavery" is to be found in the Constitution, nor the word "property" even, in any connection with language alluding to the things slave, or slavery; and that wherever in that instrument the slave is alluded to, he is called a "person"; and wherever his master's legal right in relation to him is alluded to, it is spoken of as "service or labor which may be due"—as a debt payable in service or labor. Also it would be open to show, by contemporaneous history, that this mode of alluding to slaves and slavery, instead of speaking of them, was employed on purpose to exclude from the Constitution the idea that there could be property in man.

To show all this is easy and certain.

When this obvious mistake of the judges shall be brought to their notice, is it not reasonable to expect that they will withdraw the mistaken statement, and reconsider the conclusion based upon it?

And then it is to be remembered that "our fathers who framed the government under which we live"—the men who made the Constitution—decided this same constitutional question in our favor long ago: decided it without division among themselves when making the decision; without division among themselves about the meaning of it after it was made, and, so far as any evidence is left, without basing it upon any mistaken statement of facts.

Under all these circumstances, do you really feel yourselves justified to break up this government unless such a court decision as yours is shall be at once submitted to as a conclusive and final rule of political action? But you will not abide the election of a Republican president! In that supposed event, you say, you will destroy the Union; and then, you say, the great crime of having destroyed it will be upon us! That is cool. A highwayman holds a pistol to my ear, and mutters through his teeth, "Stand and deliver, or I shall kill you, and then you will be a murderer!"

To be sure, what the robber demanded of me —my money—was my own; and I had a clear right to keep it; but it was no more my own than my vote is my own; and the threat of death to me, to extort my money, and the threat of destruction to the Union, to extort my vote, can scarcely be distinguished in principle.

A few words now to Republicans. It is exceedingly desirable that all parts of this great Confederacy shall be at peace, and in harmony one with another. Let us Republicans do our part to have it so. Even though much provoked, let us do nothing through passion and ill temper. Even though the Southern people will not so much as listen to us, let us calmly consider their demands, and yield to them if, in our deliberate view of our duty, we possibly can. Judging by all they say and do, and by the subject and nature of their controversy with us, let us determine, if we can, what will satisfy them.

Will they be satisfied if the Territories be unconditionally surrendered to them? We know they will not. In all their present complaints against us, the Territories are scarcely mentioned. Invasions and insurrections are the rage now. Will it satisfy them if, in the future, we have nothing to do with invasions and insurrections? We know it will not. We so know, because we know we never had anything to do with invasions and insurrections; and yet this total abstaining does not exempt us from the charge and the denunciation.

The question recurs, What will satisfy them? Simply this: we must not only let them alone, but we must somehow convince them that we do let them alone. This, we know by experience, is no easy task. We have been so trying to convince them from the very beginning of our organization, but with no success. In all our platforms and speeches we have constantly protested our purpose to let them alone; but this has had no tendency to convince them. Alike unavailing to convince them is the fact that they

have never detected a man of us in any attempt
to disturb them.

These natural and apparently adequate means
all failing, what will convince them? This, and
this only: cease to call slavery wrong, and join
them in calling it right. And this must be done
thoroughly—done in acts as well as in words.
Silence will not be tolerated—we must place
ourselves avowedly with them. Senator Douglas's new sedition law must be enacted and enforced, suppressing all declarations that slavery
is wrong, whether made in politics, in presses,
in pulpits, or in private. We must arrest and
return their fugitive slaves with greedy pleasure.
We must pull down our free-State constitutions.
The whole atmosphere must be disinfected from
all taint of opposition to slavery, before they
will cease to believe that all their troubles proceed from us.

I am quite aware they do not state their case
precisely in this way. Most of them would
probably say to us, "Let us alone; do nothing to
us, and say what you please about slavery." But
we do let them alone,—have never disturbed
them,—so that, after all, it is what we say which
dissatisfies them. They will continue to accuse
us of doing, until we cease saying.

I am also aware they have not as yet in terms
demanded the overthrow of our free-State con-

stitutions. Yet those constitutions declare the wrong of slavery with more solemn emphasis than do all other sayings against it; and when all these other sayings shall have been silenced, the overthrow of these constitutions will be demanded, and nothing be left to resist the demand. It is nothing to the contrary that they do not demand the whole of this just now. Demanding what they do, and for the reason they do, they can voluntarily stop nowhere short of this consummation. Holding, as they do, that slavery is morally right and socially elevating, they cannot cease to demand a full national recognition of it as a legal right and a social blessing.

Nor can we justifiably withhold this on any ground save our conviction that slavery is wrong. If slavery is right, all words, acts, laws, and constitutions against it are themselves wrong, and should be silenced and swept away. If it is right, we cannot justly object to its nationality—its universality; if it is wrong, they cannot justly insist upon its extension—its enlargement. All they ask we could readily grant, if we thought slavery right; all we ask they could as readily grant, if they thought it wrong. Their thinking it right and our thinking it wrong is the precise fact upon which depends the whole controversy. Thinking it right, as they do, they are not to blame for desiring its

full recognition as being right; but thinking it
wrong, as we do, can we yield to them? Can we
cast our votes with their view, and against our
own? In view of our moral, social, and political responsibilities, can we do this?

Wrong as we think slavery is, we can yet
afford to let it alone where it is, because that
much is due to the necessity arising from its
actual presence in the nation; but can we, while
our votes will prevent it, allow it to spread into
the national Territories, and to overrun us here
in these free States? If our sense of duty forbids this, then let us stand by our duty fearlessly
and effectively. Let us be diverted by none of
those sophistical contrivances wherewith we are
so industriously plied and belabored—contrivances such as groping for some middle ground
between the right and the wrong: vain as the
search for a man who should be neither a living
man nor a dead man; such as a policy of "don't
care" on a question about which all true men do
care; such as Union appeals beseeching true
Union men to yield to Disunionists, reversing
the divine rule, and calling, not the sinners, but
the righteous to repentance; such as invocations
to Washington, imploring men to unsay what
Washington said and undo what Washington
did.

Neither let us be slandered from our duty by

false accusations against us, nor frightened from
it by menaces of destruction to the government,
nor of dungeons to ourselves. Let us have faith
that right makes might, and in that faith let us
to the end dare to do our duty as we understand it.

ABSTRACT OF SPEECH AT HARTFORD, CONNEC-
TICUT, March 5, 1860

SLAVERY is the great political question of
the nation. Though all desire its settlement, it still remains the all-pervading
question of the day. It has been so especially
for the past six years. It is indeed older than
the Revolution—rising, subsiding, then rising
again, till '54, since which time it has been constantly augmenting. Those who occasioned the
Lecompton imbroglio now admit that they see
no end to it. It had been their cry that the
vexed question was just about to be settled—
"the tail of this hideous creature is just going
out of sight." That cry is played out, and has
ceased.

Why, when all desire to have this controversy
settled, can we not settle it satisfactorily? One
reason is, we want it settled in different ways.
Each faction has a different plan—they pull
different ways, and neither has a decided majority. In my humble opinion, the importance
and magnitude of the question is underrated,
even by our wisest men. If I be right, the first

thing is to get a just estimate of the evil; then we can provide a cure.

One sixth, and a little more, of the population of the United States are slaves, looked upon as property, as nothing but property. The cash value of these slaves, at a moderate estimate, is $2,000,000,000. This amount of property value has a vast influence on the minds of its owners, very naturally. The same amount of property would have an equal influence upon us if owned in the North. Human nature is the same— people at the South are the same as those at the North, barring the difference in circumstances. Public opinion is founded, to a great extent, on a property basis. What lessens the value of property is opposed; what enhances its value is favored. Public opinion at the South regards slaves as property, and insists upon treating them like other property.

On the other hand, the free States carry on their government on the principle of the equality of men. We think slavery is morally wrong, and a direct violation of that principle. We all think it wrong. It is clearly proved, I think, by natural theology, apart from revelation. Every man, black, white, or yellow, has a mouth to be fed, and two hands with which to feed it—and bread should be allowed to go to that mouth without controversy.

Slavery is wrong in its effect upon white people and free labor. It is the only thing that threatens the Union. It makes what Senator Seward has been much abused for calling an "irrepressible conflict." When they get ready to settle it, we hope they will let us know. Public opinion settles every question here; any policy to be permanent must have public opinion at the bottom—something in accordance with the philosophy of the human mind as it is. The property basis will have its weight. The love of property and a consciousness of right or wrong have conflicting places in our organization, which often make a man's course seem crooked, his conduct a riddle.

Some men would make it a question of indifference, neither right nor wrong, merely a question of dollars and cents;—the Almighty has drawn a line across the land, below which it must be cultivated by slave labor, above which by free labor. They would say: "If the question is between the white man and the negro, I am for the white man; if between the negro and the crocodile, I am for the negro." There is a strong effort to make this policy of indifference prevail, but it cannot be a durable one. A "don't care" policy won't prevail, for everybody does care.

Is there a Democrat, especially one of the

Douglas wing, but will declare that the Declaration of Independence has no application to the negro? It would be safe to offer a moderate premium for such a man. I have asked this question in large audiences where they were in the habit of answering right out, but no one would say otherwise. Not one of them said it five years ago. I never heard it till I heard it from the lips of Judge Douglas. True, some men boldly took the bull by the horns and said the Declaration of Independence was not true! The didn't sneak around the question. I say I heard first from Douglas that the Declaration did not apply to the black man. Not a man of them said it till then—they all say it now. This is a long stride toward establishing the policy of indifference—one more such stride, I think, would do it.

The proposition that there is a struggle between the white man and the negro contains a falsehood. There is no struggle. If there was, I should be for the white man. If two men are adrift at sea on a plank which will bear up but one, the law justifies either in pushing the other off. I never had to struggle to keep a negro from enslaving me, nor did a negro ever have to fight to keep me from enslaving him. They say, between the crocodile and the negro, they go for the negro. The logical proportion is, therefore, as a white man is to a negro, so is a negro to a crocodile, or as a negro may treat the crocodile, so the white man may treat the negro. The "don't care" policy leads just as surely to nationalizing slavery as Jeff Davis himself, but the doctrine is more dangerous because more insidious.

If the Republicans, who think slavery is wrong, get possession of the General Government, we may not root out the evil at once, but may at least prevent its extension. If I find a venomous snake lying on the open prairie, I seize the first stick and kill him at once; but if that snake is in bed with my children, I must be more cautious;—I shall, in striking the snake, also strike the children, or arouse the reptile to bite the children. Slavery is the venomous snake in bed with the children. But if the question is whether to kill it on the prairie or put it in bed with other children, I am inclined to think we'd kill it.

Another illustration. When for the first time I met Mr. Clay, the other day in the cars, in front of us sat an old gentleman with an enormous wen upon his neck. Everybody would say the wen was a great evil, and would cause the man's death after a while; but you couldn't cut it out, for he'd bleed to death in a minute. But would you ingraft the seeds of that wen on the necks of sound and healthy men? He must endure and be patient, hoping for possible relief. The wen represents slavery on the neck of this country. This only applies to those who think slavery is wrong. Those who think it right would consider the snake a jewel and the wen an ornament.

We want those Democrats who think slavery wrong, to quit voting with those who think it right. They don't treat it as they do other wrongs—they won't oppose it in the free States, for it isn't there; nor in the slave States, for it is there;—don't want it in politics, for it makes agitation; not in the pulpit, for it isn't religion; not in a tract society, for it makes a fuss—there is no place for its discussion. Are they quite consistent in this?

If those Democrats really think slavery wrong, they will be much pleased when earnest men in the slave States take up a plan of gradual emancipation, and go to work energetically and very kindly to get rid of the evil. Now let us test them. Frank Blair tried it; and he ran for Congress in '58, and got beaten. Did the Democracy feel bad about it? I reckon not. I guess you all flung up your hats and shouted, "Hurrah for the Democracy!"

He went on to speak of the manner in which

slavery was treated by the Constitution. The word "slave" is nowhere used; the supply of slaves was to be prohibited after 1808; they stopped the spread of it in the Territories; seven of the States abolished it. He argued very conclusively that it was then regarded as an evil which would eventually be got rid of, and that they desired, once rid of it, to have nothing in the Constitution to remind them of it. The Republicans go back to first principles, and deal with it as a wrong. Mason, of Virginia, said openly that the framers of our government were anti-slavery. Hammond, of South Carolina, said, "Washington set this evil example." Bully Brooks said, "At the time the Constitution was formed, no one supposed slavery would last till now." We stick to the policy of our fathers.

The Democracy are given to bushwhacking. After having their errors and misstatements continually thrust in their faces, they pay no heed, but go on howling about Seward and the "irrepressible conflict." That is bushwhacking. So with John Brown and Harper's Ferry. They charge it upon the Republican party, and ignominiously fail in all attempts to substantiate the charge. Yet they go on with their bushwhacking, the pack in full cry after John Brown. The Democrats had just been whipped in Ohio and Pennsylvania, and seized upon the unfortunate

Harper's Ferry affair to influence other elections then pending. They said to each other, "Jump in; now's your chance"; and were sorry there were not more killed. But they didn't succeed well. Let them go on with their howling. They will succeed when by slandering women you get them to love you, and by slandering men you get them to vote for you.

Mr. Lincoln then took up the Massachusetts shoemakers' strike, treating it in a humorous and philosophical manner, and exposing to ridicule the foolish pretense of Senator Douglas —that the strike arose from "this unfortunate sectional warfare." Mr. Lincoln thanked God that we have a system of labor where there can be a strike. Whatever the pressure, there is a point where the workman may stop. He didn't pretend to be familiar with the subject of the shoe strike—probably knew as little about it as Senator Douglas himself. Shall we stop making war upon the South? We never have made war upon them. If any one has, he had better go and hang himself and save Virginia the trouble. If you give up your convictions and call slavery right, as they do, you let slavery in upon you—instead of white laborers who can strike, you'll soon have black laborers who can't strike.

I have heard that in consequence of this "sec-

tional warfare," as Douglas calls it, Senator
Mason, of Virginia, had appeared in a suit of
homespun. Now, up in New Hampshire, the
woolen and cotton mills are all busy, and there
is no strike—they are busy making the very
goods Senator Mason has quit buying! To carry
out his idea, he ought to go barefoot! If that's
the plan, they should begin at the foundation,
and adopt the well-known "Georgia costume"
of a shirt-collar and pair of spurs.

It reminded him of the man who had a poor,
old, lean, bony, spavined horse, with swelled
legs. He was asked what he was going to do
with such a miserable beast—the poor creature
would die. "Do?" said he. "I'm going to fat
him up; don't you see that I have got him seal
fat as high as the knees?" Well, they have got
the Union dissolved up to the ankle, but no
further!

All portions of this Confederacy should act
in harmony and with careful deliberation. The
Democrats cry "John Brown invasion." We
are guiltless of it, but our denial does not satisfy
them. Nothing will satisfy them but disinfect-
ing the atmosphere entirely of all opposition to
slavery. They have not demanded of us to yield
the guards of liberty in our State constitutions,
but it will naturally come to that after a while.
If we give up to them, we cannot refuse even

their utmost request. If slavery is right, it ought to be extended; if not, if ought to be restricted—there is no middle ground. Wrong as we think it, we can afford to let it alone where it of necessity now exists; but we cannot afford to extend it into free territory and around our own homes. Let us stand against it!

The "Union" arrangements are all a humbug —they reverse the scriptural order, calling the righteous, and not sinners, to repentance. Let us not be slandered or intimidated to turn from our duty. Eternal right makes might; as we understand our duty, let us do it!

SPEECH AT NEW HAVEN, CONNECTICUT,
March 6, 1860

MR. PRESIDENT AND FELLOW-CITI-
ZENS OF NEW HAVEN: If the Republican party of this nation shall
ever have the national house intrusted to its
keeping, it will be the duty of that party to
attend to all the affairs of national housekeeping. Whatever matters of importance may
come up, whatever difficulties may arise, in the
way of its administration of the government,
that party will then have to attend to: it will
then be compelled to attend to other questions
besides this question which now assumes an
overwhelming importance—the question of
slavery. It is true that in the organization of
the Republican party this question of slavery
was more important than any other; indeed, so
much more important has it become that no
other national question can even get a hearing
just at present. The old question of tariff—a
matter that will remain one of the chief affairs
of national housekeeping to all time; the question of the management of financial affairs; the
question of the disposition of the public domain:

how shall it be managed for the purpose of getting it well settled, and of making there the homes of a free and happy people—these will remain open and require attention for a great while yet, and these questions will have to be attended to by whatever party has the control of the government. Yet just now they cannot even obtain a hearing, and I do not purpose to detain you upon these topics, or what sort of hearing they should have when opportunity shall come. For whether we will or not, the question of slavery is the question, the all-absorbing topic, of the day. It is true that all of us—and by that I mean not the Republican party alone, but the whole American people here and elsewhere— all of us wish this question settled; wish it out of the way. It stands in the way and prevents the adjustment and the giving of necessary attention to other questions of national housekeeping. The people of the whole nation agree that this question ought to be settled, and yet it is not settled; and the reason is that they are not yet agreed how it shall be settled. All wish it done, but some wish one way and some another, and some a third, or fourth, or fifth; different bodies are pulling in different directions, and none of them having a decided majority are able to accomplish the common object.

In the beginning of the year 1854, a new

policy was inaugurated with the avowed object and confident promise that it would entirely and forever put an end to the slavery agitation. It was again and again declared that under this policy, when once successfully established, the country would be forever rid of this whole question. Yet under the operation of that policy this agitation has not only not ceased, but it has been constantly augmented. And this, too, although from the day of its introduction its friends, who promised that it would wholly end all agitation, constantly insisted, down to the time that the Lecompton bill was introduced, that it was working admirably, and that its inevitable tendency was to remove the question forever from the politics of the country. Can you call to mind any Democratic speech, made after the repeal of the Missouri Compromise down to the time of the Lecompton bill, in which it was not predicted that the slavery agitation was just at an end; that "the Abolition excitement was played out," "the Kansas question was dead," "they have made the most they can out of this question and it is now forever settled"? But since the Lecompton bill, no Democrat within my experience has ever pretended that he could see the end. That cry has been dropped. They themselves do not pretend now that the agitation of this subject has come to an end yet. The truth is that this question is one of national importance, and we cannot help dealing with it; we must do something about it, whether we will or not. We cannot avoid it; the subject is one we cannot avoid considering; we can no more avoid it that a man can live without eating. It is upon us; it attaches to the body politic as much and as closely as the natural wants attach to our natural bodies. Now I think it important that this matter should be taken up in earnest and really settled. And one way to bring about a true settlement of the question is to understand its true magnitude.

There have been many efforts to settle it. Again and again it has been fondly hoped that it was settled, but every time it breaks out afresh, and more violently than ever. It was settled, our fathers hoped, by the Missouri Compromise, but it did not stay settled. Then the compromises of 1850 were declared to be a full and final settlement of the question. The two great parties, each in national convention, adopted resolutions declaring that the settlement made by the compromise of 1850 was a finality—that it would last forever. Yet how long before it was unsettled again? It broke out again in 1854, and blazed higher and raged more furiously than ever before, and the agitation has not rested since.

These repeated settlements must have some fault about them. There must be some inadequacy in their very nature to the purpose for which they were designed. We can only speculate as to where that fault—that inadequacy is, but we may perhaps profit by past experience.

I think that one of the causes of these repeated failures is that our best and greatest men have greatly underestimated the size of this question. They have constantly brought forward small cures for great sores—plasters too small to cover the wound. That is one reason that all settlements have proved so temporary, so evanescent.

Look at the magnitude of this subject. One sixth of our population, in round numbers—not quite one sixth, and yet more than a seventh—about one sixth of the whole population of the United States, are slaves. The owners of these slaves consider them property. The effect upon the minds of the owners is that of property, and nothing else; it induces them to insist upon all that will favorably affect its value as property, to demand laws and institutions and a public policy that shall increase and secure its value, and make it durable, lasting, and universal. The effect on the minds of the owners is to persuade them that there is no wrong in it. The slaveholder does not like to be considered a mean fellow for holding that species of property, and hence he has to struggle within himself, and sets about arguing himself into the belief that slavery is right. The property influences his mind. The dissenting minister who argued some theological point with one of the established church was always met by the reply, "I can't see it so." He opened the Bible and pointed him to a passage, but the orthodox minister replied, "I can't see it so." Then he showed him a single word —"Can you see that?" "Yes, I see it," was the reply. The dissenter laid a guinea over the word, and asked, "Do you see it now?" So here. Whether the owners of this species of property do really see it as it is, it is not for me to say; but if they do, they see it as it is through two billions of dollars, and that is a pretty thick coating. Certain it is that they do not see it as we see it. Certain it is that this two thousand million of dollars invested in this species of property is all so concentrated that the mind can grasp it at once. This immense pecuniary interest has its influence upon their minds.

But here in Connecticut and at the North slavery does not exist, and we see it through no such medium. To us it appears natural to think that slaves are human beings; men, not property; that some of the things, at least, stated about men in the Declaration of Independence apply to them as well as to us. I say we think, most of us, that this charter of freedom applies to the slave as well as to ourselves; that the class of arguments put forward to batter down that idea are also calculated to break down the very idea of free government, even for white men, and to undermine the very foundations of free society. We think slavery a great moral wrong, and while we do not claim the right to touch it where it exists, we wish to treat it as a wrong in the Territories, where our votes will reach it. We think that a respect for ourselves, a regard for future generations and for the God that made us, require that we put down this wrong where our votes will properly reach it. We think that species of labor an injury to free white men— in short, we think slavery a great moral, social, and political evil, tolerable only because, and so far as, its actual existence makes it necessary to tolerate it, and that beyond that it ought to be treated as a wrong.

Now these two ideas—the property idea that slavery is right and the idea that it is wrong— come into collision, and do actually produce that irrepressible conflict which Mr. Seward has been so roundly abused for mentioning. The two ideas conflict, and must forever conflict.

Again, in its political aspect does anything in any way endanger the perpetuity of this Union but that single thing—slavery? Many of our

adversaries are anxious to claim that they are
specially devoted to the Union, and take pains
to charge upon us hostility to the Union. Now
we claim that we are the only true Union men,
and we put to them this one proposition: What
ever endangered this Union save and except
slavery? Did any other thing ever cause a moment's fear? All men must agree that this thing
alone has ever endangered the perpetuity of the
Union. But if it was threatened by any other
influence, would not all men say that the best
thing that could be done, if we could not or
ought not to destroy it, would be at least to keep
it from growing any larger? Can any man believe that the way to save the Union is to extend
and increase the only thing that threatens the
Union, and to suffer it to grow bigger and
bigger?

Whenever this question shall be settled, it
must be settled on some philosophical basis. No
policy that does not rest upon philosophical
public opinion can be permanently maintained.
And hence there are but two policies in regard
to slavery that can be at all maintained. The
first, based on the property view that slavery is
right, conforms to that idea throughout, and demands that we shall do everything for it that we
ought to do if it were right. We must sweep
away all opposition, for opposition to the right

is wrong; we must agree that slavery is right, and we must adopt the idea that property has persuaded the owner to believe, that slavery is morally right and socially elevating. This gives a philosophical basis for a permanent policy of encouragement.

The other policy is one that squares with the idea that slavery is wrong, and it consists in doing everything that we ought to do if it is wrong. Now I don't wish to be misunderstood, nor to leave a gap down to be misrepresented, even. I don't mean that we ought to attack it where it exists. To me it seems that if we were to form a government anew, in view of the actual presence of slavery we should find it necessary to frame just such a government as our fathers did: giving to the slaveholder the entire control where the system was established, while we possess the power to restrain it from going outside those limits. From the necessities of the case we should be compelled to form just such a government as our blessed fathers gave us; and surely if they have so made it, that adds another reason why we should let slavery alone where it exists.

If I saw a venomous snake crawling in the road, any man would say I might seize the nearest stick and kill it; but if I found that snake in bed with my children, that would be another question. I might hurt the children more than

the snake, and it might bite them. Much more, if I found it in bed with my neighbor's children, and I had bound myself by a solemn compact not to meddle with his children under any circumstances, it would become me to let that particular mode of getting rid of the gentleman alone. But if there was a bed newly made up, to which the children were to be taken, and it was proposed to take a batch of young snakes and put them there with them, I take it no man would say there was any question how I ought to decide!

That is just the case. The new Territories are the newly made bed to which our children are to go, and it lies with the nation to say whether they shall have snakes mixed up with them or not. It does not seem as if there could be much hesitation what our policy should be.

Now I have spoken of a policy based on the idea that slavery is wrong, and a policy based upon the idea that it is right. But an effort has been made for a policy that shall treat it as neither right nor wrong. It is based upon utter indifference. Its leading advocate has said: "I don't care whether it be voted up or down." "It is merely a matter of dollars and cents." "The Almighty has drawn a line across this continent, on one side of which all soil must forever be cultivated by slave labor, and on the other by

free." "When the struggle is between the white man and the negro, I am for the white man; when it is between the negro and the crocodile, I am for the negro." Its central idea is indifference. It holds that it makes no more difference to us whether the Territories become free or slave States, than whether my neighbor stocks his farm with horned cattle or puts it into tobacco. All recognize this policy, the plausible sugar-coated name of which is "popular sovereignty."

This policy chiefly stands in the way of a permanent settlement of the question. I believe there is no danger of its becoming the permanent policy of the country, for it is based on a public indifference. There is nobody that "don't care." All the people do care, one way or the other. I do not charge that its author, when he says he "don't care," states his individual opinion; he only expresses his policy for the government. I understand that he has never said, as an individual, whether he thought slavery right or wrong—and he is the only man in the nation that has not. Now such a policy may have a temporary run; it may spring up as necessary to the political prospects of some gentleman —but it is utterly baseless; the people are not indifferent, and it can therefore have no durability or permanence.

But suppose it could! Then it can be maintained only by public opinion that shall say, "We don't care." There must be a change in public opinion; the public mind must be so far debauched as to square with this policy of caring not at all. The people must come to consider this as "merely a question of dollars and cents," and to believe that in some places the Almighty has made slavery necessarily eternal. This policy can be brought to prevail if the people can be brought round to say honestly, "We don't care"; if not, it can never be maintained. It is for you to say whether that can be done.

You are ready to say it cannot; but be not too fast. Remember what a long stride has been taken since the repeal of the Missouri Compromise! Do you know of any Democrat, of either branch of the party—do you know one who declares that he believes that the Declaration of Independence has any application to the negro? Judge Taney declares that it has not, and Judge Douglas even vilifies me personally and scolds me roundly for saying that the Declaration applies to all men, and that negroes are men. Is there a Democrat here who does not deny that the Declaration applies to a negro? Do any of you know of one? Well, I have tried before perhaps fifty audiences, some larger and some smaller than this, to find one such Democrat, and never yet have I found one who said I did not place him right in that. I must assume that Democrats hold that; and now not one of these Democrats can show that he said that five years ago! I venture to defy the whole party to produce one man that ever uttered the belief that the Declaration did not apply to negroes before the repeal of the Missouri Compromise! Four or five years ago we all thought negroes were men, and that when "all men" were named, negroes were included. But the whole Democratic party has deliberately taken negroes from the class of men and put them in the class of brutes. Turn it as you will, it is simply the truth! Don't be too hasty then in saying that the people cannot be brought to this new doctrine, but note that long stride. One more as long completes the journey from where negroes are estimated as men to where they are estimated as mere brutes—as right property!

That saying, "In the struggle between the white man and the negro," etc., which, I know, came from the same source as this policy—that saying marks another step. There is a falsehood wrapped up in that statement. "In the struggle between the white man and the negro," assumes that there is a struggle, in which either the white man must enslave the negro or the negro must enslave the white. There is no such struggle.

It is merely an ingenious falsehood to degrade
and brutalize the negro.   Let each let the other
alone, and there is no struggle about it.   If it
was like two wrecked seamen on a narrow plank,
where each must push the other off or drown
himself, I would push the negro off—or a white
man either; but it is not: the plank is large
enough for both.   This good earth is plenty
broad enough for white man and negro both,
and there is no need of either pushing the other
off.

So that saying, "In the struggle between the
negro and the crocodile," etc., is made up from
the idea that down where the crocodile inhabits,
a white man can't labor; it must be nothing else
but crocodile or negro; if the negro does not,
the crocodile must possess the earth; in that
case he declares for the negro.   The meaning
of the whole is just this: As a white man is to a
negro, so is a negro to a crocodile; and as the
negro may rightfully treat the crocodile, so may
the white man rightfully treat the negro.   This
very dear phrase coined by its author, and so
dear that he deliberately repeats it in many
speeches, has a tendency to still further brutalize the negro, and to bring public opinion to the
point of utter indifference whether men so bru-
talized are enslaved or not.   When that time
shall come, if ever, I think that policy to which

I refer may prevail. But I hope the good free men of this country will never allow it to come, and until then the policy can never be maintained.

Now, consider the effect of this policy. We in the States are not to care whether freedom or slavery gets the better, but the people in the Territories may care. They are to decide, and they may think what they please; it is a matter of dollars and cents! But are not the people of the Territories detailed from the States? If this feeling of indifference—this absence of moral sense about the question—prevails in the States, will it not be carried into the Territories? Will not every man say, "I don't care; it is nothing to me"? If any one comes that wants slavery, must they not say, "I don't care whether freedom or slavery be voted up or voted down"? It results at last in nationalizing the institution of slavery. Even if fairly carried out, that policy is just as certain to nationalize slavery as the doctrine of Jeff Davis himself. These are only two roads to the same goal, and "popular sovereignty" is just as sure, and almost as short, as the other.

What we want, and all we want, is to have with us the men who think slavery wrong. But those who say they hate slavery, and are opposed to it, but yet act with the Democratic party—where are they? Let us apply a few tests. You say that you think slavery a wrong, but you renounce all attempts to restrain it. Is there anything else that you think wrong, that you are not willing to deal with as a wrong? Why are you so careful, so tender of this one wrong and no other? You will not let us do a single thing as if it was wrong; there is no place where you will allow it to be even called wrong. We must not call it wrong in the free States, because it is not there, and we must not call it wrong in the slave States, because it is there; we must not call it wrong in politics, because that is bringing morality into politics, and we must not call it wrong in the pulpit, because that is bringing politics into religion; we must not bring it into the tract society, or other societies, because those are such unsuitable places, and there is no single place, according to you, where this wrong thing can properly be called wrong.

Perhaps you will plead that if the people of slave States should of themselves set on foot an effort for emancipation, you would wish them success and bid them God-speed. Let us test that! In 1858 the emancipation party of Missouri, with Frank Blair at their head, tried to get up a movement for that purpose; and, having started a party, contested the State. Blair was beaten, apparently if not truly, and when the news came to Connecticut, you, who knew that Frank Blair was taking hold of this thing by the right end, and doing the only thing that you say can properly be done to remove this wrong—did you bow your heads in sorrow because of that defeat? Do you, any of you, know one single Democrat that showed sorrow over that result? Not one! On the contrary, every man threw up his hat, and hallooed at the top of his lungs, "Hooray for Democracy!"

Now, gentleman, the Republicans desire to place this great question of slavery on the very basis on which our fathers placed it, and no other. It is easy to demonstrate that "our fathers who framed this government under which we live" looked on slavery as wrong, and so framed it and everything about it as to square with the idea that it was wrong, so far as the necessities arising from its existence permitted. In forming the Constitution they found the slave-trade existing, capital invested in it, fields depending upon it for labor, and the whole system resting upon the importation of slave labor. They therefore did not prohibit the slave trade at once, but they gave the power to prohibit it after twenty years. Why was this? What other foreign trade did they treat in that way? Would they have done this if they had not thought slavery wrong?

Another thing was done by some of the same men who framed the Constitution, and afterward adopted as their own act by the first Congress held under that Constitution, of which many of the framers were members—they prohibited the spread of slavery in the Territories. Thus the same men, the framers of the Constitution, cut off the supply and prohibited the spread of slavery; and both acts show conclusively that they considered that the thing was wrong.

If additional proof is wanting, it can be found in the phraseology of the Constitution. When men are framing a supreme law and chart of government to secure blessings and prosperity to untold generations yet to come, they use language as short and direct and plain as can be found to express their meaning. In all matters but this of slavery the framers of the Constitution used the very clearest, shortest, and most direct language. But the Constitution alludes to slavery three times without mentioning it once! The language used becomes ambiguous, roundabout, and mystical. They speak of the "immigration of persons," and mean the importation of slaves, but do not say so. In establishing a basis of representation they say "all other persons," when they mean to say slaves. Why did they not use the shortest phrase? In providing for the return of fugitives they say "persons held to service or labor." If they had said "slaves," it would have been plainer and less liable to misconstruction. Why didn't they do it? We cannot doubt that it was done on purpose. Only one reason is possible, and that is supplied us by one of the framers of the Constitution—and it is not possible for man to conceive of any other. They expected and desired that the system would come to an end, and meant that when it did the Constitution should not show that there ever had been a slave in this good free country of ours.

I will dwell on that no longer. I see the signs of the approaching triumph of the Republicans in the bearing of their political adversaries. A great deal of this war with us nowadays is mere bushwhacking. At the battle of Waterloo, when Napoleon's cavalry had charged again and again upon the unbroken squares of British infantry, at last they were giving up the attempt, and going off in disorder, when some of the officers, in mere vexation and complete despair, fired their pistols at those solid squares. The Democrats are in that sort of extreme desperation; it is nothing else. I will take up a few of these arguments.

There is "the irrepressible conflict." How
they rail at Seward for that saying! They repeat it constantly; and although the proof has
been thrust under their noses again and again
that almost every good man since the formation
of our government has uttered that same sentiment, from General Washington, who "trusted
that we should yet have a confederacy of free
States," with Jefferson, Jay, Monroe, down to
the latest days, yet they refuse to notice that at
all, and persist in railing at Seward for saying
it. Even Roger A. Pryor, editor of the Richmond "Enquirer," uttered the same sentiment
in almost the same language, and yet so little
offense did it give the Democrats that he was
sent for to Washington to edit the "States"—the
Douglas organ there, while Douglas goes into
hydrophobia and spasms of rage because Seward dared to repeat it. That is what I call
bushwhacking—a sort of argument that they
must know any child can see through.

Another is John Brown! You stir up insurrections; you invade the South! John Brown!
Harper's Ferry! Why, John Brown was not
a Republican! You have never implicated a
single Republican in that Harper's Ferry enterprise. We tell you if any member of the
Republican party is guilty in that matter, you
know it or you do not know it. If you do know

it, you are inexcusable not to designate the man
and prove the fact. If you do not know it, you
are inexcusable to assert it, and especially to
persist in the assertion after you have tried and
failed to make the proof. You need not be told
that persisting in a charge which one does not
know to be true is simply malicious slander.
Some of you admit that no Republican designedly aided or encouraged the Harper's Ferry
affair; but still insist that our doctrines and declarations necessarily lead to such results. We
do not believe it. We know we hold to no doctrines and make no declarations which were not
held to and made by our fathers who framed
the government under which we live, and we
cannot see how declarations that were patriotic
when they made them are villainous when we
make them. You never dealt fairly by us in relation to that affair—and I will say frankly that
I know of nothing in your character that should
lead us to suppose that you would. You had
just been soundly thrashed in elections in several States, and others were soon to come. You
rejoiced at the occasion, and only were troubled
that there were not three times as many killed
in the affair. You were in evident glee; there
was no sorrow for the killed nor for the peace
of Virginia disturbed; you were rejoicing that
by charging Republicans with this thing you

might get an advantage of us in New York and the other States. You pulled that string as tightly as you could, but your very generous and worthy expectations were not quite fulfilled. Each Republican knew that the charge was a slander as to himself at least, and was not inclined by it to cast his vote in your favor. It was mere bushwhacking, because you had nothing else to do. You are still on that track, and I say, Go on! If you think you can slander a woman into loving you, or a man into voting for you, try it till you are satisfied.

Another specimen of this bushwhacking— that "shoe strike." Now be it understood that I do not pretend to know all about the matter. I am merely going to speculate a little about some of its phases, and at the outset I am glad to see that a system of labor prevails in New England under which laborers can strike when they want to, where they are not obliged to work under all circumstances, and are not tied down and obliged to labor whether you pay them or not! I like the system which lets a man quit when he wants to, and wish it might prevail everywhere. One of the reasons why I am opposed to slavery is just here. What is the true condition of the laborer? I take it that it is best for all to leave each man free to acquire property as fast as he can. Some will get wealthy. I don't believe in a law to prevent a man from getting rich; it would do more harm than good. So while we do not propose any war upon capital, we do wish to allow the humblest man an equal chance to get rich with everybody else. When one starts poor, as most do in the race of life, free society is such that he knows he can better his condition; he knows that there is no fixed condition of labor for his whole life. I am not ashamed to confess that twenty-five years ago I was a hired laborer, mauling rails, at work on a flatboat—just what might happen to any poor man's son. I want every man to have a chance—and I believe a black man is entitled to it—in which he can better his condition—when he may look forward and hope to be a hired laborer this year and the next, work for himself afterward, and finally to hire men to work for him. That is the true system. Up here in New England you have a soil that scarcely sprouts black-eyed beans, and yet where will you find wealthy men so wealthy, and poverty so rarely in extremity? There is not another such place on earth! I desire that if you get too thick here, and find it hard to better your condition on this soil, you may have a chance to strike and go somewhere else, where you may not be degraded, nor have your family corrupted by forced rivalry with negro slaves.

I want you to have a clean bed and no snakes in it! Then you can better your condition, and so it may go on and on in one ceaseless round so long as man exists on the face of the earth.

Now to come back to this shoe strike. If, as the senator from Illinois asserts, this is caused by withdrawal of Southern votes, consider briefly how you will meet the difficulty. You have done nothing, and have protested that you have done done nothing, to injure the South; and yet to get back the shoe trade, you must leave off doing something that you are now doing. What is it? You must stop thinking slavery wrong. Let your institutions be wholly changed; let your State constitutions be subverted; glorify slavery; and so you will get back the shoe trade—for what? You have brought owned labor with it to compete with your own labor, to underwork you, and degrade you. Are you ready to get back the trade on these terms?

But the statement is not correct. You have not lost that trade; orders were never better than now. Senator Mason, a Democrat, comes into the Senate in homespun, a proof that the dissolution of the Union has actually begun. But orders are the same. Your factories have not struck work, neither those where they make anything for coats, nor for pants, nor for shirts, nor for ladies' dresses. Mr. Mason has not reached

the manufacturers who ought to have made him
a coat and pants. To make his proof good for
anything, he should have come into the Senate
barefoot.

Another bushwhacking contrivance—simply
that, nothing else! I find a good many people
who are very much concerned about the loss of
Southern trade. Now, either these people are
sincere, or they are not. I will speculate a little about that. If they are sincere, and are
moved by any real danger of the loss of the
Southern trade, they will simply get their names
on the white list, and then instead of persuading
Republicans to do likewise, they will be glad
to keep you away. Don't you see they thus shut
off competition? They would not be whisper-
ing around to Republicans to come in and share
the profits with them. But if they are not sincere, and are merely trying to fool Republicans out of their votes, they will grow very
anxious about your pecuniary prospects; they
are afraid you are going to get broken up and
ruined; they did not care about Democratic
votes—oh, no, no, no! You must judge which
class those belong to whom you meet. I leave
it to you to determine from the facts.

Let us notice some more of the stale charges
against Republicans. You say we are sectional.
We deny it. That makes an issue; and the bur-

den of proof is upon you. You produce your proof; and what is it? Why, that our party has no existence in your section—gets no votes in your section. The fact is substantially true; but does it prove the issue? If it does, then in case we should, without change of principle, begin to get votes in your section, we should thereby cease to be sectional. You cannot escape this conclusion; and yet, are you willing to abide by it? If you are, you will probably soon find that we have ceased to be sectional, for we shall get votes in your section this very year. The fact that we get no votes in your section is a fact of your making, and not of ours. And if there be fault in that fact, that fault is primarily yours, and remains so until you show that we repel you by some wrong principle or practice. If we do repel you by any wrong principle or practice, the fault is ours; but this brings you to where you ought to have started—to a discussion of the right or wrong of our principle. If our principle, put in practice, would wrong your section for the benefit of ours, or for any other object, then our principle and we with it, are sectional, and are justly opposed and denounced as such. Meet us, then, on the question of whether our principle, put in practice would wrong your section; and so meet it as if it were possible that something may be said on our side. Do you accept the challenge? No? Then you really believe that the principle which our fathers who framed the government under which we live thought so clearly right as to adopt it, and indorse it again and again, upon their official oaths, is, in fact, so clearly wrong as to demand your condemnation without a moment's consideration.

Some of you delight to flaunt in our faces the warning against sectional parties given by Washington in his Farewell Address. Less than eight years before Washington gave that warning, he had, as President of the United States, approved and signed an act of Congress enforcing the prohibition of slavery in the Northwestern Territory, which act embodied the policy of government upon that subject up to and at the very moment he penned that warning; and about one year after he penned it, he wrote Lafayette that he considered that prohobition a wise measuse, expressing in the same connection his hope that we should some time have a confederacy of free States.

Bearing this in mind, and seeing that sectionalism has since arisen upon this same subject, is that warning a weapon in your hands against us, or in our hands against you? Could Washington himself speak, would he cast the blame of that sectionalism upon us who sustain his policy, or upon you who repudiate it? We respect that warning of Washington, and we commend it to you, together with his example pointing to the right application of it.

But you say you are conservative—eminently conservative—while we are revolutionary, destructive, or something of that sort. What is conservatism? Is it not adherence to the old and tried against the new and untried? We stick to, contend for, the identical old policy on the point in controversy which was adopted by our fathers who framed the government under which we live; while you with one accord reject, and scout, and spit upon that old policy, and insist upon substituting something new. True, you disagree among yourselves as to what that substitute shall be; you have considerable variety of new propositions and plans, but you are unanimous in rejecting and denouncing the old policy of the fathers. Some of you are for reviving the foreign slave-trade; some for a congressional slave code for the Territories; some for Congress forbidding the Territories to prohibit slavery within their limits; some for maintaining slavery in the Territories through the judiciary; some for the "great principle" that if one man would enslave another, no third man should object, fantastically called "popular sovereignty"; but never a man among you in favor of Federal prohibition of slavery in Federal Territories according to the practice of our fathers who framed the government under which we live. Not one of all your various plans can show a precedent or an advocate in the century within which our government originated. And yet you draw yourselves up and say, "We are eminently conservative."

It is exceedingly desirable that all parts of this great Confederacy shall be at peace and in harmony one with another. Let us Republicans do our part to have it so. Even though much provoked, let us do nothing through passion and ill temper. Even though the Southern people will not so much as listen to us, let us calmly consider their demands, and yield to them if, in our deliberate view of our duty, we possibly can. Judging by all they say and do, and by the subject and nature of their controversy with us, let us determine, if we can, what will satisfy them.

Will they be satisfied if the Territories be unconditionally surrendered to them? We know they will not. In all their present complaints against us the Territories are scarcely mentioned. Invasions and insurrections are the rage now. Will it satisfy them if in the future we have nothing to do with invasions and insurrections? We know it will not. We so know because we know we never have had anything to do with invasions and insurrections; and yet this total abstaining does not exempt us from the charge and the denunciation.

The question recurs, What will satisfy them? Simply this: we must not only let them alone, but we must somehow convince them that we do let them alone. This we know by experience is no easy task. We have been so trying to convince them from the very beginning of our organization, but with no success. In all our platforms and speeches we have constantly protested our purpose to let them alone; but this has had no tendency to convince them. Alike unavailing to convince them is the fact that they have never detected a man of us in any attempt to disturb them.

These natural and apparently adequate means all failing, what will convince them? This, and this only: cease to call slavery wrong, and join them in calling it right. And this must be done thoroughly—done in acts as well as in words. Silence will not be tolerated—we must place ourselves avowedly with them. Douglas's new sedition law must be enacted and enforced, suppressing all declarations that slavery is wrong, whether made in politics, in presses, in pulpits, or in private. We must arrest and return their fugitive slaves with greedy pleasure. We must pull down our free-State constitutions. The whole atmosphere must be disinfected of all taint of opposition to slavery before they will cease to believe that all their troubles proceed from us. So long as we call slavery wrong, whenever a slave runs away they will overlook the obvious fact that he ran because he was oppressed, and declare that he was stolen off. Whenever a master cuts his slaves with the lash, and they cry out under it, he will overlook the obvious fact that the negroes cry out because they are hurt, and insist that they were put up to it by some rascally Abolitionist.

I am quite aware that they do not state their case precisely in this way. Most of them would probably say to us: "Let us alone; do nothing to us, and say what you please about slavery." But we do let them alone,—have never disturbed them,—so that, after all, it is what we say which dissatisfies them. They will continue to accuse us of doing, until we cease saying.

I am also aware that they have not as yet in terms demanded the overthrow of our free-State constitutions. Yet those constitutions declare the wrong of slavery with more solemn emphasis than do all other sayings against it; and when all these other sayings shall have been silenced, the overthrow of these constitutions will be demanded, and nothing be left to resist the demand.

It is nothing to the contrary that they do not demand the whole of this just now. Demanding what they do, and for the reason they do, they can voluntarily stop nowhere short of this consummation. Holding as they do that slavery is morally right and socially elevating, they cannot cease to demand a full national recognition of it, as a legal right and a social blessing.

Nor can we justifiably withhold this on any ground save our conviction that slavery is wrong. If slavery is right, all words, acts, laws, and constitutions against it are themselves wrong, and should be silenced and swept away. If it is right, we cannot justly object to its nationality—its universality; if it is wrong, they cannot justly insist upon its extension—its enlargement. All they ask we could readily grant, if we thought slavery right; all we ask they could as readily grant, if they thought it wrong. Their thinking it right, and our thinking it wrong, is the precise fact upon which depends the whole controversy. Thinking it right, as they do, they are not to blame for desiring its full recognition as being right; but thinking it wrong, as we do, can we yield to them? Can we cast our votes with their view, and against our own? In view of our moral, social, and political responsibilities, can we do this?

Wrong as we think slavery is, we can yet afford to let it alone where it is, because that much is due to the necessity arising from its actual presence in the nation; but can we, while our votes will prevent it, allow it to spread into the national Territories and to overrun us here in these free States?

If our sense of duty forbids this, then let us stand by our duty fearlessly and effectively. Let us be diverted by none of those sophistical contrivances wherewith we are so industriously plied and belabored—contrivances such as groping for some middle ground between the right and the wrong; vain as the search for a man who should be neither a living man nor a dead man; such as a policy of "don't care" on a question about which all true men do care; such as Union appeals beseeching true Union men to yield to Disunionists, reversing the divine rule, and calling, not the sinners, but the righteous to repentance; such as invocations to Washington, imploring men to unsay what Washington did.

Neither let us be slandered from our duty by false accusations against us, nor frightened from it by menaces of destruction to the government, nor of dungeons to ourselves. Let us have faith that right makes might; and in that faith let us to the end dare to do our duty as we understand it.